Tourism and Language in Vieques

Anthropology of Tourism: Heritage, Mobility, and Society

Series Editors
Michael A. Di Giovine (West Chester University of Pennsylvania)
Noel B. Salazar (University of Leuven)

Mission Statement

The Anthropology of Tourism: Heritage, Mobility, and Society series provides anthropologists and others in the social sciences and humanities with cutting-edge and engaging research on the culture(s) of tourism. This series embraces anthropology's holistic and comprehensive approach to scholarship, and is sensitive to the complex diversity of human expression. Books in this series particularly examine tourism's relationship with cultural heritage and mobility and its impact on society. Contributions are transdisciplinary in nature, and either look at a particular country, region, or population, or take a more global approach. Including monographs and edited collections, this series is a valuable resource to scholars and students alike who are interested in the various manifestations of tourism and its role as the world's largest and fastest-growing source of socio-cultural and economic activity.

Books in Series

Alternative Tourism in Budapest: Class, Culture, and Identity in a Postsocialist City, by Susan E. Hill

Tourism and Prosperity in Miao Land: Power and Inequality in Rural Ethnic China, by Xianghong Feng

Tourism and Language in Vieques: An Ethnography of the Post-Navy Period, by Luis Galanes Valldejuli

Tourism and Language in Vieques

An Ethnography of the Post-Navy Period

Luis Galanes Valldejuli

LEXINGTON BOOKS
Lanham • Boulder • New York • London

Published by Lexington Books
An imprint of The Rowman & Littlefield Publishing Group, Inc.
4501 Forbes Boulevard, Suite 200, Lanham, Maryland 20706
www.rowman.com

Unit A, Whitacre Mews, 26-34 Stannary Street, London SE11 4AB

British Library Cataloguing in Publication Information Available
The hardback edition of this book was previously catalogued by the Library of Congress
as follows:

Library of Congress Cataloging-in-Publication Data

Includes bibliographic references and index.
ISBN 978-1-4985-5541-8 (cloth : alk. paper)
ISBN 978-1-4985-5543-2 (pbk. : alk. paper)
ISBN 978-1-4985-5542-5 (Electronic)

Contents

Acknowledgments vii

Introduction ix

1 Tourism 1

2 Land 13

3 Work 33

4 Language, the Imaginary, and Tourism 75

5 Race 91

6 Decontamination, Reparations, Health, and Crime Issues 117

7 The Future of Vieques 125

Conclusion 133

Bibliography 137

Author Index 149

Subject Index 153

About the Author 157

Acknowledgments

First and foremost, I owe my gratitude to three students from the University of Puerto Rico at Cayey who acted as research assistants during a crucial period of the research project, in the years of 2008 and 2009: Beni Rosado, Verónica Sumpter and Myraida Rodríguez. Their insertion into the Vieques community allowed for the collection of crucial information which would have been otherwise very hard to collect and, while I assume full responsibility for the ideas and arguments contained in this book, they are in many ways intellectual coauthors of the book. I also owe gratitude to many other colleagues who either debated with me on the relevance of the preliminary findings during the early and middle stages of fieldwork, or read and commented on parts or whole drafts of the book, including Jorge Capetillo-Ponce, Timothy Sieber, Glenn Jacobs, Lorna Rivera, Julian Jefferies, Annie Fabian, Manuel Lobato Vico, Otomie Vale, Angel Rodríguez, Yves Paul, José Rosado, Christian Girault, Gustavo Gelpi, Antonio Aledo, José Andrés Dominguez, Florentino Rodao, Michael Di Giovine, Noel Salazar and Kasey Beduhn. Moreover, I also owe gratitude to several colleagues who, while holding key administrative positions at both the University of Puerto Rico at Cayey or the University of Massachusetts at Boston, provided unconditional support to this research project, making possible to accommodate my research activities and my teaching duties, including Ram Lamba, Gloria Butrón, Raúl Castro, Rafael Aragunde and Stanley Wanucha. Finally, I owe a very special gratitude to many Viequenses who acted as informants for my research project (many of whom I cannot mention by name to preserve their anonymity), as well as to key Viequense activists and community leaders who provided continuous support throughout the decade-long period of research activities. In this last category, five deserve a very special mention: Roberto Rabin, Nylda Medina,

Carmen Valencia, Zaida Torres and Penny Miller. I also thank Miguel Angel Lague for helping me with the maps that are contained in the book.

Parts of this research project were made possible through financial support from the "Fondo Institucional para el Desarrollo de la Investigación" (FIDI) from the University of Puerto Rico at Cayey.

Introduction

Vieques is an island/municipality of Puerto Rico, which in turn is an unincorporated territory of the United States. It is a very small island, serpent-like in shape, with a land area of 52 square miles (130 sq km or 33,000 acres) and a population of 9,301 as of 2010. It is located 19.62 miles (31.58 km.) from the port of Fajardo, in mainland Puerto Rico, so traveling back-and-forth between the two islands is relatively easy, with several ferries covering the route daily. The ferry takes less than two hours (one way), and, because the route is considered a "federal highway," the ferry system is subsidized by the Puerto Rican government, so the ticket cost is very inexpensive. It was two dollars per person as of 2015.

During the period 1941 to 2003, two-thirds of the island of Vieques was used as a US military base under Navy control and, while Vieques is best known for its prolonged David versus Goliath-like struggle to expel the Navy form the island (cf. Rabin n/d; McCaffrey 2002; Barreto 2002; Cruz Soto 2008; Ayala and Bolivar 2011), this work is instead interested in documenting events taking place on the island during the post-Navy period, or, more specifically, during the first decade after the departure of the Navy—roughly the period from 2004 to 2016. The physical departure of the Navy did not put an end to the struggle of the Viequenses against the US Navy and US Government, and finding solutions to the devastating environmental and health scenarios left behind after sixty-two years of bombing practices made inevitable the idea that "the struggle continues" (*la lucha continúa*) (Berman Santana 2006; Baver 2006). But the history of Vieques that we were able to capture ethnographically revealed a very different dimension of the post-Navy struggles of the Viequenses, that is, one where social conflicts are derived not so much from the Navy legacy, but rather from the introduction of a relatively massive tourism industry into the island. The development of the tourism industry is thus an inevitably important part of the history of Vieques in the post-Navy period, and this work can therefore be viewed as a micro-history of what happens to a small island during the very early stages of the introduction of a tourist-based economy, with an emphasis on its effects on the native population.

The history of the development of tourism in Vieques is unique when compared to other Caribbean islands, precisely because of the presence of the Navy on the island for over sixty years. After the 1959 Cuban Revolution, North American tourism was deprived of its favorite Caribbean destination, thus causing a diversion of tourists to other Caribbean islands that although more distant from the US mainland than Havana, became accessible as tourist destinations because of enhanced advances in their transportation industry (e.g., commercial airlines, cruise ships). The effect of the introduction of tourism into the small Caribbean islands after 1960 was massive (in terms of number of tourists) and economically beneficial (at least when measured by macroeconomic statistical indicators), but often also socially conflictive, in terms of its negative impacts on the local population. Vieques, thus, was probably the only small island in the whole Caribbean (with certainty in the US Caribbean) that was spared from the booming tourism development in the years following the Cuban Revolution. And it was, for good or bad, the presence of the Navy that prevented Vieques from taking the profitable route of tourism earlier than it did. When the Navy left, in 2003, Vieques remained (quite literally) "the last virgin territory in the Caribbean."

Thus, the exit of the Navy meant, for Viequenses, not only the end of live-bombing exercises, contamination and military presence on the island, but also the beginning of a process by which it would be forced to emulate the path previously followed by so many other small Caribbean "sister" islands, albeit with a delay of over forty years, and perhaps with the intensity that a forty-years delay would call for. In this sense, while the history of Vieques during the Navy period is unique (perhaps even exceptionally unique), the same is not true for the post-Navy period. The history of the post-Navy period is, contrariwise, so common in the Caribbean. It resembles the history of so many other small islands in the region, and around the world, after the introduction of tourism-based economies. The processes we document for Vieques during the post-Navy period are mirror images of processes that have been widely documented in the anthropological and sociological literature on tourism in the Caribbean, and that were delayed in Vieques due to the presence of the US Navy. Indeed, in many of the Caribbean islands with tourist-based economies the same history repeats over and over again. And the same is true for many other small tropical islands around the globe: be these Ibiza and Mallorca (Spain), or Java and Sumatra (Indonesia), among others.

Polly Pattullo, in documenting the history of the construction (and the opposition movements against the construction) of the Hilton Jalousie

Plantation resort, in the Pitons volcanic-hills of St. Lucia—a tourism project that Derek Walcott, the St. Lucian poet and playwright and Nobel-prize winner in literature, described as equivalent to "opening a casino in the Vatican" (quoted in Pattullo 2005: 2)—says the following:

> What is important about the story of Jalousie is that it is so typical. There are countless other Jalousies in the Caribbean and the story of the Jalousies, taken together, provokes an essential debate about tourism: Who benefits? And how? It asks questions about sovereignty (when beaches and valleys become foreign fields). It presents dilemmas about economic well-being and how profits are distributed. It generates arguments about how tourism can (or cannot) protect the environment, and speculates about the social and cultural relations between visitors and hosts . . . [the story] has been repeated time and time again. (Pattullo 2005: 4)

To be sure, Vieques is but one more of the "countless other Jalousies" in this sea of islands whose histories repeat themselves "time and time again." Cuban scholar Antonio Benítez Rojo (1996) has coined the phrase "the repeating island," or *la isla que se repite*, in an attempt to highlight the psychological and behavioral patterns that can serve to talk about the Caribbean as a culturally unified region, beneath or below the undeniable racial and ethnic diversity that characterizes the region. And, while the usage that Benítez Rojo gives to the concept is more in line with a cultural/aesthetic understanding of Caribbean peoples, we believe the concept is equally apt to describe what is happening in the multiple island microstates throughout the Caribbean with tourism economies. If there is something that unquestionably "repeats itself" in the Caribbean from island to island, it is certainly tourism, and the multiple social conflicts that result from tourism: related to jobs, price of land, water, migration, racial and ethnic discrimination, contamination, health and so on.

The introduction of tourism into the island of Vieques in the period after 2003 had a positive effect on the island's economy, at least when measured by official statistics: that is, per capita income increased from $2,997 in 2000 to $8,054 in 2010, and poverty was reduced from 73.3 percent to 42.9 percent over the same period. The unemployment rate also decreased from 16.1 percent in 2003 (the year the Navy left) to 9.2 percent in 2006, but went up again during the years of the US financial crisis, beginning in 2008. It reached a high peak of 22.4 percent in 2009, but started descending again afterward, and by 2012 it was already at a relatively low 13.9 percent.

And yet, in spite of these apparent economic changes, the dissatisfaction of many local Viequenses with the direction the island had taken in the post-Navy period was clearly palpable. This fact became particularly evident to us on March 31, 2009: on that date, the news reached Vieques (it was in the front page of all local newspapers) that the Republican congressman James Inhofe from Oklahoma had proposed that the Navy should return to Vieques, only six years after it had departed. Viequenses reacted to the news in different and interesting ways. Some took the proposition as a serious possibility, as sixty years of dealing with the Navy had taught them that anything is possible. "They have more tricks than Batman's belt" (*Tienen más trucos que el cinturón de Batman*) was the response of one of our informants. But what is interesting is the number of Viequenses who reacted, half-jokingly, by saying that they would welcome the return of the Navy; as though they had discovered that they were better off with the Navy than with the foreign tourism investors, mainly North Americans, who came after (Given that Vieques and Puerto Rico are unincorporated territories of the United States, North Americans residing on the island are not, technically speaking, foreigners. They are American citizens living in American territory. Nonetheless, Viequenses unequivocally refer to them as "foreigners" or *extranjeros.*). In any case, the comment should be taken, we believe, not so much as an indication of a true desire, but rather as a reflection of their deep dislike for the current situation.

The changes deriving from the introduction of tourism could be evidenced almost immediately after the departure of the Navy (and even before, since the decision to leave by 2003 was made public in 2001), and many of our informants publicly expressed the feeling that it took them by surprise: "No one ever thought that this would happen" (*nunca se pensó que esto iba a pasar*), or "I wasn't expecting this" (*no me lo esperaba*); were common responses from locals.

> I never thought Vieques would turn into these conditions . . . Vieques was not mentally and emotionally prepared for the exit of the Navy. I think that Vieques thought that it was . . . they thought, well, we'll go to the beach at two, and on Monday to work . . . And then, all of a sudden, this tourism process like crazy. This is crazy . . . I mean, I think we didn't assume the task of getting ready, together with the same intensity of the struggle [to get the Navy out], to foresee what Vieques would become now. We [Viequenses] are the marginalized in the island . . . I sincerely tell you, I think the people of Vieques never thought that, if the Navy left, this would be like it is. No. People form Vieques thought we would continue in that honey moon, bathing in the beach . . . No one ever thought that this would happen . . . Life hits you hard! (Activist Viequense #1)[1]
>
> I wasn't expecting this so much, when I saw the development [of tourism] after the Navy, and the Navy left and all of that . . . I was expecting that the unity [shown by Viequenses in their struggle to get the Navy out] would have been maintained, but one cannot feel it that strong. (Worker Viequense #7)[2]

The directness with which Viequenses express their complaints, with the tourism industry or any other issue, is in fact another legacy of the Navy. That is to say, that if the presence of the Navy in Vieques for a period of over sixty years helped delay the introduction of tourism development, it also helped produced a community "on the defense," and, in general terms, very active and vocal in community movements. Sixty years of struggle with the Navy has produced a legacy of community leaders and mobilization capacity that has continued to mark social life even after the departure of the Navy, and which now mobilizes against injustices resulting from the introduction of tourism. Thus, many Viequenses exhibit extraordinary abilities to defend their position vocally. Many of them are also highly articulate, and draw heavily from the terminology of civil rights, democracy and ecological movements. The Viequenses also exhibit strong attitudes of leadership. There is a high percentage of civilian participation in public hearings and community movements, and the Viequenses in general are very much informed of the events taking place in the island. One of our interviewees, an American waiter who has lived in Vieques for several years, commented on this combative attitude of the Viequenses: "Viequenses are great in that they are very in-tune with what's going on, and they are very protective of what they have" (Employee North American #5).

This particular combative trait of the Viequenses, to be sure, deepens its roots in a long history of community activism and struggle against the Navy. The legendary "David against Goliath" image[3] (of which much photographic evidence abound) of fishermen in 20-foot *yola* boats blocking the path of 130-foot US Navy ships, still remains vivid in the minds of the Viequenses. Evoking a long list of past and present leaders, one of our informants talked about Vieques as a "volcano" that may seem to remain dormant at times, but can erupt at any moment.

> Look, we return again to the same thing . . . You met . . . Ismael, and Carlos Zenon, and Prieto Ventura, and Roberto Rabin [all contemporary leaders]. But before us, we had an Adrián García that was "a man with hair in his chest."[4] We had here the three Emerizcos's brothers: Se, Adriano and Victor. We had here an Esaul Sánchez . . . [names several other leaders of the past] . . . These men had the courage of standing [on top of a small fisherman boat] right in front [of Navy ships]. That is the volcano that I'm telling you, that has always been here. (Activist Viequense #1)[5]

So, beyond the similarities that might exist between Vieques and other small Caribbean islands with tourism-based economies, Vieques is also unique in the sense that its inhabitants have endured a long history of participation in struggles and mobilizations, and tend to be very active and vocal in the defense of what they think should happen on the island. The long-held image of the Puerto Rican as "docile" and "on their knees" (*ñangotao*)[6] does not fit well with the Viequense character.

Thus, the large-scale introduction of tourism, combined with the struggles of the Viequenses to contain the negative effects of tourism, and the combative voice of the Viequenses resounding in the background conform the ethnographic context of our work.

LANGUAGE

But the voice of complaint of the Viequenses, as collected by us, was not only loud and combative, but also highly complex. The voice consisted of a multiplicity of positions, of arguments and counterarguments, carried out in a linguistic field abundant in empty signifiers, and where contradictions and paralogistic phrases were sometimes allowed. It was a voice begging for a radical exegesis—with emphasis not only on what the voice is truly attempting to say, but also on the unorthodox "forms" that are used to say it. It required an exploration into the linguistic strategies the subalterns employ to resist/accommodate injustice and make sense of their own condition, and into the broader Viequense/Puerto Rican language game in which these linguistic strategies are put into play. Attempting to decipher what exactly this voice is asking for, how it is asking for it, how it fails to get what it is asking for—and how it divagates after failing to get what it was asking for—is the main theoretical objective of this book.

Thus, on a theoretical level this book is about language or, more specifically, about the "pragmatics" of language in everyday usage. In this sense, it is distanced from other more mainstream approaches to the study of language which center almost exclusively on the "semantics" of language. Mikhail Bakhtin's distinction between the "unitary" and the "decentralizing tendencies in the life of language" is at the heart of the division between pragmatic-centered and semantic-centered approaches to the study of language.

> Philosophy of language, linguistics and stylistics [i.e., such as they have come down to us] have all postulated a simple and unmediated relation of speaker to his unitary and singular "own" language, and have postulated as well a simple realization of this language in the monologic utterances of the individual. Such disciplines actually know only two poles in the life of language, between which are located all the linguistic and stylistic phenomena they know: on the one hand, the system of a unitary language, and on the other the individual speaking in this language . . . This exclusive "orientation toward unity" in the present and past life of languages has concentrated the attention of philosophical and linguistic thought on the firmest, most stable, least changeable and most mono-semic aspects of discourse . . . that are furthest removed from the changing socio-semantic spheres of discourse. Real ideologically saturated "language consciousness," one that participates in actual heteroglossia and

multi-languagedness, has remained outside its field of vision. It is precisely this orientation toward unity that has compelled scholars to ignore all the verbal genres (quotidian, rhetorical, artistic-prose) that were the carriers of the decentralizing tendencies in the life of language, or that were in any case too fundamentally implicated in heteroglossia. (Bakhtin 1981: 269, 274)

Within the field of linguistic anthropology proper, Bakhtin's critique will find an echo in, for example, the work of linguistic anthropologist Laura A. Ahearn. In her *Living Language* (2011), Ahearn condemns the continuity of this orientation toward unity and fixed meanings in what she calls "the Chomskyan/Saussurean approach" to language that has dominated the field up to the present. Taking as point of departure the Saussurean distinction between *langue* (language as it should be properly spoken) and *parole* (language as it is spoken), the emphasis has traditionally centered on the formal study of *langue*, that is, on the rules and patterns of language, on fixed meanings and on what Chomsky will later call the "universal grammar" that is common to all human languages. Within the philosophy of language, the approach has its equivalent in the prevalent search for an "ideal language." In opposition to this approach, Ahearn instead proposes, following Bakhtin, a study of "living" language in real-life, socially charged contexts, where rules are often broken and where meaning is being constantly contested and negotiated. This book can be conceived as an attempt to follow Ahearn's invitation.

Thus, in documenting and analyzing the complaining and complex voice and language of the Viequenses in their multiple post-Navy struggles, emphasis is placed on "the decentralizing tendencies in the life of language," on its radically dialogical/relational nature, and on the conflict-ridden contexts in which it is produced. With this aim in mind, we draw from a terminology stemming from the works of ordinary-language philosophers and anthropologists like Wittgenstein, Derrida, Lyotard, Bakhtin or Ahearn: that is, living language, language games, family resemblance, phrases in dispute, *le différance*, the *differend*, heteroglossia, and so on. Particularly relevant among these terms is the Wittgenstenian concept of "language game," and deserves some explanation. Without attempting to underestimate the contributions of Wittgenstein to the philosophy of ordinary language, the usage that Wittgenstein gave to this term cannot be divorced from his interest in the truth-value of propositions, and his work never departed from the wider aim of helping philosophy find answers to key philosophical questions; and this is true for both the first and the second Wittgenstein (for those who wish to adhere to the idea of two Wittgensteins). Thus, when he spoke about "language games" and the "forms of life" which supports them, what he really had in mind was a community of speakers made up of philosophers or scientists, and not the type of human communities anthropologists usually encounter

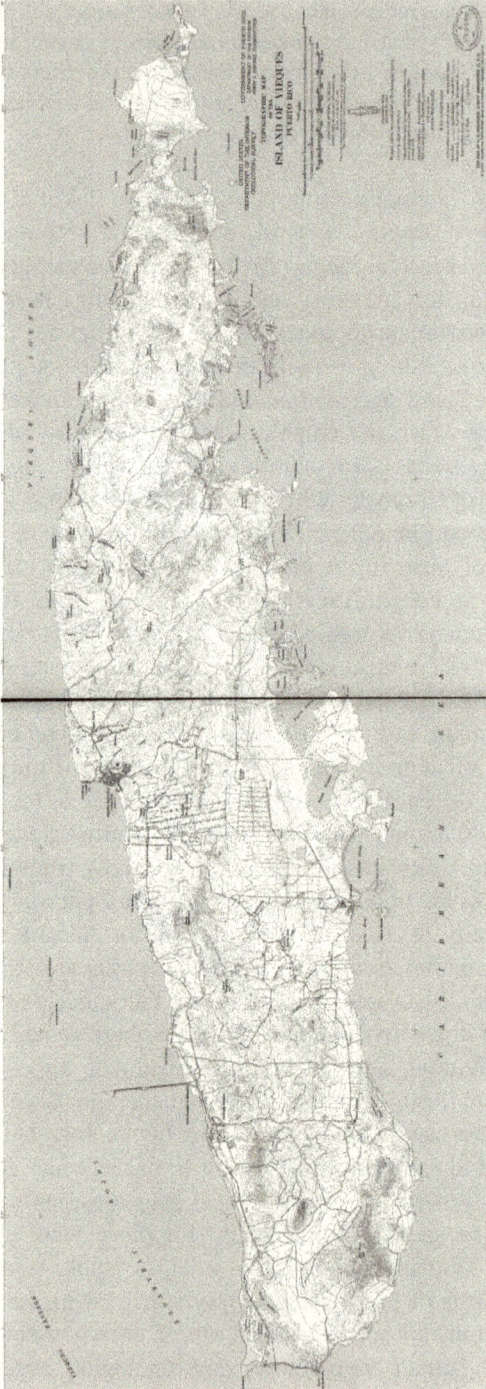

Figure I.1 Map of Vieques Island. *Source:* Geological Survey, U.S. Topographic map of the Island of Vieques, Puerto Rico. [Washington, DC: The Survey, 1951] Map. Retrieved from the Library of Congress, https://www.loc.gov/item/88693720/. (Accessed June 29, 2017).

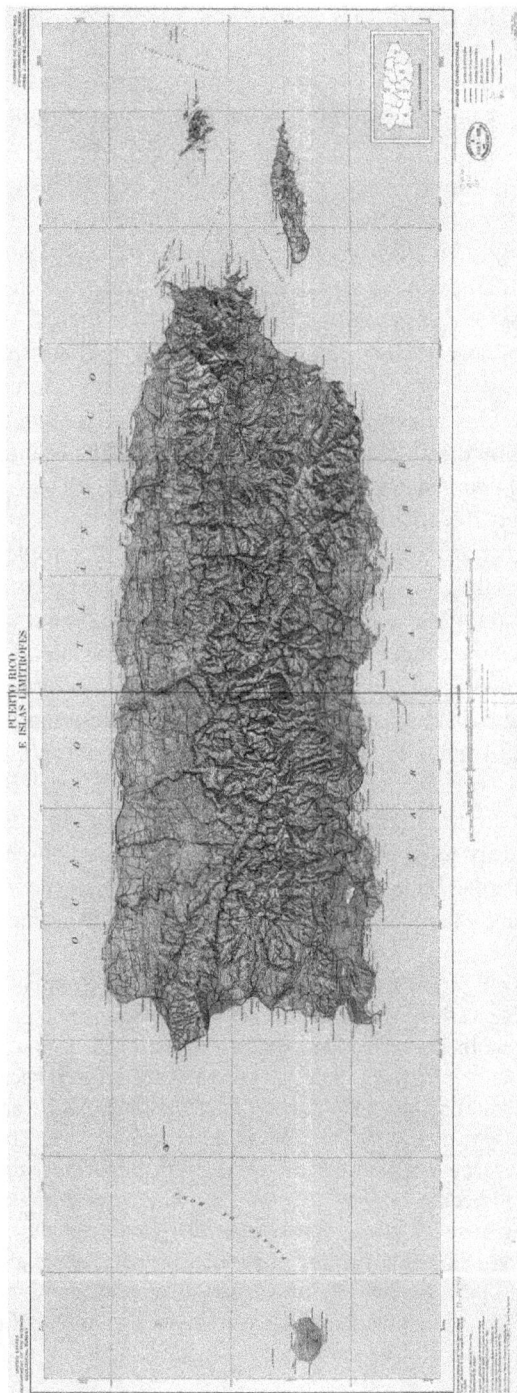

Figure I.2 Map of Puerto Rico and Surrounding Islands. *Source:* Geological Survey, U.S. Puerto Rico e islas limítrofes. [Washington, DC: El Survey; San Juan: Distribuido por el Gobierno de Puerto Rico, Departamento del Interior, 1952] Map. Retrieved from the Library of Congress, https://www.loc.gov/item/88693719/. (Accessed June 29, 2017).

in their fieldwork—and this is true despite the abundance of examples of made-up communities with exotic language games in his writings. Seen from the perspective of anthropological fieldwork, Wittgenstein's analysis holds to a too romantic and unproblematic view of human communities (i.e., the philosophical community), where linguistic exchanges are produced in contexts presumably free from external interferences, other than those stemming from the willingness and desires of two or more persons to understand each other correctly. It would be left to other ordinary-language philosophers (i.e., pragmatists, contextualists), and social scientists as well to, after Wittgenstein, assume the task of differentiating between the "semantics" of language (the study of meaning and truth-conditions of meaning) and the "pragmatics" of language (the study of meaning in used language); also to figure out how language games are played out in pragmatic- and conflict-ridden contexts; and to include within those pragmatic considerations the social fractures deriving from colonialism, slavery, racism and power struggles in general (cf. Recanati 2004; Burge 2007).

Our position on this issue is that all speech-acts are "heteroglossia," produced in "pragmatically" and "polemically" saturated contexts, and that it would be close to impossible, if not altogether impossible, to extract the pure meaning of any speech-act independent of "pragmatic" considerations. If this could be true for speech-acts produced within a community of philosophers or scientists (something we are skeptical about, as were Bakhtin and the second Wittgenstein), it would certainly not be true for the speech-acts collected by us in Vieques. In fact, we believe that, as the power struggles intensify, the meaning of speech-acts becomes harder and harder to understand. In this sense, the speech-acts collected by us in Vieques fit better the Lyotardian characterization of "phrases in dispute" than the one emerging from the more idyllic community of speakers and "language games" imagined by Wittgenstein.

A phrase "happens" . . . By its rule, a genre of discourse supplies a set of possible phrases, each arising from some phrase regimen. Another genre of discourse supplies another set of other possible phrases. There is a *différend* between these two sets (or between the genres that call them forth) because they are heterogeneous. And linkage must happen "now"; another phrase cannot not happen. It's a necessity; time, that is. There is no non-phrase . . . There is no last phrase. In the absence of a phrase regime or a genre of discourse that enjoys universal authority to decide, does not the linkage (whichever one it is) necessarily wrong the regimens or genres whose possible phrase remains unactualized? Problem: Given 1) the impossibility of avoiding conflict (the impossibility of indifference) and 2) the absence of a universal genre of discourse to regulate them (or, if you prefer, the inevitable partiality of the judge): to find, if not what can legitimate judgment . . . , then at least how to save the honor of thinking. (Lyotard 1988: xii)

And it will be in their attempt to "at least save the honor of thinking" that Viequenses/Puerto Ricans will take recourse to a complex language game where words no longer acquire their meaning simply through "family resemblance" (as was for the second Wittgenstein), but behave more like what Iris Marion Young has called "unruly categories" (1998).

In the end, it is hoped that the adoption of a "living language" approach to the case of Vieques will help us show what happens to language when it loses its capacity to carry and transmit meaning, when the "ideal" functions of language are obstructed by unequal power relations, losing its ability to "speak" in the proper sense of the term. It will help us argue, with Gayatri Spivak, that "the subaltern cannot speak" (1994). In post-Navy Vieques, we will argue, a combination of factors—colonialism, racism, the history of slavery, language barriers, tourism and neoliberalism—will conspire to make the voice of the Viequense a muted one. In this period, Viequenses will discover that the structures that prevents their voice from being heard in the post-Navy period are as strong and imposing, if not stronger and more imposing, than the ones that were in place during the 1941–2003 period.

Now, in claiming that the subalterns "cannot speak" we do not mean to say (and neither did Spivak) that they do not physically speak—in fact, they speak, and speak a lot. It only means that the circle of communication has been severed, and therefore they will not be listened to. Even while the voice of the Viequense (as we have recorded it) is a salient, combative voice, a voice with a complaint, a voice claiming for justice and marked by a desire for recognition and respect, it will not be listened to. Nonetheless, the voice will be uttered, and it will be uttered because language is the only recourse the people have left, the last tool of resistance, to express their complaints, even if their complaints will not transcend the sphere of colloquial or ordinary language, and even when nobody will listen to them. When every other attempt to be listened to has failed, people still have language itself, language for the sake of language, simply because it is possible. And even if, as Spivak has suggested, the conversation would look like a conversation between Robinson Crusoe and Friday, the conversation *faux de mieux* will take place. What we record is precisely this conversation.

METHODOLOGICAL NOTE

In order to preserve the anonymity of our informants and interviewees we have used pseudonyms. In quotations, we have identified them by their place of origin (North American, European, Puerto Rican, Viequense, etc.), and by their role in the community (i.e., activists, employers, employees, etc.), and finally by a number. Informed consent was obtained from all interviewees. (See chapter 3, footnote 2 for additional information on the subjects interviewed.)

NOTES

1. Translated from Spanish. Original statement reads: "Yo nunca pensé que Vieques se iba a poner en estas condiciones . . . Vieques no estaba preparado mentalmente y emocionalmente para cuando la Marina saliera. Yo creo que Vieques pensó . . . se pensó, pues, los domingos pa' la playa a las dos, y el lunes a trabajar. Y llegó de momento un proceso turístico a lo loco. Esto es a lo loco . . . O sea, yo creo que no asumimos la visión de prepararnos, junto con esa misma lucha intensa, para ver lo que iba a ser el Vieques ahora. Y nosotros somos los marginados en la isla . . . Yo sinceramente te digo, yo creo que el de Vieques no pensaba que, si la Marina salía, esto iba a ser así. No. Los de Vieques pensamos que íbamos a seguir de luna de miel, metiditos en las playas . . . Nunca se pensó que esto iba a pasar . . . La vida da unos cantazos." All interviews conducted in Spanish, and quoted in this book, were translated into English by the author.

2. Translated from Spanish. Original statement reads: "Eso no me lo esperaba yo tanto, cuando vi desarrollar después de la Marina, y se fue la Marina y todo eso, yo me esperaba que hubieran mantenido una unidad, que no se nota tanto."

3. The metaphor of Goliath against David is taken from Humberto García Muñiz's article by the same name. See García Muñiz 2001.

4. Puerto Rican expression, implying bravery and manliness.

5. Translated from Spanish. Original statement reads: "Mire, es que volvemos a lo mismo . . . Ustedes conocieron a Pupa, a Ismael, a Carlos Zenón, a Prieto Ventura, Roberto Rabin. Pero antes que nosotros: aquí había un Adrián García que era un hombre de pelo en pecho. Aquí estaban los tres hermanos Emerizco: Se, Adriano y Victor. Aquí estaba un Esaul Sánchez. Que antes que nosotros, antes que la prensa, esos hombres tenían la valentía de pararse ahí al frente [de los barcos de la Marina]. Ese era el volcán que yo le digo, que eso siempre estuvo ahí."

6. The definitions of Puerto Ricans as "docile" (*dócil*) and "on their knees" (*ñangotao*) are contained in two canonical texts produced by Puerto Rican intellectuals: *Insularism* by Antonio Pedreira (2001[1934]); and *The docile Puerto Rican* by René Marqués (1977[1962]). The controversy and debate generated by these two texts lingers on well into the present.

Chapter 1

Tourism

Although Vieques already had a small tourism industry before 2003, the number of new hotel rooms available in the island more than doubled during the decade-long period from 2003 to 2015. By the end of this period, Vieques had approximately 500 hotel rooms, plus a 156-room W Resort (a luxury line of hotels owned by the Starwood chain), and 88 rental villas—as well as multiple restaurants, bars, car-rentals, diving and souvenir shops, and so on.[1] The number of tourists visiting the island (measured by the people traveling by ferryboat alone) increased from approximately 500,000 to 1.2 million during the same period. Also the number of residential tourists more than doubled, from 236 to 526 between 2000 and 2010.[2]

But the model of development that evolved after 2003, or at least the one that was the cause of much social conflict, was the model of residential tourism (also often referred to as "second-home tourism"). This is due to the fact that the attractiveness Vieques had as a tourist destination (at that historical conjunction) differed significantly from that of the other more common tourism destinations studied by researchers. Vieques, for example, has no important "heritage" site, no exotic indigenous population, no autochthonous artisanal products or elements of material culture to be commercialized and no major cultural distinctiveness of touristic relevance (other than Puerto Rican culture). It does have, as one of its major touristic attractions, one of the seven bioluminescent bays in the world (discussed later). But its attractiveness for tourists in the years following 2003 derived not only from its warm and sunny climate (and its beautiful beaches) but also from the fact that it was relatively unspoiled—the last virgin territory in the Caribbean—and that the land was relatively inexpensive. The island became an attractive option for retirees who were seeking a place with warm weather in order to reside either permanently or seasonally. It became particularly attractive to North

American investors, given the fact that the land they were buying was "within their own country," and bought with American dollars.

Thus, the type of tourism that developed in Vieques after 2003, while sharing some similarities with the "sun and sand" model of other tourism destinations around the Caribbean and elsewhere, fits best the model of "second-home" or "residential" tourism model. More specifically, it responds to what Müller has defined as an "international mobility [of retired persons] from the north to the sunbelts of North America and Europe" (2011: 390). It is a phenomenon that commenced in the 1990s, and that only threatens to increase in the coming decades, as a massive generation of baby-boomers approach retirement age; and their migratory movement toward the tropics threatens to follow the route already established by their predecessors. It is estimated that by 2050 the US population over sixty-five years of age will total approximately 83.7 million people, up from 43.1 million in 2012 (Ortman et al. 2014).

Research on the phenomenon of residential tourism, and specifically on the migration of retired persons, has had a disharmonious existence within the field of tourism studies, up to the point where researchers have not yet agreed upon a proper name for the subfield. While many researchers prefer the name of "second-home tourism," others believe that the concept is inadequate to describe this growing mobility among retired householders because, as Müller has stated, in these cases "they may constitute true first homes," or because "'second-home' ownership sometimes represent a pre-stage to permanent migration" (2011: 388, 390). The phenomenon is also different from that of "weekend homes," since the geographical place of the second home is often far removed and in a different country, from the place of the first home or country of origin. The alternative concept of "residential tourism" is increasingly being used, but is also considered inadequate by some. Torres Bernier (2003), for example, has argued that the concept is "paradoxical," as a resident is not a tourist. Müller has also suggested that the reason why "second-home tourism has attracted only limited attention . . . [is] possibly . . . due to second home being considered at the edge of what is regarded as tourism," since the concept of "tourist" implies (presumably) that the visit to the host destination will be of short duration. In fact, the phenomenon of residential tourism falls outside Smith's 1978 canonical definition, broadly accepted in the field, of a tourist as "a temporarily leisured person who voluntarily visits a place away from home for the purpose of experiencing change" (1989[1978]: 2). It also falls outside the definition of tourism adopted by the World Trade Organization (WTO), according to which "Tourism is a set of activities engaged by persons temporarily away from their usual environment for a period of not more than a year" (WTO 1994). Additional terms have been proposed—"retirement tourism," "lifestyle migration"—but as yet there is no term that is universally accepted within the discipline of tourism studies to define this particular tourism niche.

Nonetheless, the phenomenon was documented as early as the late 1970s (Coppock 1977; Boschken 1975), although it was mainly during the mid- to late 1990s that it began receiving increased attention in the literature (Kaltenborn 1997, 1998; Müller 1999, 2002, 2004; Hall and Müller 2004; King and Paterson 1998; King, Warnes and Williams 2000; Buller and Hoggart 1994; Warnes 1994; William, King and Warnes 1997; William and Hall 2002; Casado-Díaz 1999, 2006; Casado-Díaz et al. 2004; Benson & O'Reilly 2009; Wong & Musa 2015; Aledo 2008; Aledo et al. 2012; Mazón y Aledo 2005; Shucksmith 1983). In the context of the Americas, the creation of communities of residential tourists has been also well documented throughout the Central American and Caribbean region—in places like Guanacaste, Costa Rica (van Noorloos 2011a, 2011b, 2013), in Pipa, Brazil (Aledo et al. 2013), in Boquete and Bocas del Toro, in Panama (Benson 2013, 2015; Myers 2009; McWatters 2009; Jackiewicz & Craine 2010; Spalding 2013) and throughout several islands within the region (Guerrón Montero 2011)—in a process defined by Müller as "rural gentrification" (2004: 393).

In general, several patterns of this second-home or residential tourism phenomenon emerge from these various cases: it creates jobs, but mostly in the construction business, and at the expense of other traditional economic activities; the guests create an enclosed "lifestyle" community, often of members from the same nationality, and have limited contact with the local population; the relation between host and guests is made problematic because of language differences, or the disruption of long-established social norms, and so on. But, above everything, it is the increasing value of the land that seems to have a particularly detrimental effect on the local community, who then lack the economic resources to acquire new land (Coppock 1977; Gallent and Tewdwr-Jones 2000). As Müller explains, "The concerns usually focus on the exclusion of the local population as a result of the increase in property prices produced by second home demand, particularly when it is perceived that local young families are unable to purchase a property" (2004: 392–393). As we will attempt to show, many of the detrimental effects associated with the phenomenon of "residential tourism" will replicate in Vieques in almost exact manner.

Thus, the type of tourism that developed in Vieques during the first decade after the departure of the Navy was related to this phenomenon of residential tourism, and it was particularly at (or about) this community of "residential tourists" that Viequenses speak when they raise their voice in protest. In fact, Viequenses in general don't seem to have a problem with the few short-term, "overnight" tourists who visit the island, and even seem to enjoy their presence—as if the "seduction of difference" that Picard and Di Giovine (2014) speak about worked both ways within the host-guest relation. We will attempt to show that the same will not be true about their relation with residential tourists.

Thus, despite the dispute about whether these foreigners are best considered as "residents" or "tourists," in our research context it would have been impossible to erase these "residents" as integral part of what one could call the tourism package, or as important actors in the broad social dynamics that evolves along tourism development.

THE DIVISION BETWEEN HOSTS AND GUESTS

Another major dichotomous polarity cutting across the tourism research field (beyond that of resident/tourist) is that of host/guest. Thus, while much of the early anthropological works on tourism focused on the host community, and on the effects of tourism on host communities, the past decades have witnessed a significant interest on the tourist as the main subject of research. At least since the publication of MacCannell's *The Tourist* (1976), much effort has been devoted to understanding the tourists from a "phenomenological" perspective: exploring their motivations for embarking on tourist trips, their search for "authentic" experiences, their inclinations to be seduced by "difference" and by "otherness," their "gaze" or sensory-visual experiences, the "liminal" and "pilgrimage-like" quality of their traveling, their consumption habits, their "practices and performances" and so on (Cohen 1979; Picard and Di Giovine 2014; Pearce 1993; Urry 1990; Graburn 1977; Wearing, Stevenson and Young 2010; Bruner 2005; Gmelch 2010[2004]; Crouch 2004). Because of their phenomenological orientations, this interest in the tourist translates, as Leite and Graburn have pointed out, into "more interpretivist than political-economic paradigms in recent years" (2011: 35). Even when the relation between "guest" and "host" has been explored, it has often been done with an interest in the former, or often based on very casual and short-timed encounters in places like markets or tours (Evans-Pritchard 1989; Salazar 2012; Greenwood 1989; Crouch et al. 2001). On the contrary, the type of encounters and interactions between hosts and guests that we witnessed in Vieques differed drastically from these short and casual encounters, as residential tourists have a continued presence in the island, and often engage in day-to-day interaction with the local population.

A more insightful view of the host/guess dynamics can be found in language-centered approaches to the study of tourism. This is also true of the literature focused on language-related phenomena like "imaginaries," "discourses," "regimes of truth" or "the hegemonic." What is insightful in this literature is that, even when they center their interests on "the tourist," there is always a recognition that the tourist's speech acts and discourses are always framed as "responses" or "contestations" to other discourses with which they have entered in dispute, and with which they are engaged in a "dialectical" or "dialogical" relation inside a "hermeneutic cycle"—inside what Di Giovine has called "the field of touristic production" (Salazar 2010, 2012, 2014; Salazar and Graburn 2014; Di Giovine 2014; Thurlow and Jaworski 2010, 2011; Aledo et al. 2013; Graburn and Gravari-Barbas 2012; Bruner 2005; Hall-Lew and Lew 2014; Moeran 1983; Gmelch and Moeran 2004). Language and the imaginary, thus, will provide the models (the master metaphors) for a new conception of the social field as multiple and fluid, forcing us at the same time to avoid producing essentialist accounts of the cultures we study. Given the complexity of the topics discussed by these researchers, as well as the relevance that their arguments have to our own work in Vieques, we have decided to explore it in greater detail later in the book, that is, along the discussions that emerge from our empirical findings in Vieques, as well as in a separate chapter (chapter 4). It will suffice to say here that the findings and interpretations of these authors greatly coincide with our own findings and interpretations of the Vieques data, and set the agenda for an anthropology of tourism sensitive to the heteroglossic dimensions of the imaginaries and discourses within the "field of touristic production."

In either case, and as Stronza has pointed out, too much emphasis on understanding either the host or the guest (one or the other) "has left us with [only] half explanations" (2001: 262). "Missing from many current analyses," Stronza will complain, "is an attempt to learn more about the dynamic of host-guest interactions by observing and talking with people on both sides of the encounter" (2001: 272). We, on the contrary, have attempted to look at both hosts and guests in their daily encounters, and to interpret their discourses and actions in their relational character, where they constitute and reconstitute each other through dialogical interaction; or, to put it in linguistic terms, as participants in a conversation between themselves, and where every speech-act is produced as a response to the other's phrase-regime with which it has entered "in dispute."

THE DIVISION BETWEEN POSITIVE AND NEGATIVE ASSESSMENTS OF TOURISM

In his review of the literature on tourism published for the past four decades, Simoni has also noticed a marked differentiation—a "black and white pendulum" (2013: 40)—between positive and negative assessments of tourism. Regarding positive assessments, many have seen in tourism development a "panacea," an ideal economic project that not only reduces poverty, but also fosters intercultural understanding and, as such, can become the foundation of a more inclusive society. It is in this sense, for example, that Burtner and Castañeda speak of tourism as a possible "force for world peace."

> Tourism as "a force for world peace" ignites the imagination of many, from Popes and presidents to academics. . . . In general there are two aspects or assumptions to this idea. First, travel brings people together in host-guest relations that foster understandings of cultural differences, goodwill, and the desire to peacefully overcome local and world problems. Second, tourism development is itself a positive force that addresses poverty, underdevelopment, conflicts, etc., by developing economic opportunities and growth for marginalized communities. Tourism thus reduces the grounds for violence, hate, discrimination, and aggression. (Burtner and Castañeda 2010)

Martha Honey has also outlined a long list of the multiple benefits that are claimed to be derived (or that can be derived) from sustainable models of tourism, and more specifically from ecotouristic models, along the same line:

> Around the world, ecotourism has been hailed as a panacea: a way to fund conservation and scientific research, protect fragile and pristine ecosystems, benefit rural communities, promote development in poor countries, enhance ecological and cultural sensitivity, instill environmental awareness and social conscience in the travel industry, satisfy and educate the discriminating tourist, and, some claim, build world peace. (Honey 2008: 4)

But it has been mainly the added element of global cultural interaction—that is an inevitable and constitutive part of the touristic experience—that has led many researchers to view tourism development in more positive terms and that has pushed the debate about tourism development to follow a somewhat different path from the path followed by the debate about development in general, where epithets like "collective delusion," "discourse fantasy," or "nightmare" are the norm (Rist 2013; Escobar 1995; Ferguson 1994; Sen 2000). Sach's general assessment of development efforts, made in 1996, is illustrative of this tendency within development studies even to this day: "The idea of development stands like a ruin in the intellectual landscape. Delusion and disappointment, failures and crimes have been the steady companions of development and they all tell a common story: it did not work" (1996: 1).

While there is a general agreement among contemporary researchers that development projects (tourism-based or otherwise) have the potential to impoverish and harm the people it originally intended to help, and that there is an ample list of examples where this indeed has happened, researchers of tourism have also been able to point to cases where tourism development—under the banner of "alternative tourism development," or "ecotourism," or "pro-poor tourism," or "tourism revitalization processes" (cf. Telfer 2009; Hunter and Green 1995; Hughes 1995; Little 1996)—has been beneficial to all the stakeholders or actors involved, including the host community. Stronza (2001) and Honey (2008), for example, have recognized the success of ecologically based tourism models, or "ecotourism"; that is, a model based on "a set of principles" that include extending the economic benefits of tourism to both land conservation and the local community, and recognizing "the participation of local residents [as] critical to maximizing the economic, environmental, and social benefits of tourism" (Stronza 2001: 278). But, as Honey warns, the path of ecotourism is "the road less travelled" within tourism development, and "genuine ecotourism is hard to find"; although one can find "some excellent examples in the field" (2008: 6, 33). Michael Di Giovine has also documented examples of tourism development where the "betterment" of all the parties or stakeholders involved has been achieved, like Hội An, Việt Nam (2009a) and Pietrelcina, in Italy (2009b; 2010); although he would also warn that "the road was not direct, nor was it terribly easy for locals" (2009a: 212). In these cases, Di Giovine argues, the key to success was the adoption of a model of tourism development guided by what he calls a "revitalization paradigm."

The concept of "revitalization," as used by Di Giovine, "does not reject 'the concept of development,' but rather reveals an alternative conceptualization" of it (2010: 274). It does reject, though, traditional paradigms of modernization and development, mainly on the grounds that they "deprive local actors of any agency" (2009a: 212). The revitalization paradigm, on the contrary, attempts to be a more equitable, sustainable, participatory model of development, based on "the contention that the primary resource which governments and tourism practitioners must manage is local 'goodwill'" (2009a: 39); and therefore focused on the empowerment of locals and on poverty alleviation" (2010: 273).

> Tourism development suffers from an unforeseen clash of cultures in its very approach—a clash which is often subtle, and which threatens to marginalize those to whom the initiatives are intended to help. It seems that what is needed . . . is an alternative paradigm . . . [one that] call upon, and valorize, locals' traditional worldviews. (Di Giovine 2009a: 218)

But the irony of the situation is that, alongside these positive evaluations of tourism development—even if only because tourism development projects are seen as more friendly to the environment and economically beneficial to the community than other realistically available alternatives—the literature is also abundant in negative assessments and critiques of tourism. In fact, much of the early anthropological studies of tourism adopted a critical stance toward tourism, and prepared the road for further critical analyses (Martínez Mauri 2010). Burtner and Castañeda, for example, have pointed out how "anthropologists began the study of tourism proclaiming tourism as a form of neocolonialism that creates dependency of developing countries, increases poverty in Third World nations, and corrupts and disauthenticates native cultures via commodification" (2010: 16). Crang has also argued that early anthropological approaches to tourism were dominated by what he has called an "erosion thesis," under which tourism was positioned "as a problem, as something that homogenizes local cultures towards one undifferentiated aggregate . . . where change is seen only as diminishing original cultures and reducing global difference" (2004: 74). Much in the same vein, Leite and Graburn have argued that the:

> Central concern in early ethnographic works on tourism . . . explored the "impacts" on social, cultural and environmental aspects of the so-called "host community." . . . Many of these studies assumed that tourist destinations in the "global South"—viewed as the powerless, the poor, the colonized—were reacting to overwhelming outside pressures from the rich metropolitan North . . . [;] and that the tourist presence was the active vector of change, with the local population a passive recipient whose traditional lifeways were irreparably altered. (Leite and Graburn 2011: 40)

To be sure, one of the problems with these early negative assessments of tourism has to do with its one-sided vision, centered on the structural aspects of the tourism industry, but paying little attention to the agency of the local subjects, to the forms adopted by the local populations to resist/accommodate these imposed structures (cf. Baldacchino 1997). It is perfectly legitimate and valid to develop a critique of the structure, whether it is the structure of tourism industry or those of neoliberalism and free market globalization; something which, in fact, has already been done by others ad nauseam. But keeping the critique at an exclusive structural level would evade the set of questions which are of relevance to us here, and to the discipline of anthropology in general: what are local populations doing to resist and adapt to these global/structural processes? How are they exerting some degree of agency in earning subsistence and in their construction of moral boundaries? What are they saying and doing about their own condition? How are they being transformed by the process?

Be that as it may, and as Simoni has argued, what emerges from a review of the literature on tourism development is the continued coexistence of positive and negative assessments side by side, with a balance of (in appearance) contradictory findings, and where it becomes difficult to determine if the benefits of tourism development outweigh the harms, or the opposite. Simoni has summarized the status of the debate as of 2013, as it emerges from the literature, in the following terms:

> On the one hand, touristic encounters and relationships appeared to be fraught by striking inequalities, highly deceptive, and a constant source of misunderstanding and reciprocal exploitation. On the other hand, they seemed to hold the promise of mutual understanding, and the establishment of positive connections between people from around the globe, notably across the North-South divide. Touristic encounters were thus said to constitute a realm of 'mere illusion' and 'make believe association,' a 'parody of human relationships' . . . where deception and exploitation prevail. Alternatively, they were portrayed as the "building block for global peace and cultural understanding . . . bringing ordinary men and women from around the world into contact with one another," and thus helping "dispel the myths, stereotypes and caricatures that often hold sway from a distance." (Simoni 2013: 39–40)

Now, in Simoni's view, the division between positive and negative assessments of tourism can be explained as resulting from misunderstandings and misinterpretations of the subjects under study, which in turn are a product of the superficial empirical grounding of much of the research done. In other words, precisely because the discourses produced by the research subjects in their ordinary usage of language (in "living" language) is often ambivalent, or heteroglossic, incorporating multiple perspectives (even contradictory) at once—that "counter univocal readings" (Simoni 2013: 52), in the face of which "we should resist the impulse to find coherence at all cost" (Simoni 2013: 51)—then, one same discourse (when only explored superficially) can serve to empirically support both positive and negative assessments of the development process simultaneously. Given this paradoxical situation, the final decision as to which type of assessment will be made (positive or negative) rests on "taken for granted idealizations," "generalizations" and "clear-cut aprioristic judgements" of the researchers themselves (consciously or unconsciously). "Thus," says Simoni, "it becomes possible to understand why touristic encounters are being assessed in contrasting, and often paradoxical, ways" (2013: 51).

But the core problem with this duality between positive and negative assessments of development, as Simoni recognizes, is related to the superficial way in which empirical data is being collected. Consequently, the only way to overcome this duality is by incorporating more in-depth and detailed observations and descriptions of host/guest encounters and interactions.

> These [contrasting] perspectives do not appear to enhance our understanding of how these encounters and relationships emerge and develop *in situ*. Instead, they run the risk of reiterating in a rather un-reflexive manner taken for granted

idealizations (when a naive stance predominates) and critiques (once cynicism prevails). The main problem is that such generalizations too often rely on deductive assumptions and clear-cut aprioristic judgments, without paying enough attention the understandings of research participants and their competing claims. In trying to counter simplistic assessments of touristic encounters, my work builds on Malcolm Crick's observation that "[t]he question of what sort of social relationships grow up in tourism encounters can only be answered by detailed and descriptive studies." (Simoni 2013: 40)

Moreover, while gathering detailed and descriptive empirical data will allow us to transcend the positive/negative assessments' dispute, it will not solve the dispute in favor of one or the other position, Simoni further warns, but will simply help show the difficulties behind claiming a "correct" and "final" interpretation of it, given its "plurality, processual character, and generative potentials" (2013: 41). Thus, what detailed and empirically grounded research will reveal (and what our own fieldwork reveals) is the existence of a plural and multivocal voice, whose complex internal nature cannot be easily reduced to a coherent whole.

From the moment that our ethnographies take us in the variety of contexts and spheres of interaction that make up a person's life, the experiences of our research participants, their claims and actions, seem to counter univocal readings, and call instead for a plurality of interpretations. (Simoni 2013: 52)

In the end, attempting to go beyond the positive/negative assessments' dispute requires not only increased engagement with our subjects of research, but also, and perhaps more important, a revision of our notions of "intentionality" and "agency" in the interpretation of our subjects' discourses and actions. It will require, as Aledo et al. have argued, a recognition that "the rationality of the social agents is limited and multiple . . . [that] their interests are not rationally predetermined nor . . . formulated in conscious manner . . . [or that] they express themselves through varied cognitive and discursive means" (2013: 8).[3] The challenge, then, is to be able to portray the reality one encounters as faithfully as possible, but without erasing its complex internal diversity and plurality.

NOTES

1. Based on the informal inventory taken from information gathered through different sources, including tourist guides and the internet. Inventory was taken in 2014.

2. According to data from the Puerto Rican Tourism Company, Vieques registered an increase in hotels and hostels occupancy rate during the post-Navy period. The

occupancy rate went from 47.1 percent in 2003 to close or above the 50 percent mark for the period 2004–2008 (with a high-peak of 54.6 percent in 2005 and a low-peak of 49.2 percent in 2006). In 2008, after the US financial crisis, the occupancy rate dropped sharply to 44.5 percent in 2009 and 39.2 percent in 2010, returning to levels above 50 percent in 2011 and afterward (53.7 percent in 2011 and 52.5 percent in 2012). In any case, this information is based on a very small and statistically unrepresentative number of hotels registered as "paradores" within the Tourism Company, and real numbers are with all probability significantly higher. See *Caribbean Business* "Vieques tourism surging in FY 2012" (March 16, 2012): http://caribbeanbusinesspr.com/news03.php?nt_id=68832&ct_id=1.

3. Translated from Spanish. Original text reads: "encubre una cierta concepción utilitarista del individuo . . . Es importante recordar que la racionalidad de los agentes sociales es limitada y múltiple. Sus intereses no están predeterminados racionalmente ni tampoco se formulan de forma consciente . . . se expresan por medios cognitivos y discursos variados (Aledo 2013: 8).

Chapter 2

Land

The impact of tourism on land resources is almost always problematic; the case is particularly true of small islands like Vieques, where land scarcity is already imposed by geographical accident. The only thing differentiating Vieques from other small Caribbean islands with tourism economies is that, as stated earlier, in Vieques the introduction of tourism was delayed, when compared to the rest of the islands, by a period of approximately forty years.

The departure of the Navy in 2003 unleashed what economic journalist Miguel Díaz Román labeled a "speculation bacchanal" (*bacanal especulativa*) or "real-estate *boom*" (*boom inmobiliario*) (2013: 26): hundreds of wealthy North American investors and residential tourists flooded the island with the intention of buying and speculating with land, offering Viequenses "irresistible" quantities of money for their houses and properties. This in turn caused a series of "land rescuing" movements led by locals, and fueled by the conviction, in the locals' minds, that "Americans want to take over Vieques," or the fear that soon Vieques will become an island without Viequenses:

Americans want to take over Vieques. A Viequense has a house, sells it, they go and spend the money, and return broke. The thing is that they are dumb. We Puerto Ricans are dumb. (Worker Viequense #12)[1]

There is also a certain feeling that they are losing the island a little bit, and that things are reaching a level where they will not be able to do anything, that they will not be able to compete unless something radical happens, which is scary but the truth. That has happened in other islands. People from Vieques, and from Puerto Rico in general, have to return to Culebra also . . . the fact that, let's say, they should have made some sort of history of Caribbean islands, so that you see how many things repeat themselves, and they are going to make the same errors, and that one thing . . . pap, pap, pap . . . [while snapping fingers] one thing leads to another. (Worker Viequense #7)[2]

In the long run they are going to take us out, little by little they are going to
take us out. What are we going to do? We leave the island to the gringos, "buy
everything and you stay." No, shit, let them go to hell! (Worker Viequense #1)[3]

Perhaps the best way to measure the intensity with which the speculation
bacchanal took place is by the drastic increase in the value of land registered
throughout the period, as measured by actual sales. Based on conversations
with local Viequense businessmen, Díaz Román suggested an increase of
3,000 percent for the period 2003–2012. Díaz Román's calculations are,
though, based on the two biggest (and most talked about) sales for the period
2003–2012: an eight-acre plot in Puerto Real sold for $800,000 (precisely
$100,000 per acre); and a villa in Martineau Bay Resort sold for $1.5 million
(see Díaz Román 2013: 26). Before the Navy left, the general, standard price
for an acre of land in Vieques was three thousand dollars. Thus, it presumably went from 3,000 to 100,000 dollars almost immediately. But Díaz
Román's calculations are based on sales that are not representative of the
more common residence market. Our own calculations, based on a sample
of forty-seven actual sales that took place in the period between 2003 and
2009, revealed an increase of 318 percent,[4] which is probably a more accurate
estimate for regular homes.

Several factors can account for the intensity with which the sales occurred
(and continue to occur) and the absurdity of the prices being paid for land
during the "speculation bacchanal." The departure of the Navy was indeed
an influential factor, as was the natural beauty of the island and its beaches.
Moreover, with two-thirds of the island already declared a wildlife refuge,
and with most of the beautiful beaches that the tourists frequent located
within that wildlife refuge, the preservation of that pristine state for these
two-thirds of the island is guaranteed for many years to come. Any overdevelopment that could potentially take place in Vieques will be restricted
exclusively to the one-third of the island reserved for civilian population.
Finally, one additional factor leading to the "speculation bacchanal" comes
from the fact that Vieques is a US territory, and is thus more attractive to
North American investors in comparison with other non-US small Caribbean
islands. In Vieques they are investing, after all, *inside their own country*.

The same is true for the several other small US islands/possessions in the
Caribbean, like Culebra and the US Virgin Islands (including St. Thomas,
St. John and St. Croix). Yet Vieques, in contrast with all these other US
Caribbean territories, experienced the real-estate boom much later, and the
contrast between them is evident, at least in the eyes of our interviewees and
informants. Vieques is thus seen (by both locals and foreigners) as the last
US Caribbean enclave that remains underdeveloped, and Culebra, St. Thomas
and St. John the models, in people's minds, of what extreme overdevelopment

is—a peek at what Vieques might look like in the near future. The rationale behind investing on land in Vieques, as it exists in the minds of foreign investors, was explained to us by an informant in the following terms:

> [Vieques is] the last US territory in the Caribbean that is available. St. Thomas and St. John are just full-up, and it's expensive. And then you have the fact written that, in the next ten years some 70 million Americans are going to retire. . . . So I see that they are either going to go to Central America, anywhere in a half a dozen places down there, or they are going to go to the Caribbean. And like I said: St. John is way too expensive, over there, and St. Thomas is what it is. . . . I wouldn't want to live over there, because being in Charlotte Amalie with 35 thousand people on a day . . . and there's a lot of crime there too. (Employer North American #4)[5]

In any case, stories about actual cases of sales were abundant in our interviews. The structure of these stories was always the same: a Viequense sold his or her property to a North American for a given amount, and in a few years the North American was able to resell the property for an amount three or four times over the buying rate. In all estimates, the increases reported in actual cases tended to reflect an increase of between 300 and 500 percent (which is close to our own estimate of 318 percent).

> Well, where I live, the guy, an American, he bought the house in $193,000, seven or eight years ago, 193 thousand *pesos* [Puerto Ricans indistinctively use *dolar* or *peso* to refer to the US dollar], in the beach in Bravos de Boston, and the house is now worth 1 million *pesos*, only because it is beach-front. The guy made the deal of a lifetime. He bought it for 193 thousand pesos, and the guy who bought the house before him, he also was an American also, that bought it for even less than that. (Worker Viequense #1)

> Look, that house was bought in [19]96 for 125 thousand pesos, to the inheritors of Don Vigilio Ortiz. That one over there [pointing to another house] . . . in 2000 it was sold for 485 thousand. Now it is worth 1.4 million dollars. The guy in the corner [pointing to yet another house], he is from Vieques, he is selling for 3 million pesos. My neighbor from up here, the house immediately after ours, sold for 1.1 million pesos. But because I, I have never seen a 500 dollar bill . . . This other one [pointing to another house] is stuck in court. He has not been able to collect. But in here everybody is selling like crazy. LIKE CRAZY! (Other Viequense #1)[6]

While many Viequenses were tempted to sell but didn't, many others actually did sell. And yet, the lives of those who sold and left the island were never mentioned in our interviews. A huge portion of those people who did sell were people who, as one informant described them, "had never seen a 500 dollars bill" and suddenly saw themselves with hundreds of thousands of dollars deposited in their hands. What have they done with the money and with their lives? Did they leave Vieques? Did they squander all the money and are now houseless and broke? Are they happy with their new lives? If they could turn back time, would they sell again? One thing is for sure: while many of the Viequenses who sold undoubtedly benefited from real-estate boom prices, many Viequenses who did not sell still feel that these foreign investors actually took advantage of them, since they were then able to resell for even higher prices.

> Because, you know, never ever we thought that in Bravos de Boston properties could be worth 500 thousand pesos, 1 million pesos, because of the beach, you know . . . because the beach is everywhere here, you know. We never thought that the land was worth that much. But in the eyes of the Americans it was worth more than what we wanted. And basically they took advantage of the fact that we were ignorant and didn't know the value of the land, and they bought from us all they could. (Worker Viequense #1)[7]

In any case, the intensity the "speculation bacchanal" reached can also be evidenced visually when one drives through the isolated inner roads in the central mountainous regions of Vieques, where one can see many big luxury houses spread throughout the landscape. The houses built by North Americans can be easily differentiated not only by their size and their luxury (many have swimming pools, and at least one has a tennis court), but also by their general aesthetics. Moreover, in some barrios, their close proximity with smaller and more humble-looking Vieques houses creates a dramatic contrast, allowing one to easily discriminate between one and the other. And the gentrification-like process that is taking place in Vieques at an island-wide level is perhaps best evidenced here.

Many of these houses belong to residential tourists who use them as second homes, and therefore do not live in the house all year round. While the houses are empty, many are rented on a weekly basis to big groups, as some of them are big enough to accommodate as many as twenty people. In 2010, we were able to count a stunning number of 88 villas that were available for rent in Vieques. Viequenses are fond of repeating rumors about who some of these villa owners are, offering names from the top ranking "rich and famous":

> There are a lot of people here. The governor of New York has two properties here, he has a house and a property . . . his name is Pataki. And some artists also have . . . I think Jeniffer López and Mark Anthony . . . I believe they have a property here. They have it in Martineau, in the villas in Martineau. Ricky Martin himself has a villa here too, I think . . . and others that are looking . . . the thing is that they keep quiet. All of a sudden they show up and then leave, you know . . . Benicio del Toro was here last year, you know . . . I don't know

if he has a property here but he was walking around here, you know, Benicio del Toro walking by here, you know . . . and Chuck Norris was also around, walking by the Bar Plaza . . . Willie Smith was here, he came in a big boat. He didn't touch land but he was here. He came for the wedding of Hillary—did you see Fresh Prince?, there was the actress that played Hillary—she got married in Vieques. (Worker Viequense #1)[8]

But perhaps an even better indicator of the intensity with which the speculation bacchanal took place is the fact that many of the North American buyers were willing to buy under extremely risky circumstances, namely in situations where the Viequense seller did not have a land title to the property being sold.

LAND TITLES

Many Viequenses do not have legal ownership over the houses and properties where they now live, since most of them are descendants of land squatters (or were squatters themselves) who never acquired formal ownership of the land. The history of Vieques is full of episodes of mass evictions and land squatting movements (cf. Santiago Ríos 2007), and the memory of these episodes are very much alive in the historical consciousness of Viequenses.

A good portion of the Viequense population is made up of descendants of sugarcane cutters and workers from the sugar plantations that were operating in the island up until the late 1920s. As was the case in many other sugar plantations in Puerto Rico, in Vieques' plantations workers were allowed to live on plantation lands, but they would not have legal ownership over the land they lived on. As Robert Rabin has explained for the Central Playa Grande,

> The plantation workers lived in the lands of the plantation itself, in neighborhoods called "colonias," or "areas surrounding and on the outskirts of the factory, were the cane was grown and where the tenant farmer and mill workers lived." The workers that lived in these areas built homes, farmed the land and raised animals, but had no title to the land as it was all owned by Don Juan Ángel Tió. (Rabin 2011: 34)

By the time the Navy arrived, in the early 1940s, all sugar plantations in Vieques had already ceased operations, but the plantation workers who were left jobless continued to live on the plantation lands, even though it was owned by their former employers. Thus, it was these big land owners from whom the Navy expropriated the land, and not the workers. The workers were subsequently removed by force by the Navy from the lands as they "illegally" inhabited it. As Rabin explains,

The US was able to acquire the land with very few transactions with landowners as the majority of the land was owned by the sugar mill and plantation owners. Ten principal ownerships accounted for 92 percent of the land procured. These large land owners received compensation but the workers were removed from the land and their houses demolished without much legal obstacles or compensations. (Rabin 2011: 34–35)

The Navy acquired in this way control of approximately 26,000 of the 33,000 acres that make up Vieques. Many of these expelled workers were forced to either migrate (many migrated to mainland Puerto Rico, but many also migrated to the island of St. Croix, which is part of the US Virgin Islands) or remained living on the island with few options beyond continuing squatting within the portion of the island that was left for the civilian population, or in areas within the "buffer zone" (that is, areas under Navy control but adjacent to the civilian zone). Many of the *barrios* that exist today in Vieques were formed in this manner, including the legendary Monte Carmelo. (cf. Hopgood Dávila 2013)

By the time the Navy left, many of these squatters (or their descendants) had already been able to obtain formal titles for their properties, but most had not. Thus, when foreign investors came offering money for their properties, the transaction was complicated by the absence of ownership title. This fact, though, seems to have not prevented these foreign investors from buying. Many of them purchased without a title, and have been able to obtain the title after the purchase. All transactions where there was no land title had to be performed in cash, as banks wouldn't grant credit without one. It is common, thus, for Viequenses to be suspicious of how North Americans have been able to obtain a title so fast (after the purchase), since they were never able to get one themselves, despite many attempts.

The price of land is too high and is being sold without land titles. There are no land titles. A piece of land in Monte Carmelo that I have doesn't have a land title, if a foreigner comes and offers to buy it and I sell it to him because of some necessity, I assure you that in less than one and a half month he is able to get a land title. How do they do it? He buys it. That happens all the time, foreigners buy pieces of land and the land titles miraculously appear. (Other Viequense #5)[9]

In any case, the historical legacy of land squatting movements, and the historical consciousness of these movements, provided the know-how behind new waves of land squatting mobilizations, or "land rescues," that will emerge in the very early stages of the post-Navy period in Vieques.

THE LAND RECOVERY MOVEMENTS

The intensity with which Viequenses perceived the speculation bacchanal, and the generalized fear that "the Gringos want to take over Vieques," provoked the emergence of several land recovery movements. We were able to document three major independent but interrelated land recovery movements in Vieques during the period 2005–2007: Verde Vieques, La Hueca and El Monte.

The particularities of these post-Navy land squatting movements are difficult to understand independent of the processes of land devolutions that were taking place with the departure of the Navy. Even prior to its official departure, in 2003, the Navy had already transferred a good portion of the land to federal and local civil authorities. Already by 2001, the Navy had transferred 8,100 acres from the western side of the island, as well as approximately 15,500 acres from the eastern side, totaling approximately 23,600 acres. Out of these 23,600 acres, approximately 18,000 were turned into a wildlife refuge and transferred to the US Department of Wildlife Service (USFWS). An additional 4,250 acres were transferred to the municipal government. The particularity of the post-Navy period land squatting movements, and what distinguishes them from previous land squatting movements, was the fact that in all contemporary movements, the lands invaded were contained within the 4,250 acres transferred to the municipality, and already in the hands of the municipal government. When the land squatting movements commenced, in 2005, the municipality had not yet developed a strategic plan for the utilization of those recently acquired lands. Moreover, the move was strategically planned by squatters, since the Major (then Damaso Serrano) was seen a weaker opponent than what could have been the USFWS or the Navy.

VERDE VIEQUES

In 2005, Vieques experienced the first land squatting movement in the post-Navy period. Under the leadership of Alba Encarnación (better known as Pupa), a "controversial" community leader of Vieques, a group of approximately 300 Viequenses invaded the land in the northern side of the island, in a place that is now referred to by the same name of the movement, *Verde Vieques* (Green Vieques). The motivations behind the movement were recounted by Pupa as follows:

> Look, I have a project. It's called Verde Vieques [Green Vieques] . . . But here everybody is selling [the land] like crazy. *like crazy!* . . . Vieques had four

expropriations between [19]38 and [19]42 . . . well, we're going for the fifth one now . . . So then I said to myself: "Wait a minute . . . if things continue like this" (*Esperate . . . Si esto sigue así . . .*). (Pupa Encarnación)[10]

Thus, a group of squatters led by Pupa invaded a strip of land in the northeastern side of the island. Afterward, they engaged in a two-year struggle with the municipal government, culminating in 2007 with the transfer of 330 acres to a communal corporation named Verde Vieques. Several conditions were imposed in order to qualify to receive land under the agreement: only poor Viequenses who do not already possess land would be eligible. Moreover, individual land plots could not exceed 900 sq m, and during the first twenty years after purchase the land would be owned communally, so residents cannot sell the land to anybody other than the corporation (at the original purchase price) during that period. The communal corporation would assume the responsibility of running with the qualification process.

The squatters' rationalization of their actions can be summarized as follows: when their Viequense children grow up and wish to become independent, they will not be able to acquire property in Vieques at "post-real-estate boom" prices, so they will need to leave the island. With the passage of time, and as the older generations pass away, Vieques will be emptied of Viequenses. Thus, the expulsion of the civil population that was the primary ambition of the Navy for sixty years would now be achieved de facto, in the post-Navy period, within a period of one or two generations.

> In twenty years, when I'm no longer here, they will become aware that Verde Vieques, it's only purpose was to guarantee that Viequenses remain in Vieques. Because otherwise they will be expelled. And they won't know they are being expelled. (Pupa Encarnación)[11]

Pupa went on to compare the current land situation in Vieques with the Navy V-C Plan during the seventies (better known in Vieques as *Plan Drácula* or "Dracula Plan"): that is, a plan that proposed the removal of all civil population (and their buried relatives) from Vieques, and the transfer of the totality of the island to the Navy. It was called "Dracula Plan" because it contemplated the digging of the graves in the cemetery and the relocation of the human remains somewhere else in mainland Puerto Rico.[12] Pupa thus describes the current land situation as a disguised version of the Dracula Plan.

> The Dracula Plan of the Marines in the decade of the seventies, do you know what it was? To expel the people from Vieques, and to dig out the dead. That was the Dracula Plan. Well, [what exist today is] almost the same . . . They [Viequenses] don't realize that. (Pupa Encarnación)[13]

For Pupa there was only one option left: to invade the land. This would entail, Pupa thought, giving a very small portion of the land recently transferred by the Navy to the municipal government to "qualified" poor Viequenses. What they got was 330 acres, which represented 8 percent of the 4,250 acres transferred to the municipality. The mayor could easily dispose of a small fraction of those lands without much loss, preventing at the same time a political conflict with his constituents. Pupa adds:

> Well, the mayor was mad . . . but he passed them [330 acres] to me, with some conditions: for residents of Vieques, who don't own a home. Is it mine? No, it belongs to the corporation for twenty years . . . Look, the Mayor gave me 330 acres. Too bad he didn't give me 600. I would have given him people from Vieques for twenty more years . . . He fought so much to give them to me . . . but he had 4,100 [acres]. What happened was the he gave us those [330 acres] to shut up our mouths. (Pupa Encarnación)[14]

LA HUECA

The movement of Verde Vieques was actually preceded by a smaller and less-articulated land squatting movement in the southern side of the island, in a place called La Hueca. While there are some controversies over the dates the invasions began for each movement, they seem to have emerged almost simultaneously, both in 2005, with only days or weeks apart; but independently. In any case, the movement of La Hueca started with only four squatters. One of these original four, Sombra, told us about the early history of the invasion:

> I have [land] in La Hueca, right there, man . . . Nobody can take me out of there . . . No, I've been in that land since the moment I said I would invade there. Not only the land . . . I went to the Department of Land and everything, and I looked at the maps and: "Here, this doesn't belong to anybody." From there we started, some close friends, my brother, another close friend, like four more friends, and we took over the area. Later on Verde Vieques emerged, and we said: "Hey, we need to fence the area because there are other people coming." (Sombra)[15]

The movement grew, and new squatters joined the La Hueca movement, until it reached a total of 123 people. Eventually, when the issue of Verde Vieques was about to be resolved, the lands invaded in La Hueca were also included as part of the 330 acres granted to the Verde Vieques corporation, and both strips of land were included in the same deed, as belonging now to the Verde Vieques. Mayor Serrano, instead of dealing with two public corporations, fused both land strips into one single corporation, Verde Vieques.

There was nothing essentially wrong with fusing the two groups into one single deed, but frictions between the two groups emerged immediately. The source of the friction was (presumably) due to the fact that it was the people from Verde Vieques who would assume the task of screening squatters according to the eligibility criteria, and there were (also presumably) some squatters from La Hueca who did not meet the eligibility criteria. In fact, there was a latent fear among the squatters from La Hueca that the people from Verde Vieques Corporation would want to decide who gets what, and even who gets in or out. The limit of 900 sq m per individual seems to have been also a source of friction between the two groups. Pupa, the leader from Verde Vieques, was vocal on the conflictive relation between the two groups.

> We have had, yes, difficulties, because they [i.e. squatters from La Hueca] don't recognize Verde Vieques, but they are in the deed. Then, I had to talk to Rosa [a leader from La Hueca], not to take anybody out, but it had to be 900 [squared] meters for each one, people from Vieques who don't have a house. As long as they comply with that. (Pupa Encarnación)[16]

In any case, by 2013 (that is, eight years after the original invasion and four years after legal acquisition of the land) the squatters from Verde Vieques and La Hueca still do not live in the land they invaded. For financial reasons squatters have been unable to either build their houses or prepare the land for construction (i.e., building roads, getting water and electric power connections, etc.). Many of the problems that the Verde Vieques and La Hueca movements face came to the forefront in a 2011 meeting of residents of La Hueca, which we attended.

LA HUECA MEETING IN 2011

A meeting of squatters from La Hueca was called on March 2011. The meeting revealed that frictions between them and the people from Verde Vieques were still very much alive. They accepted the fact that, since they were already in the Verde Vieques deed, they needed to comply with the eligibility criteria that appear in the deed. They were, though, distrustful about the fact that it would be people from Verde Vieques who would be evaluating the eligibility of everybody from La Hueca, so they hired their own lawyer to oversee the process. Following lawyer's recommendations, the two groups reached an agreement: files of all La Hueca squatters would be sent to Verde Vieques, but in packages of ten cases, with a second package of ten more cases delivered only after the first ten have been reviewed and accepted/ rejected. As of the date of the meeting, Sunday, March 15, 2011, the first group of ten files had not yet been delivered.

The meeting also revealed the internal financial problems of the group: many people were overdue on their fees, which was supposed to be used to pay for preparing the land for construction. These costs were to be paid by the squatters, since the only thing the municipality gave over was the land.

The meeting finally ended with a plea to all members of the group: "Please start building your houses. That's the only way they can't kick us out of here!" Yet, it is doubtful that construction of house could realistically start any time soon. The poor Viequenses (to qualify you have to be poor) are told they need to come up with thousands of dollars to pay for the infrastructure for water and electricity, for roads and plots measurements, but the reason they are invading land in the first place is because they are poor. So houses never get built, and squatters risk being expelled from the corporation if within a certain period of time they cannot prove they are using the land for the purpose for which it was granted: that is, to live on it. The same problems are present in Verde Vieques and are understandable given that these costs are significantly high.

Thus, by 2011—that is, four years after the Verde Vieques Corporation acquired the land, and six years after the original invasion—the process of qualification had not even started. When we last visited the site in 2016, only very rustic houses (where nobody was living) could be seen, and the vegetation was threatening to overtake the whole area. To what extent will squatters be able to raise the money needed to build their new houses is a big "question mark" overshadowing the movement. And the same is true for Verde Vieques, although some houses have been built there.[17]

EL MONTE

After the Verde Vieques and La Hueca movements had managed to acquire the land in dispute, another group of seven or eight (we were never able to determine exactly how many) young Viequenses invaded a beautiful spot in the central-western region of the island with very difficult access (accessible only through a really broken road), and which, for lack of a specific name, was always referred to as "El Monte" (the mountain). According to one of the invaders, Berito, the invasion of El Monte started even before Verde Vieques. In fact, Berito claims he and the others had already cleared the land before 2005 (i.e., before the Verde Vieques and the La Hueca invasions), but abandoned it to join the Verde Vieques movement, only to return to it after Verde Vieques had succeeded in their struggle. Berito tells the story of the motivations that led him to become a squatter:

What happened was that I had a lot in Villa Borinquen . . . I had it for seven years. Then, I already had the form of the house marked, and I had built a fence there, then [mayor] Damaso came and sent me a *buldoza* [bull dozer] and they sold it, to some guy . . . Then the guy started to build another house . . . when I went there the house was already almost finished and everything . . . "A house built in my lot!" Then, everybody told me:"Hey, go and fight that because they took your lot in Villa Borinquen. And then I said to myself: I am going to look for a lot somewhere else. But instead of looking for it in Villa Borinquen, I said, I'm going to the west because in the west there are lots from the municipality that are abandoned, so there is nobody there, there is no movement there, and I went in hiding there. That's when I started the movement, and to build my house and all of that . . . And when they found out that I was there they came to talk to me, saying that it was rented. (Berito)[18]

Even though the land Berito invaded belonged to the municipality, as was the case with Verde Vieques and La Hueca, the person who came to talk Berito out of the property was not the mayor, but rather a wealthy Viequense businessman called Richard. Richard explained to Berito that he had rented the land from the municipality, and so the land was his, technically. From then on, the issue became one of proving to Berito that the place was indeed rented by Richard. Berito refused to move unless it was shown to him that the land was actually rented (Berito often refers to Richard as Richard's Café because he owns a business with that name in Isabel II):

They had it rented, but none of the ones that came had the papers [showing] that he had it rented, so I said: "Well, if you don't have the papers I'm not leaving." So then Richard came and talked to me, telling me it was not his problem that I needed land somewhere else, that I needed to leave there one way or another. Then came Pablo [O'Connelly] from the government to tear down the house. A couple of weeks later we reached an agreement, and he tells me: "If you don't leave the government will bring you to court." Then, I said: "Well, I'm staying here and the government can take me to court." Then nothing else happened. Then the mess of Verde Vieques got started, and after that they never took me to court, until now, when Richard Café is suing me for being there. (Berito)[19]

Thus, in 2009 Berito finally received a citation to go to court. By then, Berito had already built a small cement structure on the land, and was not living the place but would occasionally spend the night there. The citation came with a copy of the rental agreement between Richard and the municipal government, dated October 17, 2008. But because Berito claims he has been there since 2005, his legal argument (presumably consulted with his lawyers) was that Richard cannot take action against him because he rented the property after the invasion, and not before.

But Richard's Café never took possession of those lands until the 17 of October of 2008, and I've been there since 2006. You know, I don't know why he was saying that he had those lands, because he didn't have them . . . I don't know what else I can tell you. I went to court on the eighth, to see what was happening . . . My lawyers say that he [Richard] is not supposed to be able to do that, because he had no control of the land when I was there. I'm supposed to do alright in the [court] case, I'm supposed . . . but one never knows, because he is doing it for some reason . . . we're going to keep fighting up there. (Berito)[20]

Berito also was suspicious of the content of the rental agreement which specifies the use Richard will make of the land during the rental period—a passive park for picnics, with ponies. The ultimate suspicion was that it was all a facade covering something bigger, perhaps a mega hotel.

I am sure that the reasons he has for gaining control [of the land] are different from what they really are going to do up there. That is a façade . . . because it doesn't make sense. Because what you want to do up there can be done in any other place. You know, you don't need a view that great [*cabrona*] to make pony rides, you know . . . You want that view to make a fucking big hotel, or many houses . . . like the rumors that were going around that they wanted to make 60 villas and each villa would be worth 1 million pesos . . . You know, that this is a façade . . . I can't tell you, I really don't know what they have in plan . . . But they have something, . . . I don't know what it is. I think that it's not legal. (Berito)[21]

ETHICS OF THE LAND FOR THE LAND

With the speculation bacchanal evolving in leaps and bounds, and with land squatting movements flowering everywhere, some of the Viequenses interviewed by us voluntarily provided what they believe would be a solutions to the problem:

You can have more development, but don't go on expropriating families. The problem comes when you want to take too much space, because you can have your business in a considerable space, but when you start wanting two or three *cuerdas* (acres), these are things that should not be allowed, because you may have the money to buy but there should be some ethical and moral laws that prohibited that from happening. We don't have the capital to invest but whoever has it cannot buy everything. (Other Viequense #5)[22]

I think a law should be passed that prohibits selling to an outsider. If you are going to sell to somebody it has to be a local, to a local or to a Puerto Rican from the mainland, you know, not to an American or to a foreigner from outside. Or, if you can sell it, you know, put a tax on the sale, you know, for the government, a tax that is almost impossible for a person from the outside to buy. . . . They are not going to do it, you know, because it sounds a little bit like, I don't know, like dictatorial, like it is something not democratic. But the truth is that's the only way you can put a stop to this. And they are anyway going to buy all the land eventually, because the people have money: "A tax, fine, I will pay it, no problem." They don't care because they have millions. But at least it would hold back the process a little bit. (Berito)[23]

To be sure, many independent countries and autonomous territories in the Caribbean with important tourism economies have placed restrictions on the flow of international capital, workers and ownership of land, in arrangements similar to the ones proposed by our informants. But Vieques is not an independent country, and neither is Puerto Rico; and the North Americans who are buying the land in Vieques are not "foreigners" in the strict sense of the term, since they are US citizens purchasing land in US territory. The arrangements proposed by our informants, to be sure, would be unviable under the American flag. This is, to be sure, one line of argumentation which will not be listened to.

As an alternative solution to these unviable recommendations, the 2004 "Master Plan for the Sustainable Development of Vieques, Part II" proposes the creation of a zoning system under which a part of the land would be placed in perpetual trusts, to be used exclusively for satisfying the needs of Viequenses, including the housing needs of the poor. Section 10.1 (p. 103) of the 2004 "Master Plan" says the following about the zoning and land trust system:

A useful mechanism for dealing with the problem of hoarding and speculation with the purchase and sale of land is the application of a zoning system in accordance with that public interest . . . a governmental intervention could be articulated that has as a result, to curb the increase in the price of land, to reduce speculation in the field of real estate and to insure reasonable cost of land.[24]

The idea acquires a more concrete form in the 2008 "Area Plan for the Municipality of Vieques," where the zoning and land trusts system are described as "the legal tool" (*herramienta legal*) by which Vieques can provide solution to the problems of "illegal occupation of land" and land speculation. The document states that this end could be achieved by:

Creation of one or more public trusts over the land . . . With this instrument the Municipality retains ownership over the land permanently . . . [Moreover,] where the objective is to provide social housing, the trust should be communitarian and with limited ownership. In this way the housing developed in the place remains accessible to low income groups.[25]

Thus, the idea of "land trusts" was already in the mind of urban planners and governmental administrators way before the Verde Vieques Trust was created, although the Verde Vieques Trust differs from the Land Trusts system contained in the Area Plans in important ways. First, while the Verde Vieques Trust retains ownership of the land for a period of twenty years, in the Land Trusts ownership is retained perpetually by the municipality. Moreover, and perhaps more importantly, while the Verde Vieques Trust requires as part of the eligibility criteria to be both poor and Viequense, in the Land Trusts the eligibility criteria for social housing does not differentiate between Viequenses and non-Viequenses, although it does require them to be from the "low income groups."

FINAL REMARKS

The idea of an "ethics of the land for the land" proposed by some of the Viequenses we interviewed is destined to not be heard, much like the voice of Spivak's subalterns who "cannot speak." Moreover, the debate over land often pushes Viequenses to move the conversation to a higher level of critique: to an existential level. In here, tourism is conceived as a new disguised version of the Dracula Plan because, as the original Dracula Plan, it threatens not only to mute their voice, but also, and more dangerously, to make them landless, force them out of the island, and with time made to disappear. In these discourses over land, it is the fear that "Americans want to take over Vieques"; the fear of a new Dracula Plan which threatens to leave Vieques without Viequenses is what worries Viequenses the most. Thus, when talking about land issues, Viequenses interviewed by us frame their struggle not merely as a struggle for the right to participate and share in the wealth produced by tourism, but rather as a struggle for the right to exist as a distinctive community, period. To be sure, one cannot think of a better way of excluding the Viequense population from benefiting from the wealth produced by the tourism economy, and of muting their voice once and forever, than by forcing them out of the island.

NOTES

1. Translated from Spanish. Original statement reads: "Los americanos se quieren quedar con Vieques. Un viequense tiene una casa, la vende, se van y se gastan el dinero, y viran pa' atrás pelaos. Es que son brutos también. Nosotros los puertorriqueños somos brutos."

2. Translated from Spanish. Original statement reads: "También yo creo que hay cierto sentido de que están perdiendo la isla un poco, y que está llegando a un nivel

donde no van a poder hacer nada, que no van a poder competir a menos que algo radical pase, que eso asusta pero es una realidad. Eso pasó en varias islas. La gente de Vieques y de Puerto Rico en general tienen que volver a Culebra también, al hecho de que, ponte, deberían hacer una clase de historia de islas caribeñas, para que tu veas cómo se van a repetir un montón de cosas, y van a cometer los mismos errores, y una cosa . . . pap, pap, pap . . . esto llevó a eso."

3. Translated from Spanish. Original statement reads: "A la larga nos van a sacar, poco a poco nos van a sacar. ¿Qué vamos a hacer? Le dejamos la isla a los gringos, compren todo y quédense ustedes. No, mierda es, que se vayan pal carajo."

4. Our own calculations, based on a sample of forty-seven actual sales that took place during the period 2003–2009, revealed an increase of 318 percent in the price of land. This figure coincides with anecdotic stories of sales provided by our informants.

5. The figure of 70 million Americans retiring in the next ten years, provided in this quotation by one of our interviewees is wrong. By 2030, the total population over sixty-five years of age in the United States is expected to total approximately 72 million, and that is probably what our informant meant to say. In any case, this represents a significant increase in that segment of the population, up from approximately 40 million in 2010.

6. Translated from Spanish. Original statement reads: "Mire, esa casa en el 96 la compraron en 125 mil pesos, a los herederos de Don Vigilio Ortiz. Aquella que está allí. En el 2000 la vendieron en 485 mil. Ahora vale 1.4 millones de dólares. El de la esquina, que es de Vieques, está vendiendo en 3 millones de pesos. Mi vecino de aquí arriba, el próximo que nos sigue a nosotros, vendió en 1.1 millones de pesos. Pero como yo, no ha visto nunca un billete de 500 pesos. Este está pillao porque le vendió la mitad al canadiense, que dicen que la esposa mato en el Viejo San Juan. Usted sabe que el papá paró, y eso está en litigio. Por eso él no ha cobrao. Pero aquí to' el mundo está vendiendo como loco. ¡Como loco!"

7. Translated from Spanish. Original statement reads: "Bueno, donde yo vivo, el chamaco, un americano, él compró la casa en 193 mil pesos, hace siete u ocho años atrás, 193 mil pesos, en la playa en Los Bravos de Boston, y ahora la casa vale 1 millón de pesos, solamente porque está en la playa. El tipo dio el palo. La compró en 193 mil pesos, y el tipo que la compró antes de él, también era un americano también, que la compró más barata que eso. Porque, bueno, jamás y nunca nadie pensaba que en Los Bravos de Boston valían las propiedades 500 mil pesos, 1 millón de pesos, por la playa, tu sabes . . . porque la playa está en todos lados aquí, tu sabes. Nosotros nunca pensamos que los terrenos valen tanto. Pero a los ojos de los americanos valen más de lo que nosotros queríamos. Y básicamente ellos se aprovecharon de que nosotros éramos ignorantes y no sabíamos lo que vale el terreno, y nos compraron casi todo lo que pudieron."

8. Translated from Spanish. Original statement reads: "Hay mucha gente aquí metida. El gobernador de Nueva York tiene dos propiedades aquí, tiene una casa y tiene una propiedad . . . se llama Pataki. Y un par de artistas que tienen . . . yo creo que Jeniffer López y Mark Anthony yo creo que tienen propiedades aquí. La tienen en Martineau, en las villas de Martineau. El mismo Ricky Martin tienen una villa aquí también, yo creo . . . y par de gente que están buscando, lo que pasa es que están

callaos. Llegan así de momento y se van, tú sabes . . . Benicio del Toro estaba aquí el año pasao, tu sabes . . . no sé si tiene propiedad aquí pero estaba caminado por aquí, tu sabes, Benicio del Toro caminando por ahí, tu sabes . . . y Chuck Norrys estaba por ahí también, caminando por el Bar Plaza . . . Willie Smith estuvo aquí, vino en un bote gigante. No estuvo en tierra pero estuvo por ahí. Vino a la boda de Hillary - ¿tu vistes de Fresh Prince?, estaba la actora que hacía de Hillary, se casó aquí en Vieques."

9. Translated from Spanish. Original statement reads: "Los terrenos están a precios elevados y te los venden sin título de propiedad. Aquí no hay título de propiedad. Un terreno en Monte Carmelo que tengo no tiene título de propiedad, si viene un extranjero y me ofrece comprarlo y se lo vendo por alguna necesidad, yo te aseguro que en menos de mes y medio consigue el título de propiedad, como lo hace?, lo compra. Eso pasa todo el tiempo, los extranjeros compran los terrenos y aparecen los títulos, títulos que no había aparecen."

10. Translated from Spanish. Original statement reads: "Mire, yo tengo un proyecto. Se llama Verde Vieques. Ese proyecto surge, pues . . . las casas . . . Pero aquí to el mundo está vendiendo como loco. ¡Como loco! . . . Monte Carmelo, Bravos de Boston, que comenzó en el 56, y después fue que en el 60 cogió fuerza, ese acantilado norte, puedo apostar, es más – pero almuerzos y esas cosas – apostar un almuerzo con usted que solamente hay una persona de Vieques residiendo que se llama Marcos Perez. Todo el mundo vendió, todo ese acantilado norte, preciosísimo. Y la gente de Vieques ahora mismo está sin acceso allí. Ahí está La Lanchita metida en el agua, y solamente hay uno, se llama Marcos Pérez. Perdieron eso también. Se metieron a Bastimento a principios del 90, y busque, en Bastimento, no hay diez familias de Vieques . . . Vieques tuvo 4 expropiaciones del 38 al 42, pues vamos pa la quinta."

11. Translated from Spanish. Original statement reads: "En 20 años, cuando yo no esté, se van a dar cuenta que Verde Vieques, su única función era garantizar que el viequense siguiera en Vieques. Porque si no los van a sacar. Y ellos no saben que se van."

12. For a detailed history of the Dracula Plan, see Evelyn Vélez Rodríguez (2002).

13. Translated from Spanish. Original statement reads: "El plan Drácula de la Marina en la década del sesenta, ¿tú sabes cuál era? Que sacaran a los de Vieques, y que se llevaran a los muertos. Ese era el Plan Drácula. Pues, es casi . . . Ellos no se dan cuenta."

14. Translated from Spanish. Original statement reads: "Bueno, le estuvo mal al alcalde, al que se fue, pero me las traspasó, con unas cláusulas: residentes de Vieques, que no tengan casa. ¿Y es mío? No, es de la corporación por veinte años . . . Mira, el alcalde a mí me dio 330 cuerdas. Qué pena que no me dio 600. Le iba a meter por veinte años la gente en Vieques. Pero como peleó tanto pa' dármelas . . . pero tenía disponibles 4,100. Lo que pasa que él nos dio eso pa' callarnos las bocas."

15. Translated from Spanish. Original statement reads: "Yo tengo en La Hueca, ahí, mano . . . De allí no hay quien me saque . . . No, yo llevo allí desde el 2003. Yo estoy en ese terreno desde que yo dije que iba a invadir allí. No solo el terreno, yo había ido al departamento de tierras y todo, y había "chequeao" los mapas y: - "Aquí, esto no es de nadie." De ahí empezamos unos cuantos panas, mi hermano, otro panita, como 4 panas más, y cogimos el área. Después vino lo de Verde Vieques, y ahí nosotros: - "Eh, hay que cercar porque ya viene gente por ahí."

16. Translated from Spanish. Original statement reads: "Hemos tenido, sí, dificultades, porque ellos no reconocen a Verde Vieques, y la escritura está. Entonces tuve que hablar con Rosa (Menes), no para sacar a nadie, pero que sean 900 metros para cada uno, gente de Vieques que no tenga casa. Después que eso esté . . . "

17. The death of community leader Pupa Encarnación on March 11, 2012 was an additional setback for the movement, and the search for a committed leadership still remains among the greatest challenges the movement will need to overcome in the years ahead.

18. Translated from Spanish. Original statement reads: "No, lo que pasó fue que yo tenía un terreno en Villa Borinquen, entonces . . . por 7 años lo tenía. Entonces tenía ya marcada la formación de la casa, y tenía una verjita puesta, entonces vino Dámaso y me tiró una "buldoza" [bull dozer] y lo vendieron, a un tipo ahí . . . Entonces el tipo empezó a construir la casa . . . cuando yo fui la casa estaba casi terminá y to . . . "¡una casa en el terreno mío!" Entonces todo el mundo me dijo, oye ve y pelea eso porque cogieron tu terreno en Villa Borinquen. Entonces yo dije: Yo voy a buscar un terreno en otro lado. Pero en vez de buscarlo en Villa Borinquen, yo dije, me voy pal oeste, porque en el oeste hay terrenos del municipio que están abandonados, entonces no hay nadie, allí no hay movimiento, y me fui escondido para allá. Ahí fue que empecé el movimiento y a hacer la casita y eso . . . y cuando averiguaron que yo estaba allí vinieron a hablar conmigo, pero lo tenían alquilado."

19. Translated from Spanish. Original statement reads: "lo tenían alquilado y eso, pero ninguno de los que venía tenían los papeles de que lo tenían alquilado, y yo dije: "Bueno, si no tienen los papeles yo no me voy de aquí." Hasta que vino Richard y habló conmigo, y él me decía que no era problema de él que yo necesitara una tierra en otro lado, que me fuera de allí como quiera, y yo le dije que me iba a quedar. Entonces vino Pablo (Oconelly) del gobierno a tumbar la casa. Un par de semanas después llegamos a un acuerdo, que me dice: Si no te vas el gobierno te va a llevar a la corte. Entonces yo dije: "Bueno, pues yo me quedo aquí y que el gobierno me lleve a la corte." Entonces no pasó más nada. Entonces empezó el revolú de Verde Vieques, y después nunca me llevaron a la corte hasta ahora, que Richard Café me está demandando por estar allí."

20. Translated from Spanish. Original statement reads: "Pero Richard Café nunca tuvo posesión de esas tierras hasta el 17 de octubre de 2008, que fue los otros días, y yo llevo allí desde el 2006. Tu sabes, yo no sé por qué él decía que tenía esas tierras, porque él no las tenía . . . No sé qué más te puedo decir de eso . . . Yo fui a la corte el día 8, a ver qué pasa con eso . . . Los abogados dicen que se supone que él no puede hacer eso, porque él no tuvo el control de las tierras cuando yo estuve allí. Se supone que yo salga bien en el caso, se supone, pero uno nunca sabe, porque cuando él lo hace es por algo . . . vamos a seguir luchando allá arriba . . . "

21. Translated from Spanish. Original statement reads: "Yo estoy seguro que las razones que él tiene para tener el control son diferentes a lo que de verdad van a hacer allá arriba. Eso es un tape lo que tiene . . . porque no hace sentido. Eso que tú quieres hacer allá arriba lo pueden hacer en otro lado. Tú sabes, tú no quieres una vista así de cabrona para hacer "rides" de ponis, tú sabes . . . Tú quieres esa vista para hacer un hotel bien hijo de puta, o muchas casas . . . como los rumores que habían que querían

hacer 60 villas y cada villa valía un millón de pesos . . . Tu sabes, que esto es un tape . . . No sé decirte, no sé en verdad que tienen planeao ahí . . . Ellos tienen algo, yo no sé lo que es, yo creo que legal no es."

22. Translated from Spanish. Original statement reads: "Se puede elaborar más pero que no vayan a desalojar familias. El problema es que quieras acaparar mucho espacio, porque tú puedes tener tu negocio en un espacio considerable, pero cuando ya quieres dos o tres cuerdas ya son cosas que no se deben permitir porque puedes tener el dinero para comprar pero debe de haber unas leyes éticas morales que impida que se pueda hacer. No tenemos el capital para invertir pero el que lo tenga no se puede apropiar de todo."

23. Translated from Spanish. Original statement reads: "Yo creo que deberían pasar una ley que tú no puedas venderle a una persona de afuera. Si vas a vender a alguien tiene que ser a un local, a un local o a un puertorriqueño de la isla, tú sabes, que no sea un americano o un extranjero de afuera. O si lo puedes vender, tu sabes, poner un tax en la venta, tu sabes, pal gobierno, un tax que sea casi imposible para una persona de afuera comprar . . . Pero que no lo van a hacer, tu sabes, porque suena un poquito más como que, no sé, como que dictadura, como que no es algo democrático. Pero en verdad es la única manera que tu puedes parar esto. Y como quiera te van a comprar todas las tierras eventualmente, porque la gente que tiene chavos: "Un tax, está bien, yo te lo pago, no hay problema." No les importa porque tienen millones de más. Pero por lo menos se aguanta un poco el proceso."

24. "Plan Maestro para el Desarrollo Sustentable de Vieques, Parte II: Recomendaciones," commissioned by the Grupo Interagencial de Vieques y Culebra, p.103, http://www.suagm.edu/umet/pdf/cedes/pdf/segndo_ informe_vieques2.pdf). Original text reads: "Un mecanismo útil para atender el problema del acaparamiento y especulación con la compra y venta de terrenos, es la aplicación de una zonificación acorde con ese interés público . . . se puede articular una intervención gubernamental que como resultado, frene el alza en los precios del terreno, reduzca la especulación en el campo de las bienes raíces y asegure costos razonables para terrenos."

25. Plan de Area, Parte III (p. 86). Translated from Spanish. Original text reads: "se crearán uno o más fideicomisos públicos de la tierra . . . Con este instrumento el gobierno municipal mantiene la tenencia de la propiedad permanentemente . . . cuando el objetivo fuere el proveer vivienda social, el fideicomiso debe ser comunitario con equidad limitada. De esta manera se mantiene la vivienda que se desarrolle en el lugar, accesible para grupos de bajos ingresos."

Chapter 3

Work

Simultaneously with the "speculation bacchanal," there emerged in post-Navy Vieques a "job boom" within the tourism/service sector. The opening of multiple hotels, restaurants and other tourism-oriented businesses on the island created a broad job market which many Viequenses attempted, with different degrees of success, to enter. Its impact was strong enough to increase per capita income by 62 percent (from $2,997 to $8,054), and reduce poverty by more than 30 percentage points in one decade (2000–2010).

Several initiatives were developed with the intention of integrating the Vieques community into the nascent tourist economy. The local public high school opened a program in hostel management ("Hostelería") that provides training in the skills basic to the tourism and hospitality industry to young Viequenses. There was also, beginning in March 2009, a program to provide language and entrepreneurial skills, as well as financial aid to locals wishing to open small businesses. The "Incubadora de Microempresas Bieke, Inc.," a not-for-profit community organization providing guidance and funding to local Viequenses wishing to open a business, also opened its doors in 2008; and by 2011 it had some fifteen small businesses under its umbrella.[1] But, based on the information collected by us, the general experience of Viequenses attempting to get into the tourism economy has been conflictive, and so to the dissatisfaction of most.

Viequenses are, in general, not satisfied with the working conditions imposed on them within the tourism industry, nor with the conflictive and confrontational form that the employer-employee relations are increasingly assuming. Moreover, and given that in most cases of employer-employee relationship the former is a North American and the latter Viequense, the conflict often assumes a racial dimension: it is perceived as a conflict between North American gringos and Viequenses.

We were, by 2004, already able to document the existence of discourses about labor-related conflicts in Vieques. In fact, by then they had already acquired what Clifford Geertz would have called a "public life"—and a very robust and healthy life at that. They existed in conversations in the Bar La Plaza or in the Mambo Minimarket, certainly to a greater degree than what one could find in any other Puerto Rican municipality. Everybody seemed to have already constructed an informed (or semi-informed) opinion on the subject, and everybody was more than willing to articulate his or her opinion in a discursive manner, often extensively.

The debate would reach its most vivid expression in conversations where the accusation that Viequenses are lazy (*vagos*) was brought up. No other characterization incites more resentment among Viequenses than that of being called *vago* and the moral indignation locals felt about accusations of laziness only helped to fuel the voice of our informants, and to infuse strong feelings and emotions into their speech acts. It became evident from very early stages of fieldwork (already by 2004) that we had struck upon what anthropologist Katherine Browne has called a "cultural hot button," that is, a topic of conversation that is "hot," recurrently brought up in conversations, and where one's true position on the subject "is not easily hidden once the button is pressed" (Browne 2004:134).

With the intention of capturing these discourses about work ethics and laziness in a more systematic and formal manner, we conducted a series of semi-structured interviews over the labor conditions inside the tourism economy of Vieques during the year 2009.[2] The interviews revealed a whole community intensively engaged in a debate over the allegedly problematic work ethics of Viequenses, and often (as we will attempt to show) posed in a language that was potentially insulting, unapologetic and often bordering on racism and political incorrectness—coming from all sides of the debate.

DISCOURSE ABOUT THE LAZINESS OF
VIEQUENSES PRODUCED BY FOREIGNERS

In the discourses produced by Viequenses about their own laziness, it is the North Americans who are blamed for making the accusation ("the gringos say we are lazy"; or "los gringos dicen que somos vagos"). And indeed, the assertion was upheld by most of our "foreign,"[3] mostly North American, interviewees (tourism investors and workers alike) with different degrees of intensity, but always in an open and unapologetic manner.

In the case of North American employers talking about their perception of the Viequense employees, they would produce a dual response: that is, they would often start expressing great satisfaction with the Viequense employees *they currently have*, but would then move to a criticism of Viequenses working attitudes based on past experiences. Speaking exclusively of their current Viequense employees, some North American employers said the following:

> I can boast a little bit that we have some of the best [Viequense] employees, I think, than anybody on the island, and stable. We have people who have been with us since we got here, seven years ago. That's pretty long in the restaurant business. (Employer North American #3)

> It has always been our policy [to employ Viequenses]. . . . We have one gringo. But he lives on Vieques and has for many years. And he speaks Spanish. But, in thirteen years, we have had very little turnover. (Employer North American #1)

> We have had the same [Viequense] people for many, many years. They come here and never go away, because they are treated well. So they never leave their job. And if a new position opens up, they usually try to get a relative or friend to come in. (Employer North American #2)

But, having said that, the response of foreign business owners and managers would then shift to narratives of bad experiences they have had in the past, and to a critique of Viequenses' work ethics in general. Thus, hand in hand with the positive discourse about current Viequense employees, there was also a strong (actually, stronger and more emphatic) discourse, from the foreign employers, about the problematic work ethics of former Viequense employees.

The interviews produced a long list of specific practices that these foreign employers consider problematic: that is, asking for a job and never showing up on the first day of work; working for a short period and abandoning the work after the first or second paycheck; excessive absenteeism; and, finally, the lack of social skills required for the service industry and poor performance in the work place.[4] Particularly acute was the criticism of the problem of labor mobility or turnover. The phenomenon has been amply documented in the literature on tourism (Johnson 1981, 1985; Denvir and McMahon 1992; Lashley and Chaplain 1999). Riley, for example, will point to the recurrence of these "vociferous complaints . . . about the managerial 'hassle' of coping with high labor turnover" (2004: 136) emerging from administrators in tourism contexts and reiterates that it has been amply documented in the literature. In the case of Vieques, labor mobility is closely associated to what one of our interviewees defined as "attrition," meaning by this the practice of working for a short period of time, usually for a set monetary goal, and once that goal is achieved never return to work. One of our local informants defined the logic of the system in the following terms:

In here it's been always like this, that if you want something you save, you add up, and then you buy [and never return to work] . . . Part of the enchantment of living in a small island is that, that you live day by day, and you live the moment.[5]

This practice is highly reminiscent of that attitude defined by Max Weber as "traditionalism," where "a man does not 'by nature' wish to earn more and more money, but simply to live as he is accustomed to live and to earn as much as is necessary for that purpose" (Weber 2009 [1905]: 29). In our recorded interviews, foreign employers talked about this specific practice of Viequenses in some depth.

So the mentality is they work as far as they need to go to pay that week's bills, and they don't come back. There is no long term need. And so culturally, in Vieques specifically, it is very difficult to find people who are interested enough in generating a career for themselves. They just want to live for the day. It's a problem of the Caribbean all over because it is more of a laid back society any-way. The values are all different. They don't see as . . . getting ahead and getting rich and buy boats and all things that we want as really important to them. It's not. (Employer North American #5)

They leave the work after working for a short period of time. . . . I've been with company for two and a half years. . . . and we probably have gone through eight or ten people. . . . what happens a lot of times, in the restaurant, [is that] I would always try to hire Viequenses, but there would always be a high rate of "attrition": they will be gone in 2–3 weeks. They make some money, they get excited, and then they're gone, and then will go somewhere else. So [they] wouldn't stay for long term. Let's say, in two years, out of ten Viequenses I had, only two stayed permanently. . . . out of the ten, only two stuck around. (Employer North American #7)

In this discourse, foreign employers were emphatic about the fact that there is a "difference" between the work ethics of Viequenses and their own (or the one they expect from their workers). Moreover, they acknowledge the existence of a social tension around this issue, and broadly perceive the employer/employee relationship as becoming increasingly "antagonistic," "hostile" or engaged in an "us and them mentality." Commentaries about the problematic work ethics of Viequenses coming from foreign employers (and some foreign employees as well) were many, and some of them are worth quoting extensively.

In my experience, the last four years . . . there is an absence of "willing labor," you know, like a lot of the youth here: (A) have never been in the retail industry, so they don't know how to do it; (B) the culture that their parents grew them on is not a very working culture, meaning that they haven't had to work, you know. (Employer North American #7)

I mean, I have a different work ethics that I was brought up with, than they have. I get frustrated. What's the matter with these people? (Employer North American #4)

It's a huge problem, because there is no work ethics in Vieques. One of the big fallouts of the policies of the Navy and the federal government has been to provide income to people when the economy was taken away from the sugar cane. They basically kept giving people money, so the work ethics is gone . . . the working segment of the Vieques population I think is doing very well, and some of them are getting quite wealthy, because if you have a work ethics, it's here. And so it's very beneficial in that regards. How do you incorporate the entire population of the island into it? It's going to be very difficult, long term, because of the culture of dependency created by the policies. (Employer North American #5)

I don't know what the solution is. I don't even know if we need one, I mean, the people are not unhappy. Do you know what I mean? I don't necessary need to see change here. I don't know if they need rescuing particularly, because they are not unhappy. They are happy people. You know, who am I to tell them they got to get up to go work every day? I do it, but they don't have to do it. (Employer North American #5)

This people just don't have no reason whatsoever to be any other way. . . . They don't care, as long as they keep getting their welfare, and coupons and something. . . . They know everything way in the world to beat the system. They are experts at beating the system. . . . The majority of this island, the poverty level is very high, and they are on "generational welfare." . . . From generation to generation. If they finish high school—most of them drop out. . . . It's just a shame that they don't have the opportunity, and they don't have the willingness, they don't have the need to go in their minds. They are well. They are cared for. And that's generational welfare. We can't get them off of here. It's just a shame. . . . The people who live in here, we call it the Vieques "maleie." It's sort of a . . . it's a mentality, that "Ay bendito!"—which is one of your [i.e., Puerto Ricans] favorite expressions, which I hate, because it doesn't do anything. . . . It's a very bad mentality, if you can afford to do it, but. . . . But you know, I have been here twenty-two years and, it hasn't changed, and it never will. (Employer North American #6)

Viequenses are nice, but irresponsible. They only work when they don't have another choice. If they can choose to not work . . . they will not work. (Employee European #3)[6]

We have other employees who approach work differently. That's not because they are Viequenses, that's because they are human beings. Now, there are differences in values. . . . We were talking yesterday about family. Family is sometimes more important for Viequenses that it would be for a lot of workers in North-America. So, as an employer we have to make adjustments for the fact that sometimes someone doesn't come to work, and it's because there is a child sick, and we have to figure out what to do about it, which probably under the same situation would not happen in the United States. But I don't have a problem with Viequenses as workers. . . . But, we as outsiders have to recognize that people have slightly different reactions to things and slightly different needs. In here family does come high up, people will skip work because a family member is sick. When I was working in the United States I wouldn't do it. I'm not sure that one of those things is better than the other, it's just different. And we have to understand that it's different. And they have to understand that it's pretty demanding if I want people to be here. (Employer North American #3)

People [foreigners] come here with expectations of finding people who would work the same way as they work back where they come from, and it just isn't the case, so until you adapt your expectations for people, and start treating them accordingly, they are going to feel that you are treating them badly because they don't understand why, and you're going to have a hostile relationship. . . . You can't change the whole culture from one generation. You have to deal with it to a certain extent. And if you don't you won't be successful. (Employer North American #5)

In general, in the discourses produced by our "foreign" informants and interviewees, the general idea shared is that the causes of the economic disadvantages and poverty in Vieques are to be found in the moral failings of the Viequense working subjects themselves. The expressions of these foreigners bear the clear import of discourses from the US continental sociopolitical arena, where the mainstream tendency was to place the blame for social problems on the moral vices of victims. It is a tendency that deepens its roots in Oscar Lewis's idea of a "culture of poverty"—a concept which Lewis developed from fieldwork conducted in city slums in Puerto Rico and Mexico City in the 1960s and 1970s (Lewis 1968; 1975), and which became the dominant conceptual tool for the understanding of this phenomenon of work-avoiding attitudes in the postwar era.

In fact, the theory of Lewis is of special relevance to the case of Vieques because accusations of laziness emerge precisely in the middle of a job boom, when the opportunity to find work was available. According to Lewis, it was when one experiences structural impediments to work (the absence of jobs) intensively and for a prolonged period of time that the conditions for the culture of poverty to emerge and flourish are established. Once these structural conditions extend in time for periods that transcend generations (as happened in Vieques after the closing of the sugar plantations and throughout the period of military occupation), then the problem of poverty will cease to be structural and become cultural, that is, a part of a set of values and attitudes that are transmitted from parent to children. Thus, once a new generation gets accustomed to these anti-working values and attitudes, the individual members will continue to avoid work even after the structural impediments that originally caused the problem have been removed. Thus, the argument is of special relevance to the case of Vieques because, as is suggested in the discourse of foreign interviewees, the job boom was not capable of erasing the work-avoiding attitudes of Viequenses, as Lewis would have predicted.

Thus, despite the fact that Lewis's theory of a culture of poverty is no longer accepted by the sociological community, the general arguments behind the theory continue to inform the expressions produced by our foreign interviewees, and becomes evident in expressions like "generational welfare," or in statements about "the culture that their parents grew them on."

A VIEQUENSE RESPONSE

Viequenses are well aware of the existence and contents of these negative discourses about their work ethics, and the fact that "the gringos say we are lazy" is common knowledge. Confronted with the accusation of being lazy, and in an effort to search for respect and to resist the negative effects of tourism, Viequenses produce a discourse that is evidently a counter stance, that is, one that is oppositional or a contestation. They complain about the injustices and exclusions that they endure within the tourism working sector (e.g., they are given the worst-paid jobs; the jobs are seasonal, part-time or on-call; they don't get benefits, or vacation days; they work during holidays; they work odd hours). Their complaints reproduce the generalized complaints of workers within tourism economies everywhere. The complaints, though, acquire a special significance in the Caribbean context, given the striking similarities shared with the traditional complaints of sugarcane cutters in the region during a great portion of its modern (postslavery) history, a fact which has led observers to establish similarities and continuities between the structural working conditions within tourism economies and the conditions that prevailed in the plantation economies that preceded them—and in fact, to refer to tourism economies as "neo-plantations" (Taylor 1993), or as the "new plantations" (Strachan 2002). Strachan, for example, has identified the major similarities between the two: the businesses are foreign owned; it's an export industry of a product sold to First World markets; both require a monopolization of land (shorelines in tourist economies, farmlands in the plantation economy); both provide only seasonal work. In the context of the Caribbean, Chamber adds, tourism also requires a form of servitude toward the wealthy (mostly white) tourist that is often associated with power/racial relations typical of the slave plantation.

> Adjustment to tourism employment might be especially difficult where providing service to outsiders is likely to be associated with involuntary servitude, particularly if that servitude has in the past been imposed along the lines of racial or ethnic difference. In much of the Caribbean, for example, tourism has

been characterized as a form of neocolonialism, serving to replicate many of the social and economic relationships of a racist past. Factors such as these can have important implications for workers' attitudes toward tourism employment. (Chambers 2009: 42)

But perhaps the most problematic of these similarities is the fact that both the sugar plantation and the tourism industry provide only seasonal work for the local population, who are therefore forced to search for an alternative means of subsistence during the low season. This is probably the most important factor preventing a smooth and peaceful entry of locals as workers into the tourist economy, in Vieques as elsewhere. As Chamber has documented,

> In many places, tourism demand is also subject to considerable seasonal fluctuations. Popular recreational and beach areas sometimes operate at full capacity for only a few months out of a year. In these cases, employment in the tourist industry might not be a reliable form of employment for locals, who need year-round incomes. Tourism jobs are then taken up by transient workers, contributing less to the local economy. (Chambers 2009: 37)

Moreover, it has also been argued that the problem with seasonal jobs—or more specifically with "the inevitable manipulation of labor supply by management in response to constant demand shifts" (Riley 2004: 137), often referred to in the literature as "flexibility"—is that it encourages high job mobility among workers, or the phenomenon of "attrition" to which we referred earlier (Riley 1990, 1999, 2004; Riley Ladkin and Szivas 2002; Baldacchino 1997; Gmelch 2003; Lockwood and Guerrier 1989). Riley, for example, has argued that it is the flexibility problem that creates this job mobility: "It is the need to push and pull people in and out of the market that creates this fundamental dynamic on which labor mobility is built" (2004: 137). But the irony behind this whole affair, as Riley has also argued, is that, while the argument has been convincingly put forward that "when the big companies offer employment packages that encourage stability, eventually the market itself stabilizes to the benefit of all the employers"; the reality is that, no matter how convincingly "its advocates may have won the argument, . . . they have not won support" from tourism employers (2004: 142).

THE VIEQUENSE ACCEPTANCE OF THE ACCUSATION OF LAZINESS AS VALID AND TRUTH

But there is also a unique element in the discourses of Viequenses that separates them from discourses produced in other tourism destinies. While their discourses have a clear oppositional tone, the fact is that a significant majority of our Puerto Rican and Viequense informants and interviewees were in agreement (with a lot of "buts," but nonetheless in agreement) with many of the assertions about the laziness of Viequenses and Puerto Ricans. In other words, Viequenses feel morally insulted when being accused of laziness, but simultaneously accept the accusation as valid. Expressions like "there is a reality that they are lazy" (and the like) were common among our Viequense informants and interviewees.

Thus, while it is mostly "foreign" (mostly North American) tourism investors and managers, and residential tourists in general, who initially produce the accusation (or who are blamed for initially producing the accusation) of laziness, the reception of the accusation by Viequenses is ambiguous, and, after much divagation, *generally ends with an acceptance of the accusation as valid and truth.* Even when responses produced by Viequenses were initially cautious and exculpatory of the working subject, there was always in the end an explicit recognition that Viequenses are lazy; or that Viequenses' laziness is "a phenomenon that is real." Thus, it was not only North Americans who adopted negative discourses about the work ethics of Viequenses, as our interviews revealed many Viequenses (and Puerto Ricans working in Vieques) adopting the same discourse, and using words even stronger than those used by foreigners to criticize the work-avoidance attitudes of Viequenses.

This general phenomenon has been also documented by other researchers in the tourism field. Bunten, for example, has described it as a tension between "sharing culture or selling out" (2008). And Salazar and Graburn have characterized it as governed by "two different logics at work simultaneously: a logic of differentiation that creates differences and divisions; and a logic of equivalence, that subverts existing differences and divisions" (Salazar 2014: 117). Salazar and Grabur have described the tension, following Bruner in the following terms:

> When indigenous people can control the images that they wish to meld into visitor's imaginaries, the images are favorable to the "marginalized people," often countering the negative images that have long inhabited dominant worldviews. . . . However, when the power imbalance is steep, . . . they may try to live up to the role thrust upon them (perhaps unconsciously). . . . They may be acting out (consciously) this newly acquired part of the global stage, while protecting their inner beliefs and private lives, struggling against selling out. (Salazar and Graburn 2014: 15)

Simoni has also provided a specific example from his research in Cuba, where subjects simultaneously accept and deny being a *jinetero*:

> Manuel, for instance, expressed outrage at being framed as a *jinetero*. But in other contexts of interaction, like when gossiping with his Cuban friends and

peers, he was also able to brag about his jinetero/a-like feats at the expenses of his foreign partners. (Simoni 2013: 12)

In the case of Viequenses, the archetypical structure of this type of argument usually commences with a denial of the accusation ("Viequenses are not lazy"), and even of expressing outrage at the accusation; but then moves on to provide explanations as to why Viequenses de facto don't work, or don't like to work, and so on. The argumentation ends with either an outright acceptance of the accusation or a return to the "denial" mode.

There is a phenomenon that is real, that they say people from Vieques don't like to work. . . . I don't know if you have heard that. . . . People don't understand that this is a society where there used to be no jobs, in the past there were 250 people working and the rest of the people got used to make a living without working. They don't know the discipline of work. Then, if you give them a job, I'm not saying that it's right, but I can understand why because I try to see one step further, that if you give them instructions they get mad because they live in a society that went without working, there were no jobs. It's not that they are lazy. (Worker Viequense #2)[7]

I have had problems, which is a shame for me to say it, regarding this problem that we have in all of Puerto Rico as a colony, I see they have done a good job in bringing up lazy people. This system that we have, giving them all the benefits without them having to work. Then they don't want to keep their jobs because they lose all those other benefits that are given to them for not having a job. They live better not working than working. That is the biggest problem I have had here to maintain workers. . . . The moment that the revision of aids from PAN[8]:"I have to quit because they take away my food coupons." I believe that if you work you don't need food coupons, and the government should be more strict in that, but I don't think they are going to do it because that is what they use to scare them off every four years. (Employer Viequense #16)[9]

It is not that they are lazy. What happens is that they don't have initiative in finding a better job or getting ahead a little bit. They are happy with what they already have. And that is also good, but you cannot allow others who come from the outside to step on you, you know. (Worker Viequense #1)[10]

The problem is that they are too laid back. They work for two or three months. They start with a lot of enthusiasm, all of a sudden, enough. If one is not on top of them they don't work. And that's it, two or three months, if they don't quit to go collect [government aid]. (Employer Viequense #11)[11]

This is a culture of parasites. The youth have a tendency towards leisure, of dependency . . . if they can copy it from their parents, why would one do it, it's always the same. It's what you see in Vieques society. (Other Viequense #5)[12]

I prefer to hire somebody from here, that I know he/she will be here, and not a person that comes and goes. Because then I need to bring the person back again. One is better off having a person that one trains from here than . . . as long as he/she is good. . . . But what happens here is that people are lazy. Ja! In general, in Puerto Rico, people are lazy. It's true. Including myself also, ja, ja, but it's true, Boricuas are lazy. It's not a lie. Most of them are lazy. (Employer Puerto Rican #12)[13]

At least the last ones [employees] we have had are young, and they don't have the responsibility of what is really a job, sincerely, there is a reality that they are lazy. Many work and many are lazy. (Worker Viequense #4)[14]

Even when, initially, the condition of work-avoidance is made to rest in colonialism, slavery, military occupation or anywhere else in history, in the discourses of Viequenses the final blame is also (as is in Oscar Lewis's case, and as is among our foreign interviewees as well) laid on the Viequense working subjects.

Without attempting to erase its broad internal complexity, we can identify several elements that can help illuminate the intricacies of this Puerto Rican/ Viequense language game in which ambiguous and contradictory statements of this sort are allowed. For purpose of analysis, we have divided these elements into five, as follows:

FIRST ELEMENT: THE DISCOURSE OF VIEQUENSES IS NOT AN ANTI-WORK DISCOURSE

The first contradiction one encounters in the analysis of the Viequenses discourse is a contradiction between what they say and what they do. In fact, Viequense workers (mostly blue collar) interviewed by us were for the most part hardworking individuals, and some had shown outstanding entrepreneurial attitudes for persons of their social status and cultural capital. They speak of work with a sense of duty, or at least as something that has to be done, and that will be done.

The experiences of Viequenses attempting to enter the tourism economy were diverse. Beyond several salaried workers in hotels and restaurants, we were also able to observe several Viequenses engaging in independent businesses targeting the tourist population, but most of them were small and informal (e.g., street vendors, food vendors, artisans selling in the Malecón during weekends, renting extra rooms in their houses) and probably not very profitable. Many times, these activities were performed as *chivos*, that is, economic activities that provide a small source of extra income to complement a bigger salary from an official job, or to complement the earnings of a family unit.

There was, though, one economic niche which some young male Viequenses were able to exploit quite successfully and profitably, and which provides the most extreme form of entrepreneurial initiative we could evidence in

Vieques among former blue-collared workers: that is, working as tour operators on trips in kayaks to the Mosquito Bioluminescent Bay at night.

One of the most important tourism attractions of Vieques, beyond its pristine beaches, is the Mosquito Bioluminescent Bay, commonly referred to as
the Bio-bay. It is one of only seven bioluminescent bays in the world (one
each in the Bahamas, Borneo, Hawaii, Japan, and two others in mainland
Puerto Rico); and, according to the Guinness Book of World Records, the
brightest of them all. The bay is inhabited by microscopic organisms called
Dinoflagellates (*Pyrodinium bahamense*) that burst into light at night, when
the water is shaken.

There are basically two ways of visiting the Bio-bay. There is one company, Island Adventure, that brings guests from Fajardo (in mainland Puerto
Rico) by sail-boat. They sell a package that includes a round-trip by sail-boat,
dinner, a presentation about the Dinoflagellates, a trip to the Bio-bay in an
electric motor boat, all packed into one night. According to one of the managers we interviewed, the company has been operating in this way for ten
years, and brings up to fifty people per night in the peak season, often having
to make two trips in one night.

The other way of visiting the Bio-bay is in kayaks, and it is this niche area
that a group of young Viequenses have been successfully able to penetrate
as independent workers. It is a line of business that requires little investment
(a cell phone, a truck to drive tourists, some kayaks, flyers to give around
to tourists and an insurance policy). It is also a business where there is no
intermediary, so the money goes directly from the tourist's pocket into local's
hands, most of the time in cash.

Working in the Bio-bay can also be very profitable. The price ranges from
thirty-five to sixty dollars per person. The biggest group we were able to
observe during fieldwork in 2009 was a group of seventy-five students from
the University of Puerto Rico (locally referred to as IUPI), and which immediately became the talk of the town. Being Puerto Ricans and students, they got a
heavy discount. The next day, one of our interviewees (unrelated to the kayak
industry) commented the following about the profitability of the kayak tours:

> There are times when the bus makes three trips, with 32 persons, at 35 pesos
> [each]. Last night, 75 persons at $18. That's $1,350. That was only one [tour
> operator], this Saturday, with a group from the IUPI [short for University of
> Puerto Rico]. They were 75, and because they were from the IUPI he left it at
> 18 pesos. (Other Viequense #4)

Normal groups tend to be much smaller than seventy-five persons, but it
is not uncommon during high-season to have groups of twenty-five or thirty
people every night and often making two or three trips per night.

We were able to identify some eight young Viequense men (and several other on-call assistants) working as tour operators in the Bio-bay. It is a tough job that requires much strength to carry twenty or thirty kayaks from the truck to the water and back every night, rowing throughout the lagoon, and so on. But the hardest part of the job is finding new customers, which they achieve by spending a lot of their free time handing out flyers to the tourists visiting Malecón. (In fact, it was from seeing each other so often in the Malecón that we were able to become friendly with these guys, and to conduct intensive research on their working lives.)

Working in the Bio-bay also requires a lot of trust. While they work independently, they function as a collective group, often sharing transportation for tourists, lending kayaks to each other, and such like. They have also developed standard rules for splitting the money between themselves, which can basically be summarized as follows: one fourth for the person who contacted the client; one fourth for whoever drives the tourists back and forth from/to the hotel; one fourth for the owner of the kayak; and one fourth for the person who gives the actual tour. While, under ideal circumstances, one tour operator provides all four services, there are many occasions where help is needed and earnings need to be split between one or more operators. Because of this, the business of kayak tours can only function under a high degree of trust between operators. Knowing each other for a long time, sharing communal and familial ties and being close friends, are significant elements that contribute in the construction of trust. One cannot survive in this business without knowing that there is always somebody who can lend you extra kayaks when you have a big group, or go pick up your customers at the hotel when your truck breaks down, or watch out for your kayaks while you are driving or returning customers to their hotels, and so on.

In any case, these groups of Bio-bay tour operators were of interest to us because they were deriving significant earnings from the tourism sector, and had exhibited the greatest entrepreneurial attitude we were able to witness within the working class sector of the community. It was precisely within this group that we also witnessed what we can perhaps call an incipient form of capitalist greed.

On one occasion, Benito, one of our Bio-bay tour operator informants, revealed to us something he had held as a secret: "I have an eight-steps plan to earn my first million dollars." He revealed this to me with the conviction of an Amway vendor: "It's simple. . . . You first need to save $7,812.50. I am saving and have part of the money already. . . . You need $7,812.50 to get started. Once you have that money, you then need to find a way of doubling that original saving, to turn the $7,812.50 into $15,625. In this second step, you have to find a business or a form of investment to double the amount." The third step would then be, Benito continued, to double the $15,625 in the same way, and so on until reaching a million dollars. It would take eight steps to get from $7,812.50 to one million. Benito then wrote in a napkin the impeccable mathematics of his eight-step plan:

Step 1: $7,812.50
Step 2: $15,625
Step 3: $31,250
Step 4: $62,500
Step 5: $125,000
Step 6: $250,000
Step 7: $500,000
Step 8: $1,000,000

Benito then explained he had already been able to save about 3,000 dollars, and was hoping to reach the full $7,812.50 soon after. "I still have no idea of how I will invest the first $7,812.50," he added. He later said he read it in a magazine, and couldn't remember if it was a *Reader's Digest* or another one. As I was contemplating the idea, I was unsure of the relevance of this revelation for the research project. I was unsure whether to feel happy for, or disappointed at, Benito. The first thing that came to my mind, unintentionally, was the history of Taso (Anaustacio Zayas), who was Sidney Mintz's main informant while he was working on his Cañaberal ethnography of sugarcane cutters in Puerto Rico back in the early 1950s (Mintz 1956).

After Mintz completed his ethnography on Cañaberal sugarcane cutters and published it in 1956, he left the island, only to return during the latter part of that decade to begin a project he had wanted to pursue for years: a biography of Taso (Mintz 1992[1960]). Taso was a unique worker among his peers, and it was precisely this uniqueness which led Mintz to choose him as his main informant. Taso was actively involved in political and labor movements, was a member of the Puerto Rican Socialist Party and was active in the sugar workers' union. In Mintz's view, he was one of the very few workers who had developed a "class consciousness." But when Mintz returned to Puerto Rico in the late 1950s to finish Taso's biography, he found a very different person from the one he had left behind: Taso had converted to a Pentecostal sect! "Nothing," wrote Mintz then, "had prepared me for this fundamental displacement" (1992[1960]: 63).

To be sure, there are many similarities between the early Taso and Benito. Benito is a very intelligent young man with a lot of energy. He may be an unskilled blue-collar worker with no formal higher education, but exhibited a natural wisdom and good leadership qualities. He is also, as many Viequenses, very articulate with words and keeps a sharp critical eye over what is happening in his island. He actively participated in the struggle to get the Navy out of Vieques, as well as in land recovery movements in both Verde Vieques and El Monte, and expresses views and ideas in defense of his participation in the land recovery movements that emphasize a more "communitarian," as opposed to an "individualistic," ethical worldview. Benito was also hardworking, and one of the few Viequenses who have successfully exploited the Bio-bay economic niche through the kayak tours, while at the same time keeping jobs in other places, mainly within the construction and landscaping industries.

In his activism and his going-forward attitude, Benito resembles the early Taso. But I could not feel the same disappointment for Benito's plan to become a millionaire which Mintz felt for Taso's conversion. To be sure, wanting to be a millionaire is not the same as converting to a Pentecostal sect, unless one wishes to talk about the transition from a "traditional" to a Protestant work ethic as a form of conversion. Moreover, any feeling of disappointment toward Benito's plan could be also conceived as sharing a latent complicity with the "new" Dracula Plan for Vieques: that is, a plan to deprive Viequenses like Benito of the ability to share in the wealth produced by the tourism industry in their own island, and in the only way that is culturally accepted and legally allowed, that is, through hard work. To what extent a feeling of disappointment implies an underlying desire to keep the primitive hero primitive by keeping him poor? This might not have been a question that anthropologists like Mintz would have to answer in the 1950s, but it is a question to which contemporary anthropologists cannot remain indifferent. In any case, one thing is certain: in his desire to become a millionaire, Benito reveals a profound internalization of the American Dream. In this sense, there is a significant difference between Benito's aspirations and those documented for American blue-collar workers (Lamont 2000), who are keeping a safe distance from the American Dream, or who have simply abandoned the American Dream altogether.

Caribbean anthropologists have documented similar forms of entrepreneurial attitudes among young men in other Caribbean islands with tourist-based economies. L. Kaifa Roland (2011), for example, has documented the business activities of the *jineteros* (or *luchadores*, as they prefer to be called) in Cuba, individuals who endured the economic hardships of the Special Period (and beyond), and whose business attitude resembles in many ways that of the Viequense tour operators researched by us. Katherine Browne has even gone further, claiming there is a pan-Caribbean male-exclusive work ethics that is widespread in the region, which she labels "creole economics." In her view, this "creole economics" is derived from the experience of slavery, and therefore different versions of that same phenomenon can be found everywhere in the Caribbean where sugar plantations flourished (as was the case of both Cuba and Vieques). The ethics finds its most vivid expressions in working-class males who exhibit savviness in their economic endeavors, at least within the expectations of their class. In the French Antillean island of Martinique, Browne is able to find an example of this "creole economics" in the figure of the *débrouillard*. But the economic behavior of the *débrouillard*, is different from that of the Cuban *luchadores* or the Viequense Bio-bay tour operators, as it "reaches well into the illicit zone of resourcefulness, to include ideas of cunning, dishonesty, and trickery" (2004: 131). The concept of the *débrouillard* is associated with a very long list of not only positive behaviors, including autonomy, freedom, being your own boss, working outside the formal sector, moonlighting, resourcefulness and cleverness; but also petty theft, opportunism, trickery, slyness and deceit, among others. In spite of the negative connotations some of these behaviors might have, the *débrouillard* is clearly not considered a thief, and in fact gains respect and is admired in the community for his special abilities.

To be sure, the economic behavior of Benito (and the Bio-bay tour operators in general) does not equate with those negative connotations associated with the Martiniquais *débrouillard*. In this sense, they resemble more the Cuban *jineteros*, who are defined by Roland as "nonthreatening hustler who are merely trying to acquire global capital for individual and family sustenance," and that in fact "might constitute a future business class, given their customer orientation and entrepreneurial spirit" (2011: 97–98). These Bio-bay tour operators are conducting arm's-length transactions with their clients, and are not interested in taking from them more than what is the standard price in the market for a tour. If there is something in which the Viequense tour operator's economic behavior can be perceived as deceitful, or as approaching that of the *débrouillard*, it is in the fact that they were operating without official permits to enter the lagoon (which was a protected area under the supervision of the Puerto Rico's Department of Natural & Environmental Resources, or DRNA by its Spanish acronym), and perhaps in not filing tax returns on all the money they were earning. But by then, the DRNA was looking the other way, and the tour operators were ignorant of the licenses and paperwork that they needed to have a legally compliant business.

Toward the end of the decade-long period ending 2014, access to the lagoon became restricted. Already by 2009 the Government of Puerto Rico announced that it was studying the possibility of turning the Bio-bay into a "sanctuary." The tour operators of the Bio-bay received the news with concern, realizing this could mean the end of the Bio-bay as an economic niche accessible to them (at least in the informal manner in which it had been accessible until then). While the government remained inactive at first, an unfortunate and fortuitous event in 2011 finally gave the Puerto Rico's DRNA and other governmental agencies the "excuse" to intervene in the mostly underground kayak tour business. On Tuesday, August 16, 2011, a shark, estimated to be six feet long, bit a US tourist while she was swimming in the bioluminescent bay at night. The shark was unable to tear the flesh out, and only left the imprint of its teeth on her leg, with substantial damage to nerves and muscles. The woman suffered a wound about 10 inches long that ran from below her knee to the ankle. This was all authorities needed to clamp down on the kayak business. The *Caribbean Business*, in its August 19, 2011 digital edition, reported that:

> Puerto Rico's Department of Natural & Environmental Resources [DRNA] is investigating what company, if any, organized the kayak trip, spokeswoman Ana María Ramos said. . . . People are prohibited from swimming in the biolumines-cent waters of Mosquito Bay to protect the ecosystem, and the company could face a penalty of up to $5,000 or even lose its license, she said. Despite the regulations, kayak operators often allow visitors to swim there. (*Caribbean Business* 2011)

By 2013, the DRNA was already requiring official permits and doing ran-dom checks on kayak operators on the shore of the Bio-bay. On one occasion, we were able to witness one particular instance where a tour operator was intercepted by a DRNA official upon arrival at the Bio-bay shore with a group of approximately twenty-five tourists. Because he was unable to provide the required permits, he was forced to return the money to the tourists and drive them back to their hotels.

With the access into the Bio-bay restricted, the lives of the kayak opera-tors began to change in predictable ways. Several of the guys, for example, traveled to the US mainland to find jobs, and stayed there for an extended period time. Interestingly, studies of labor migrants have helped to dissipate the biological and deterministic explanations of the presumably pathologi-cal Caribbean male work-avoidance ethics by showing that migrant workers do perform jobs in their country of work that they would not accept in their country of origin. While accepting certain jobs in the country of origin would represent a loss of status in their community, the absence of this community in the country of work eliminates the impediment for accepting these jobs. And, in the Caribbean, jobs within the tourism and service industry have traditionally been conceived as socially degrading, given the similarities and continuities between plantation and tourism economies (Strachan 2002; Taylor 1993). In fact, and as Chambers has documented for migrant work-ers employed in tourism jobs in Singapore, this often results in a preference among employers for migrant workers over locals:

> [migrant] workers have often lost the support of their personal networks and escaped the ascriptive criteria for social relations that are imposed by the tourism facilities. This provides, of course, another reason that the manager of tourism facilities might prefer outside labor over employing locals. (Chambers 2009: 43)

William Boyer has documented the exact same phenomenon among US Virgin Islanders. In speaking of discourses about laziness, lack of industriousness and moral failings in the context of the US Virgin Islands (USVI), Boyer points to the issue of "loss of status in the community" as a key defining factor in the refusal of workers to accept farm and menial jobs. By looking at the work ethics of Virgin Islanders who migrated to the US mainland, Boyer is able to conclude that "it is not true that native Virgin Islanders shunned menial and service work, because they willingly performed such work on the mainland. To undertake such work in their homeland, however, would have resulted in the loss of status" (2010: 300).

The irony behind the migratory patterns of the Viequense tour operators is that, by 2015, they had all returned back to Vieques and continued working in the Bio-bay. The long-term effect of the shark attack was that it forced them to get their permits and licenses in order, and they were now all back in their original businesses and operating with all their permits in order and with many tourists to prey on. The ones who had left to the US mainland had now returned, and had reopened their businesses. They were all still hardworking, and their entrepreneurial spirit showed no signs of waning.

But the point we wish to highlight is that the first thing one encounter in the discourse of Viequenses about laziness is a contradiction between what they say and what they do. How can these workers accept the accusation of laziness while leading such hardworking lives? Moreover, their discourse is not an anti-work discourse, but rather exhibits what Levitan and Johnson have labeled "the fundamental human ambivalence toward work" (1982: 36), where the desire for work does not erase an equal desire for leisure.

SECOND ELEMENT: THE LINK BETWEEN WORK AND *PASARLA BIEN*

In the discourses of our Viequense informants, statements about their working lives and about laziness are inseparable from discourses about their lives beyond work, or leisure life. More specifically, they are inseparable from ideas of happiness and *pasarla bien* (having a good time). In the discourses produced by Viequense workers there is, thus, an additional element of strong Caribbean import: the centrality attributed to *pasarla bien*—to "having a damn good time"—in their lives. In emphasizing the importance of *pasarla bien*, Viequenses make true Derek Walcott's assertion that "the Creole idea of life . . . is simply to have a damn good time, and that's it, basically . . . have a good time, period" (cf. Hirsh 1985: 113).

Expressions produced by Viequenses like *pasarla bien* and "happiness" are hard to define, but *pasarla bien* is broadly conceived as something that is properly achieved during one's leisure time, therefore entering in competition with "work" as a preferred vehicle toward "happiness." One of our informants, while talking about the benefits of working in the Bio-bay, had been very emphatic about the value of free (leisure) time for him:

> I like [working in the Bio-bay] because I have much time free, and my time, for me it is like money; also, because there are things that I want to do, spend time up there [in the land he invaded in El Monte]. . . . And for me that counts. And if I want to go surfing or something, well I have the time to do it. All I need to do is turn off the cell phone [the main way to contact new customers] and that's it. (Benito)

In their discourses about *pasarla bien*, Viequenses reproduce the tendency, also documented for contemporary blue- and white-collar workers in contemporary industrialized nations in general, of elevating the conversation about work and laziness to a wider existential level, and speculating about the conditions under which work can become a vehicle to a higher existential end, which they place in happiness and "having a good time." Lamont (2000), for example, has documented how French and American workers also place as a cardinal ethical command in their lives the "enjoyment of life" or "*joie de vivre*," which they claim to fulfill by sharing the warmth of interpersonal relations with family/friends or community contexts, that is, away from the world of work. In doing this, Lamont further argues, workers "have no choice": that is, should these workers decide to use work (more specifically, income) as an adequate measure of moral worth, they would then be forced to look upon themselves as morally lacking, given their low-income position. Workers thus have no option, in order to retain dignity and self-respect, but to construct a dignified persona around their extra work or leisure time activities. These workers, as Goldthorpe et al. have also commented, "are selling their work to the highest bidder while turning their emotional commitments towards family [and community] life" (1969, in Lamont 2000: 30). In other words, they have abandoned "work" and "earnings" as the standard for measuring moral worth, and have replaced it with "happiness" and ideas of *pasarla bien*. This is also the reason why Viequense workers will project an idea of themselves as happy, fun-loving and party-going people, drawing in this way a moral boundary between themselves and the hardworking, money-driven (and presumably less happier) North Americans who are "above" them.

In any case, because most of our close informants were male, young and bachelors, their ideas of *pasarla bien* were surely crossed by gender and age group preferences and cultural biases. Thus, the entrepreneurial and hardworking attitude that they exhibited were combined with an explicit desire to enjoy life, to practice surfing, participate in the Vieques nightlife, pick-up girls (maybe gringas), drink beers with friends, travel to the Big Island for concerts, organize parties at the beach, go fishing and so on.

But the expression of *pasarla bien* acquires a special nuance when related to nightlife, to partaking in the drinking and dancing and socializing that takes place in the Malecón at night (or anywhere else where there is a party). One of the problems with documenting leisure life, as opposed to documenting working life, is that leisure is something that is best captured through ethnographic observation and unstructured interaction than through formal interviews. Thus, while the feeling of dissatisfaction with the conditions of working life, for example, are well captured through words, feelings like *pasarla bien* fall within a much more elusive and ineffable dimension of existence. It is one of those things that are easier done than said. Therefore, a narrative of an improvised party at the beach in April 2009, in the form of what Clifford Geertz has called a "thick description" (1973), can provide a better understanding of the meaning of "having a damn good time" or *pasarla bien* for a Viequense, certainly more than one extracted from a recorded interview (at least for the age group of these young male Viequense workers and entrepreneurs).

On the evening of that day I received a phone call from Vero (a research assistant) telling me that Tomás had organized a party at El Cayo. There will be food and drinks, and live music. Tomás is the bouncer at Duffy's, one of the most popular bar/restaurant in the Malecón area, but he was off that night, and felt like partying. It was a slow night and there was not much else to do, plus the weather was good. The occasion was perfect for a party at El Cayo.

Because the night ended somewhat dramatically (for reasons that will be explained further down), I was unable to go to sleep afterward, and instead invested my time writing down a narrative of the events of the night, to which I later added commentaries about the working lives of men in the party, and so on. The resulting narrative provides a more integral and revealing view of the ethic, aesthetic and ludic values of Puerto Rican/Viequense working men, as they are played out in quotidian life, than any recorded conversation could.

El Cayo is a strip of land with some bushes and small coconut trees, roughly forty feet wide, and with water on both sides of the strip. It is the point where the extreme corners of two contiguous semicircular bays (Esperanza and Sun Bay) meet, forming a small peninsula-like strip of land that sticks out into the sea, dying in a big rock formation. It is an ideal place for hanging out at night for several reasons. Because there is a strong wind current between the two bays, there are no mosquitoes. Moreover, the place is close enough to Esperanza to walk back and forth, but far enough for the very loud music to be heard by anyone in Esperanza at late hours of the night. On top of that, it is an absolutely beautiful place. The word rapidly spread around, and in a matter of one or two hours the party was going. Several of the guys who usually work and hang around in the Malecón were also there.

Tomás and Feliú went to buy the food and drinks for the party. I left my hotel at around 6:30 p.m. and walked all the way through the beach to El Cayo—a ten-minute walk at the most. When I got there, around 7:00 p.m., there was a group of approximately ten people at the party. There was Beni, Jorge, Feliú, Tomás, Hatillo Rasta, Tito Miel, Micky, Vero and Melanie. Others would arrive later. The only women there were Vero, an assistant researcher, and Melanie. These guys have girlfriends and/or wives, but they don't bring them to this kind of party. The same rules that apply for women in the Malecón apply to beach parties.

These guys, who seem to be very modern in every other aspect of their lives, still live under these very conservative rules when it relates to their public life with their official female partners. Vero and I had experienced these conservative attitudes in a more drastic manner several days before. We were walking down the Malecón and encountered three young male Viequenses we both know well. We stopped to say hello and talk for a while. They all shook hands with me but make absolutely no gesture to salute Vero. We kept talking, and after a few seconds we noticed they would not even look at Vero in the eyes, and acted as if she was not there at all. Vero immediately reacted and said: "Hey, what's the matter with you guys? You're not going to say hello to me." They immediately said hello, laughed at Vero's reaction and apologized. They then provided an explanation for their behavior which, at least to us, sounded awkward. They explained that in Vieques you never say hello to your male friends' girlfriends, not to give the impression that you have (or want to have) "something with her" (algo con ella). The fact that Vero and I were not a couple made no difference. In any case, the point is that, while it is perfectly normal for two girls from San Juan (like Vero) to go to beach parties at night, in Vieques it is almost a men-only event. And while the way of life that these young men live seems to be modern in almost every way one can imagine, there seems to be a preference towards the conservative Viequense women when it comes to choosing one's "official" wife or girlfriend.

Tito Miel was the only guy from the group who was not invited, but was already there when we arrived. He is a forty-something man, slightly older than the rest of the group. When we arrived, he already had set up a hammock between two palm trees. He greeted us. He explained he had quarreled with his wife and was kicked out of the house for the night. Thus, he was planning on spending the night there in a hammock. He already had a BBQ lit up, since he was planning on cooking for himself. He also had several bottles of honey, since he is an apiculturist (that is why they call him Tito Miel, "miel" meaning honey in Spanish). He always carries honey with him because people in the street are always asking him for it. He has a formal job in a security company, but makes some extra bucks in an informal manner by selling his honey around. He assured me the bees he uses feed on natural flowers, so I bought two bottles from him, at three dollars each.

Tomás immediately prepared the area for the party. He has an old SUV which is perhaps better defined, even by him, as a "movable home." He has a big music equipment, two power generators (one gas- and one wind-powered), a tent, several hammocks, an awning, two coolers, tools of all kinds, BBQ, surfboard, fishing rods, laptop for the music, extra clothing, and tons of other stuff in boxes and bags. As he explains, his philosophy is that one must always be ready for when the occasion appears. Although he has a real home to go to, he sleeps on hammocks or in his tent many nights in any beach spot he can find, and loves doing that. He tied the awning to the branches of trees, turned on his gas-generator and lit up a light-bulb, and hooked up his music equipment, including two big speakers which he carries out of the truck and places on the floor. It was a little bit excessive, I thought. We had technology there to put up a party for 200 people, but we were only like a dozen.

Micky had also brought his computer, as well as his electric guitar together with amplifier and speaker, and was hooking up cables and microphones. Micky's father is from Vieques, but he was born and raised in the East Cost of the US mainland. He came along with his brother Mark (who was not in the party) back in the early 2000s to participate in the protests against the Navy occupation, and liked it so much that never left. They both look white, speak perfect Puerto Rican Spanish (as well as perfect English), and share also a Puerto Rican lifestyle in almost every other way possible.

Mark, Micky's brother, works for the Vieques Conservation and Historical Trust as Director of Community Affairs and Marine Life Exhibit. The Trust keeps a small but nice museum and information center in the Malecón. Mark is also very much involved in community affairs. Micky, on the other hand, is more informal. He plays the electric guitar, and works mostly as a musician. He has a band called "Micky Miers and the Rustics," and he travels to Cape Cod every summer to work there playing in pubs. He returns to Vieques during the winter-time, and lives mostly out of the money he brings from Cape Cod.

Afterwards, Tomás and Feliú brought out the stuff they bought. What they got for food was somewhat disappointing. Being experienced fishermen, at least to the extent that all Viequenses are, one would have hoped for a BBQ of fish and lobster, but hamburgers and hotdogs is what they got. Two bags of Holsum sandwich bread, two packs of Oscar-Meyer's hotdogs, and a box of hamburgers of some American brand I cannot recall. There were also two or three bags of potato chips and chicharrones (pig skin). For drinking, they got two boxes of the local Medalla beer. Since Tito Miel already had a fire going in his BBQ, we agreed it would be easier to put more wood in it, and then cook our food in his BBQ. Tito Miel immediately assumed control of the seasoning and cooking tasks, including the cooking of what he calls his specialty: hotdog with honey, which I found totally disgusting. He would also sprinkle the hamburgers and hotdogs with that Adobo Bohio seasoning that Puerto Ricans put on almost everything they eat, and that Tomás brought out from his truck/movable home.

It's almost 7:30 p.m., and Jorge explains he has some clients to bring on tour to the Bio-bay. He has four Gringas on schedule at $25 each, and needs to pick them up at their hotel by 7:30 p.m. So Jorge prepares to leave and, as he is pulling back, Berito Rasta arrives. He just came to see what was going on, as Beni had left a message in his cell phone letting him know about the improvised party. But Berito Rasta also needs to leave right away, as he also had four other tourists to bring to the Bio-bay, and also had to go pick them up at their hotel at 7:30 p.m. Both Berito and Jorge work bringing tourists on kayaks to the Bio-bay. But Jorge is tired and wants to stay in the party, so he entrusts his four Gringas to Berito Rasta. Berito then left to pick up the two 4-persons groups, total 8 persons, at $25 per head. While there will be a redistribution of the earnings afterwards, it was not necessary to spell out the arrangement then and there, nor even talk about it, since it is already taken for granted by both. Feliú volunteered to go help out with the big group, and it was assumed a helpers standard rate of two or three dollars per head to compensate him. So Berito Rasta left with Feliú, and the party continued without them.

I talked to Melanie for a little while. She is an Asian-looking girl whom I've seen around, but have never formally met. So this was the first time we talked. Her family is from Vietnam, but she was born and raised in Washington State. She likes to take walks along the beach at night, because she sunburns easily during the daytime—and that's how she ended up in the party. She has been living in Vieques for seven months, and was still mastering her Spanish. Somebody passed her a Philly, and she had a quick smoke. She said it helped her with her Spanish. She stayed around for a while, but then left. Her fluency in Spanish is still poor enough to make her feel displaced in a place where everybody is speaking Spanish.

A half-gallon of Pitorro suddenly appears on the scene. Pitorro is a form of Puerto Rican Moonshine. It was perfect to help swallow Tito Miel's totally disgusting hotdogs with honey. I seemed to be the only one who disliked his specialty plate, because everyone else was devouring them as if taste was not an important part of the eating experience. Regarding the Pitorro, the immediate problem was that we had not brought cups. But Tomás, who is a carpenter by profession, brought out of one of the boxes he keeps in his SUV three wooden cups that looked like chalices, and that he had made himself in the lathe. They served the purpose. The Pitorro was sweet and smooth, and very strong – as all Pitorros are. As Pitorro is drank in very small quantities, returning to the bottle every half an hour or hour for another shot, the bottle and Tomas's wooden chalices remained on top of the cooler throughout the night, and one could notice its content slowly diminishing with the passing of the hours.

Hatillo Rasta was dancing to Reggae music near the speakers. He is from San Juan, but works as a bartender in one of the bars in Esperanza. He is white, at least by Puerto Rican standards, but wears Rasta dreadlocks and always wears surfer clothing. He originally arrived there not because of the party, but to check on the waves near El Cayo. He wanted to do night surfing, and had his surfboard in the back of his pick-up truck, ready to go. But since waves were not good, and Mickey had finally been able to put everything together and started playing, Hatillo Rasta couldn't resist the temptation and started dancing. Since that moment on, and throughout the rest of the night, he virtually never stopped dancing. His dance had a trance-like quality to it. I made a comment about it to one of the guys, and he told me Hatillo had presumably taken some hallucinogenic mushrooms that grow on cow dung, and that is used by locals to get high. The eating of this mushroom is also popular in other Caribbean islands as well, and is a central attraction in the so-called Full-Moon Parties popular in the British Virgin Islands. Whatever the case, the truth is that Hatillo Rasta remained in his trance-like dance pretty much all night.

By around 10:00 p.m. Beni and Jorge started complaining that all the food was gone, and suggested we get more food. Jorge joined him soon after, but suggested instead that we made a serrucho (a collection in which everybody puts whatever they can), and they would go buy more hamburgers and hot-dogs. The rest of the crowd didn't seem too hungry, so nobody paid attention to them. But they didn't give up, and kept sporadically bringing up the idea for like another hour, eating in the meantime the bags of potato chips and chicharrones (pigs skin) that were left. But people were still uninterested, including myself. This all changed when Carmelo and El Gringo showed up, and Carmelo expressed that he was hungry too. The first thing Carmelo asked as he approached the group was if there was any food left. With these additional supporters, Beni and Jorge were able to move people to give them some money to go buy more food. Those who had any money would pinch in two or three dollars each.

Tito Miel had said that the fire of the BBQ had already faded out, and that he needed more wood to get it started once again. So, while Beni and Jorge were out buying food, Carmelo and El Gringo went around looking for wood and dry leaves. Within minutes Tito Miel had set the fire going again, and also within minutes Jorge and Beni arrived with the food – more hamburgers *and hotdogs. They had also bought more stuff to drink: one case of Medalla beer, one liter of Don Q Cristal rum, and a bottle of Pineapple juice to be used as mixer. But, once again, they forgot to bring cups, so Tomás' wooden chalices once again came in handy. Since there were not enough chalices for everybody, rum drinks automatically became collectively-owned, and were constantly passed around.*

Beni, after eating, went to sleep in one of the hammocks. Beni is not drinking alcohol because he is taking some prescribed pills he cannot mix with alcohol, so he drinks water and Sprite. The pills he is taking also make him sleepy, so he couldn't help falling asleep in one of the hammocks after eating. Nearby, in another hammock, was Carmelo talking to Hatillo Rasta and Vero. I couldn't hear what he was saying, but it must have been interesting judging from Hatillo Rasta and Vero's faces of astonishment.

I spoke to El Gringo for a while: a skinny, blondish, long-haired American, in his late twenties or early thirties, with the hair gathered in a ponytail. He was wearing old worn-out jeans, a baseball cap, and a pair of construction boots, instead of the more typical sneakers or sandals. His hippie-looking, red-neck appearance contrasts sharply with his work discipline and entrepreneurial spirit. He works in construction and as handy-man. He has been doing that in Vieques for ten years, and claims he is earning good money. At the moment, he has a contract with the W hotel to install 160-odd locks on doors at $40 each. He can do like twenty in a day, so he makes like $800 a day doing that. In eight days he will make $6,400. He also earns extra income by watching over North-American-owned "vacation" houses while they are not there. He subcontracts Viequenses to work for him, as he cannot do everything by himself. Carmelo is one of the Viequenses being subcontracted by El Gringo, at $10 an hour.

Micky was with the computer, selecting songs to play. At this stage he had passed from being the guitar man to being the DJ. I asked Micky to show me his music files, and stayed awhile looking at what he had. It was mostly Reggae music. I asked if he had any Salsa music, and he said of course. He then directed me to his Salsa files, and I checked them out. He had very good stuff. At my request, the music changed from Bob Marley to Ismael "Maelo" Rivera, the sonero mayor of the Salsa world.

Berito and Feliú arrived around 10:30 p.m. from the Bio-bay. It took them like three hours to run the tour. There were hamburgers and hotdogs left, and the work had made Berito hungry. He grabed a hamburger and a beer and started eating. Feliú did the same, but he is drinking water. He does not drink alcohol. They talk about the pretty gringas in the group. There was particularly one that, in the words of Berito, estaba bien buena (was gorgeous). Someone talks about having bad luck with seducing gringas. Most agreed that Alexis (who is not in the party – Beni called him, but he didn't answer), was the luckiest of the group in getting laid with gringas. Someone else suggested that half of Alexis' presumed sexual encounters with gringas are made-up. For these guys, any subject is a good excuse to tease each other. In fact, the constant teasing and teasing-back is one of the mechanisms these guys constantly use to draw group solidarity and boundaries. Knowing who to tease, knowing what to tease him or her about, achieving the familiarity necessary to enter into the teasing exchange, being able to understand what the teasing is about—all of these serve as mechanisms that allow to distinguish insiders from outsiders.

After eating, Berito, Feliú and Jorge gathered apart to settle accounts for the night. I sneaked in, just to watch the transaction. They put in action the informal and unwritten rules by which these self-made tour operators distribute the earnings, based on assigned percentages to different tasks and the use of equipment. They know I am interested in this as part of the research, so they spell out for me what they're doing. There were eight persons in the group, at $25 each, which adds up to $200. Half of that belongs to Berito, since four of the clients were his, and he provided all the service. The remaining $100 would be split in half between Jorge and Berito. Jorge gets his first 25 percent of the total (only for his 4 customers) because he brought in the costumers; and an additional 25 percent because they did the tour on kayaks owned by him. This adds up to 50 percent for Jorge. Berito, on his side, collects his first 25 percent for picking the tourists up and returning them to their hotel, and an additional 25 percent for doing the actual tour; which also adds up to 50 percent. So, out of the $200, Jorge gets $50 and Berito $150. They then both agree that Feliú will be paid $3 per customer for helping out, which adds up to $24, but is rounded to $25. Jorge gives him $5 and Berito $20. Done deal.

In the end, Berito was able to cash in $130 in approximately three hours of work. But it is no easy job: working at night, carrying kayaks up and down from the top of the truck, fixing the bus that is used to transport tourists, going into the water, rowing, etc. Jorge was perhaps the one that came out better, since he earned $45 for doing nothing. He could have made $100, but he was tired and could afford the loss. He explained that, during the past Spring Break season, he was bringing in two and three groups of 20-30 people each in one single night. He could earn as much as $2,250 in one single night. He also talks about two groups that have made reservations with him for next week: one of 25 persons and the other of 30. He doesn't complete the mathematics, but I do in my head. At $25 each, that means he will make $1,375 in two days.

Actually, Jorge seems to be doing quite well, within the norm. He started talking about the 20-feet yola (a locally-made wood boat typically used by Puerto Rican fishermen) he had just bought for $1,500, and that he had found *a new Evinrude 150 de paquete ("still in the box") for $2,500 in the Big Island, an unbelievably good deal. He expressed some concern that it might be stolen, because the price is too good to be true. That motor regularly costs $12,000. But he's not asking questions. He plans to use the boat for snorkeling tours in the daytime, and then continue doing the bio-bay tours in kayaks during the night. But beyond that, he is also looking forward to using the boat to do other things he likes to do for fun, like diving and fishing, and bringing the family out for a ride.*

As for Feliú, he earned only $25. Feliú also works with Mark (Micky's brother) at the Vieques Conservation and Historical Trust on a voluntary basis, but also runs a hamburger stand at the Malecón during weekends, where he is now famous for his "Triple-Burgers." He is much younger than the rest of the guys, and doesn't have family responsibilities, so he gets by with much less.

Around 11:30 p.m., Jorge said he had to wake up early next day, and left. At this stage, everybody had scattered around. Beni was still sleeping in one of the hammocks. Hatillo Rasta had moved his ritualistic dancing farther near the water, somewhat apart from the group, and was there all by himself. The fact that the music had changed from Reggae to Salsa didn't seem to have altered much the structure of his dance. Vero and I were talking. Tomás was with Tito Miel drinking Pitorro, sitting on the hood of Hatillo Rasta's car.

When we left, around midnight, Tito Miel started cleaning up the area, but was doing a scrappy job. At the beginning of the party, I looked for a bag and hanged it from a tree branch, but it seemed I was the only one using it. Instead, they were all throwing the trash and beer cans on a designated spot on the floor, near the cooler, with the intention of picking it up once the party was over. When I left, at around midnight, I did so worrying that some of the trash will be inevitably left back at the beach. A real shame, I thought.

On our way back to our hotel, we had to go through the food-stands area where a gringo-owned food stand called Danny's Burger was located, in order to reach the Malecón. As we were approaching this area, we started hearing the firemen's siren, and could see what seemed to be the remains of a fire in that same area. Once we got there we discovered what had happened. Somebody had set Danny's Burger on fire. The whole structure was completely reduced to ashes.

Several times after the 2009 party, the subject comes out in casual conversations within the group who attended. Somebody says: "Do you remember the party at El Cayo?," and everyone unanimously agree that "la pasamos muy bien," with a marked emphasis on the "muy bien." In a small island with no movie theater, no shopping center and no fast-food chains, the beach is often the setting of events over which people will later say that "la pasamos bien."

But the danger behind emphasizing this discourse about *pasarla bien* too much is that, in their encounter and "dispute" with discourses imported from continental US, they will be judged by a rigid either/or logic, where any minimal allegory to *pasarla bien* could potentially be equated with "anti-working" values, and thus muted.

This fact, though, seems to not have had a strong impact on our informants' lives, as by 2015 they were pursuing *pasarla bien* with the same impetus as in 2004. This fact became evident to me when I encountered Benito one summer day in 2014. I was driving with my family toward the beach at about 11:00 a.m. and had stopped at the Mambo Minimarket, which was on the way, to buy provisions for the day. I met Benito there, standing in front of the door with his surfboard next to him, waiting for somebody to give him a ride to El Cayo. He tied his surfboard to the rack on top of our car, and we gave him a ride. We talked along the way. He was working in a construction project, but they ran out of cement and were awaiting a shipment that would come on the cargo ferry at around 3:00 p.m. "That gives me a four hour break, so I decided to go surfing. I should have enough time to surf and be back at work by 3:00 p.m.," he said. I felt tempted to ask Benito about his plan to become a millionaire, but the surfboard on top of my car was all one needed to understand that, at least for the time being, the tension between leisure and work is being kept in balance.

We arrived at the beach and one of my sons (who is fond of Benito) insisted we wait to see him surf. Benito jumped in the water with the board, went under a wave, got wet, and came out hollering: "Ooooooo!" He then started swimming toward the waves. We watch him for a while. No doubt he was "having a damn good time," and only with much difficulty could one define him as having a Protestant work ethic of the type described by Weber—despite his plan to become a millionaire.

There is, thus (and beyond what a one-night party may reveal about the broader significance of *pasarla bien* in daily life in general), a strong connection between *pasarla bien* and ideals of a worthy, deserving and dignified lifestyle—this latter guided by both economic and noneconomic motives. The idea that "lifestyle factors" play an important role in determining the motivations of small-scale entrepreneurs has been also documented in the tourism literature (Shaw 2004; Dewhurst and Horobin 1998; Ateljevic and Doorne 2000). Shaw, for example, has argued "there is increasing evidence to show that lifestyle factors and non-economic motives are significant, and that the definition of the entrepreneur needs to be more inclusive of these ideas" (Shaw 2004: 126). Dewhurst and Horobin have similarly argued that, for these small-scale entrepreneurs, "success might best be measured in terms of a continuing ability to perpetuate their chosen lifestyle" (1998: 30).

THIRD ELEMENT: THE PUERTO RICAN TRADITION
OF TALKING ABOUT THEIR OWN LAZINESS

Elsewhere we have written about the *near-obsessive Puerto Rican and Caribbean tradition of talking about their own laziness* (cf. Galanes 2007). Puerto Ricans, and Caribbean peoples, in general, tend to speak in open and unapologetic manner about their own laziness, and it is possible to recover scriptural traces of these discourses dating as far back as the 16th century. As Edgardo Rodríguez Juliá has stated, "[t]he great artists and writers of the Caribbean coincide in wanting to talk about this *drowsiness*, or *taedium vitae*, so characteristic of the *tristes tropiques*" (2002: 3).

Rather than exploring the multiple instances in which this tradition finds written expression throughout Puerto Rican and Caribbean history, for the purposes of this book it will suffice to say that by 1934 Puerto Rican scholar Antonio Pedreira had already elevated the trait to the category of "national character." In his canonical essay *Insularismo*, from the same year, Pedreira would refer to this aversion to work by the name of *aplatanamiento*: a word he borrows from popular Puerto Rican argot, and where the plantain fruit acquires a metaphorical meaning associated with work-aversion (synonymous with lazy or *vago*).

> The hot climate melts our will and causes a rapid deterioration of our psychology. . . . From its weakening effects comes that national characteristic that we call *aplatanamiento*. To be *aplatanao*, in our country [Puerto Rico] means to suffer from a special kind of inhibition, a mental drowsiness, a lack of entrepreneurship. . . . It is to acclimatize oneself to the tropical effeminacy. . . . The *musa paradisiaca*, the scientific and ineffable name of the plantain, is a rhetoric symbol of our vegetative spirit. (Pedreira 2001[1934]: 39)

At a broad Puerto Rican level, this cultural tendency to talk about their own laziness would evidence an upsurge in the period 2006 and afterward, this time motivated by the publication of two independent reviews of Puerto Rican economy coming out in that same year: the first one, a study conducted by the Brookings Institution in conjunction with the locally based Center for the New Economy, published under the title *The Economy of Puerto Rico: Restoring Growth* (Collins et al. 2006); the other a special column published by *The Economist*, under the title "Trouble on Welfare Island" (2006). Both studies concluded that the most important obstacle preventing the economic development of Puerto Rico was the lack of willing workers, as evidenced by its low labor force participation rate (i.e., the proportion of men and women of working age in the overall population who are employed). The study conducted by the Brookings Institution would point to the fact that Puerto

Rico has a participation rate that is the lowest in the Americas, and "possibly the lowest in the world."[15] *The Economist* would similarly conclude that the island is "full of low income and idle hands" (2006: 25). In 2007, another major study of the Puerto Rican economy commission by *Caribbean Business* expressed the same concern.

While the reports of the Brookings Institution, *The Economist* and *Caribbean Business* all warned about the presumably critical levels of Puerto Rican participation rate in the present, the downward movement of the rate, as Puerto Rican economic historian James Dietz has shown, actually began much earlier. According to Dietz, the participation rate of Puerto Rico began its downward move with the implantation of the program for industrialization of the island's economy in the 1960s, under the name of "Operation Bootstrap" (*Operación Manos a la Obra*). Operation Bootstrap was devised on two major premises: that agriculture alone could not provide an economic viable base for the country at large; and that it was thus required to transform the Puerto Rican economy from one based on agriculture to one based on manufacture and industry. But "the defect of the development program," Dietz argues, "was that it stretched too much the premise . . . that agriculture was a too fragile base," thus reducing agricultural production to a minimum (Dietz 2002[1989]: 293). The participation rate in the workforce reached its postwar-period peak in 1951, with 55.5 percent, and then started decreasing until reaching its minimum in 1983, with 41 percent. And, as Dietz explains, "[t]his general reduction indicates that the disposition of workers to enter the job market started to decline just at the moment that the industrialization program was taking off" (2002[1989]: 294).[16]

In any case, if the 2006–2007 publications served as a warning to Puerto Ricans of the need to mend their ways, or face the enforcement of economic reforms that would be implemented by the government to solve the situation (i.e., the reports specifically recommended significant cuts on welfare spending, reducing governmental employee payroll, adopting a "Puerto Rican" minimum wage lower than the federal minimum wage, etc.), by 2009 Puerto Ricans got to witness first hand, and in very dramatic manner, the impact of these economic reforms. In this year, the pro-statehood NPP candidate, Luis Fortuño, was elected Governor of Puerto Rico. Unlike most Puerto Rican politicians, including most politicians from his own NPP party, Fortuño is a confirmed conservative, with formal ties to the US Republican Party, who publicly claims his sympathy with the economic views of former president Ronald Reagan. Thus, Fortuño entered office in 2009 with a clear plan in mind: making the government small. In the case of Puerto Rico, the first and most important step taken in that direction would be a dramatic reduction of the governmental employee payroll. Law 7 was then passed, calling for the immediate cessation of over 40,000 public employees. That meant for Vieques some seventy-three public employees.

Thus, with Fortuño, Puerto Ricans experienced the implementation of neo-liberal policies in a manner unlike anything they had witnessed in their recent past. If the publication of *Restoring Growth* and "Trouble on Welfare Island" in 2006 served as a reminder to Puerto Ricans of what the future holds for welfare-dependent individuals, that future became a reality in 2009 with the passing of Law 7. Without a doubt, the saliency of debates about the laziness of Viequenses in 2009 was partly but evidently motivated by these political events taking place at a Puerto Rican-wide level. In fact, our interviews were made while the firings had just begun, and it was very much present in the mind of our interviewees.

> Viequenses are facing, the 30th day of this month [March 2009] . . . the municipal government is leaving in the street 130 employees, without an alternative in terms of where to look for a job, and the next month they will lay off 130 more. . . . I mean, that in reality the unemployment here is above 50% without taking into consideration these layoffs of these two months. (Other Viequense #2)[17]

Thus, while the debates about the work-avoiding attitudes of Puerto Ricans are not new to the island (nor to the Caribbean region in general), in the period 2006 and after, the debate acquired a public saliency and intensity unlike anything the island had experienced in the recent past, which was exacerbated by the extensive coverage that *Restoring Growth* and "Trouble on Welfare Island" received in the media, repeatedly making the front pages of local newspapers, or the topic of conversation in TV and radio programs. Thus, the debate over the laziness of Puerto Ricans had also become a "cultural hot button" at a broad Puerto Rican level by this same period. In general, Puerto Ricans reacted to the contents of these publications in a manner similar to the way Viequenses reacted to accusations of laziness: with indignation.

The deteriorating conditions of the island's economy in the years following the publications (the US financial and real estate crisis of 2008, the cessation of 40,000 governmental employees in 2009, the exodus of industries, loss of jobs, massive migration of workers into the US mainland and "brain drain," etc.) only helped to make conditions for workers harsher, and to helped fuel the debate even further. The debate seemed to have reached the status of a national crisis; what Alvarado Vega and Díaz characterized as a "frenzied concern" (2011: n/p).

With the participation rate showing a downward trend in the years following 2006, the debate reached another climactic moment in 2011 when the legendary salsa orchestra *El Gran Combo* was commissioned by the local bank Banco Popular to rewrite, as part of a bank's promotional campaign, the title and the lyrics of their acclaimed 1960s song "I don't do anything else" [*No hago mas na'*]—leaving the music untouched. This is a very popular song where the lyrics document in a quasi-ethnographic manner, and with a dose of picaresque humor, the laziness and dependency of Puerto Ricans. The song has, as most Puerto Ricans would immediately agree, achieved the status of, if not the official manifesto celebrating the most baroque expression of their own culture, at least a manifesto to which Puerto Ricans would surrender when induced by the trance-like qualities of salsa dancing any given *Viernes Social* (Friday Night Spree), aided most probably by great quantities of "Medalla" beer and "Don Q Cristal" rum. The "Chorus" of the song, and some of its most telling lines, read as follows:

Chorus: How good is to live like this/eating and not working!
Lines: Listen to me / I have never moved a finger / and don't waste your time / I'm not going to change / No way! . . . / How good is to live life / eating, sleeping and not doing anything—Listen brother, do you know what is like to be / in a rocking chair / rocking and rocking? / Waiting for the food coupons / and the Social Security / Anyone can do that!

The song then ends with a punch line that evidences the stubbornness with which Puerto Ricans intend to hold on to this tradition in unconditional manner: "Who will work? / Who, me? / Find someone else / I already did what I was going to do." In 2011, then, *No hago mas na'* was rewritten with lyrics that said exactly the opposite to the original 1960s version, and with a new title, *Echar pa' lante* (Going Forward). The new lyrics read as follows:

Chorus: How good is to live like this / With desire to work: I wake up in the morning / I leave the house all dressed up / ready to move ahead / Never backwards / When it's time to leave work / I can remember it as if it was yesterday / the words of my mother / Saying "My son, you have to work / Heads on and never backwards" / How good, how good is to live one's life / going forward, never backwards.

The ending punch line changes from the "Who's going to work? . . . Find someone else" in the original version to the more optimistic "We need to go forward!" in the 2011 version. In any case, and even when the intention of Banco Popular or *El Gran Combo* might have been to contribute to a national project aimed at overcoming a harsh economic crisis, the prescriptive tone of this new "Going Forward!" song also had the effect of forcing Puerto Ricans to confront, once again, their own laziness; and salsa-dancing halls ceased to be a refuge where the debate could be evaded or delayed. It would be fair to say, then, that in the post-2006 period the debate about the laziness of Puerto Ricans transcended the intellectual circles and became something to be talked about seriously, soberly and in a rational manner, by all members of society.

Since the publication of *Restoring Growth* and "Trouble on Welfare Island," in 2006, the debate over the problematic work ethics of Puerto Ricans became more salient, more acute, more public and more rationalized. To put it in different words, by 2011 its impact was strong enough to transform a salsa orchestra of the stature of *El Gran Combo* from popular chronicler of Puerto Rican culture to political reformers of Puerto Rican "pathological" culture. With this move, perhaps, *El Gran Combo* ceased doing what salsa orchestras usually do or are presumably meant to do: being popular chroniclers of Puerto Rican way of life, even in its problematic dimensions, and then proposing dance as a solution. In here, the playing of the drums ceases to serve the function it has historically served since the times of the plantations: being an instrument of resistance.

Regardless of the impact that the new 2011 version of *No hago mas na'* might have had, the reality is that Puerto Rican participation rate kept decreasing and, by September 2012, it reached its lowest historical level ever of 39.6 percent. It was also the first time in Puerto Rican history that the rate went below the 40 percent threshold (Díaz Román 2012:6). By 2013, it remained slightly above that threshold, at 41.2 percent.

Thus, it is impossible to attempt to explain the saliency and form that debates about laziness acquired in Vieques outside of this broader context. But what is important to recognize is that, regardless of what might had been the causes that ignited the upsurge of these negative discourses in Vieques, the accusation of laziness would nevertheless find in the context of Vieques (and Puerto Rico) fertile ground for its reception and dissemination. In this context, the near-obsessive Puerto Rican tradition of talking about their own laziness served the function of, at the very least, granting individuals exceptional permission to talk about an issue which, because of its sensitive and potentially shameful character, social etiquette would have otherwise mandated discreetness or silence.

FOURTH ELEMENT: THE ACCEPTANCE OF THE ACCUSATION USING THE THIRD-PERSON PLURAL

And, if social etiquette grants Puerto Ricans exceptional permission to talk about their own laziness, it will also suggest the proper linguistic and orthographic forms that can be used at the moment of the speech act. One such suggested form, widely adopted by our informants, was the use of the third-person plural. That is, the acceptance of the accusation of laziness is always posed using the third-person plural "They" (*Ellos*), instead of in the more logical or convenient first person plural "We" (*Nosotros*); and without dwelling on the fact that they themselves are Viequenses and Puerto Ricans. Thus, while the response of Viequenses to accusations of laziness is self-critical on the part of the subject who produces the discourse (there is an acceptance of his/her own faults), there is also this very peculiar trait of the Puerto Rican language game which, at least at the level of the speech act, allows the subject to evade or transfer the guilt beyond himself/herself. The pervasiveness of this speech trait seems to be so strong that, on one occasion, one of our informants was forced to clarify in a very odd manner:

> What happens here is that people are lazy. Ha! In general, in Puerto Rico, people are lazy. It's true. Including myself also, ha, ha . . . but it's true, Boricuas are lazy. It's not a lie. Most of them are lazy. (Employer Puerto Rican #12)

The informant begins by adopting a "me-they" dichotomy, thus giving the impression that he wishes to exclude himself from "the rest of Puerto Ricans." This is followed by a clarification: "Including myself." Finally, after the clarification, the subject returns to the third person plural once again. To be sure, there is a big semantic difference between saying "we are lazy" and saying "They are lazy, including myself." The simple fact that he feels the need to clarify, accompanied by the multiple "it's true" and "it's not a lie," speaks about the pervasiveness of this peculiar speech trait of Puerto Ricans.

FIFTH ELEMENT: CLASH BETWEEN DISCOURSES SEPARATED BY *LE DIFFÉREND*

The saliency and forms that these discourses about laziness would assume in Vieques in the post-Navy period must be understood as the result of a clash between two major opposing discourses, one imported from the mainland US by the many North American residential tourists who moved into the island in the post-Navy period; the other feeding on local notions of work, happiness and *pasarla bien*. The first one is usually referred to in the academic literature, following a Weberian terminology, as a "Protestant work-ethics." It rests on the idea—first put forward by Calvin as a religious command, and later secularized by Hegel and Marx—that there is dignity behind the act of work. This idea was contrary to Catholic doctrine (as it then existed), which held a view of work as a necessary but undesirable task.

As is well known, sociologist Max Weber, in his *The Protestant Ethics and the Spirit of Capitalism* (2009[1905]), has traced the origin of this debate (of this clash of discourses) back to the Protestant Reform, coinciding in time with the advent of modernity and capitalism. In fact, according to Weber, capitalism was one of the major forces leading to a radical reevaluation of the activity of labor, which would be stripped from all its negative connotations and reinterpreted as a primordial human activity, in stark opposition to the ancient/medieval conception. The emergence of the Protestant ethics, in Weber's account, would then become "the spirit of capitalism," that is, the ideological force (in this case under the guise or a religious command) upon which capitalism could develop and flourish. Not ironically, the historical moment of Protestant Calvinism coincides in time with the emergence of the concept of "lazy," and its Spanish equivalent *vago*, in their modern meaning.[18] Nonetheless, it is with the works of Hegel, and later Marx, that the ideas of work as a dignified human activity and laziness a moral fault would be secularized, and eventually become part of Western common sense.

But the idea of a "Protestant work ethics" did not remained unchallenged in its struggle for hegemony. In fact, it was Max Weber himself who also devoted, in his *The Protestant Ethics and the Spirit of Capitalism*, a significant number of pages to describe the "stubborn resistance" with which this new notion of work would meet in its aim of achieving some degree of hegemony. "Wherever modern capitalism has begun its work of increasing the productivity of human labor by increasing its intensity, it has encountered the immensely stubborn resistance of this leading trait of pre-capitalist labor" (Weber 2009: 29); and it remained, Weber would recognize by 1905 (the time he was writing, and approximately 400 years after the Protestant Reform), as "the most important opponent with which the spirit of capitalism . . . has had to struggle" (Weber 2009: 28). Marx would also encounter this resistance to the modern idea of work, particularly when confronted by other Marxist thinkers who had quite literally transformed Marxism into an anti-work philosophy. The most evident example was his dispute with French Marxist Paul Lafargue (Marx's own son-in-law) who, in his *The Right to be Lazy* (1883) had argued that work-avoidance was a natural human "instinct" which bourgeois society had tried to suppress through "the dogma of love of work." One of the functions of the proletariat revolution, in Lafargue's view, was to abolish this dogma, proposing instead one of the earliest formulations known of a postwork society in the modern era. Lafargue will argue as follows:

> A strange delusion possesses the working classes of the nations where capitalist civilization holds its sway. This delusion drags in its train the individual and social woes which for two centuries have tortured sad humanity. This delusion is the love of work. . . . The proletariat, betraying its instincts, despising its historic mission, has let itself be perverted by the dogma of work. (Lafargue 1883, n.p.)

Marx expressed his opposition to Lafargue's views in energetic terms. In fact, and as is well known, it was precisely while engaged in this controversy that he said his often quoted phrase: if what Lafargue (and others) proposes is true Marxism, then "I am not a Marxist." In saying this, Marx was adhering to the position of Hegel (himself a graduate from a Protestant seminary), who viewed work as a central activity behind human development and self-actualization.

While it is true that our interviewees and informants would doubly frame the problem in religious terms, as a clash between Catholicism and Protestantism, the religious/philosophical debate simply conforms the origin of a struggle that began with the Protestant Reform (according to Weber), but that its echoes are still resounding 500 years later in many places around the world, Vieques among them. The degree to which this polarized model between Protestants and Catholics still informs mainstream thinking became evident in the recent dispute surrounding the Euro crisis, given that all the European countries in danger of forfeiting on their debts where countries of Catholic heritage, whereas all those who were not in danger of forfeiting were instead Protestant. It became a trend (even within formal economic debates and in the economic literature) to refer to the former as PIIGS, following the first letter of each of these countries: Portugal, Ireland, Italy, Greece and Spain—all of Catholic heritage. To be sure, the nonarbitrary (and unfortunate) combination of letters chosen to refer to this group of countries reveals not only the hegemony this binomial Protestant/Catholic construction still retains within contemporary economic thought, but also, and more importantly, how polarized these two views still are. The two discourses are separated by what Jean-François Lyotard (1989) has termed *le différend,* that is, by a radical inaccessibility of, or untranslatability from, one mode of discourse in dispute to the other. The case of Vieques is just but one more example of this clash of discourses about work and laziness that are as old as Protestantism and capitalism, and which continue to make themselves present in places like Vieques and Puerto Rico, and almost everywhere in the globalized world.

And yet, it must be added that, in the discourses produced by Viequenses, the line separating the two opposing views are in fact often blurred. The collective discourse they produce is too ambiguous to be classified on either side of the divide. In here, binomial categorizations of the world are rejected in favor of multiplicity of opinions, of gradations of laziness and of ambiguity and uncertainty.

Taken collectively, the discourses produced by Viequenses are far from anything one could call a unified, coherent voice. What they produce is a very complex discursive corpus (a form of broad public debate) made up of multiple arguments and counterarguments, proceeding through multiple deviations and off-roads, all inserted in a Gramscian interplay of agency and hegemony. Because of this, one will find in it multiple contradictions: for example, contradictions between what is said and what is done; or contradictions between what was said one day and what was said the next day (or five minutes later); or above all, contradictions and misunderstandings resulting from the fact that, in these discursive practices, key recurring words like "work" and "lazy" and "justice" become floating signifiers, shifting meaning every time they are uttered, impeccably following the Wittgenstenian principle that the meaning of words is in their use. On occasions, some of these words have been transformed into what Iris Marion Young would have called "unruly categories" (1997).

Discourses produced by Viequenses, and particularly those produced regarding their own laziness (or lack of it), fit perfectly the characterization of heteroglossia, as this concept is used by Bakhtin. They reveal the radically dialogical, relational and tension-full nature of "living" language, as well as the multiple interconnections between discursive regimes, and between phrases in dispute. In this sense, they are not different from what happens to human utterances all the time:

> Indeed, every concrete discourse (utterance) finds the object at which it was directed already as it were overlain with qualifications, open to dispute, charged with value, already enveloped in an obscuring mist. . . . The word, directed towards its object, enters a dialogically agitated and tension-filled environment of alien words, value judgements and accents, weaves in and out of complex interrelationships, merges with some, recoils from others, intersects with yet a third group: and all this may crucially shape discourse, may leave a trace in all its semantic layers, may complicate its expression and influence its entire stylistic profile. (Bakhtin 1981: 276)

Moreover, in the specific utterances of one single individual (when talking to the researcher) are also depositories of the tensions and contradictions of the social arena in which they are produced, and therefore equally exposed to "the virulets and droplets of social heteroglossia" (1981: 263). In them one can discern their "double-voicedness," made up of utterances that are "half-ours and half-someone else's," immersed in "an intense struggle within us for hegemony among various available verbal and ideological points of view, approaches, directions and values" (Bakhtin 1981: 345, 346). It is a voice that finds mimetic resemblance, as Bakhtin will point out, in the characters of the novels of Dostoyevsky and Tolstoy.[19]

FINAL REMARKS

Thus, it is when discourses imported from the US mainland clash with local notions of work, where the possibility of translating from one discursive corpus to another is obstructed by their *différend*, where power relations between opposing groups is highly unequal, where the debate is carried out in a linguistic field charged with empty signifiers and "unruly categories," and where language is the only resort left to voice out their indignation toward the accusations of laziness, that Puerto Ricans and Viequenses will recur to this language game in which pendulum movements between opposing stances (work versus laziness, work versus *pasarla bien*, we versus they), third person plural forms, and cultural/ideological contents derived from centuries-long near-obsessive debates about their own laziness, are welcomed. And it will be also in this context, under the rules of this Puerto Rican language game, where "indignation over" and "acceptance of" accusations of laziness can be alternatively held, and where ungrammatical and paralogistic statements like "Boricuas are lazy, including myself" are possible, and *can be said* (despite the fact that they won't be listened to, and despite the fact that Wittgenstein would have not approved of them as appropriate for philosophical discourse).

Some anthropologists have also encountered ambivalences and contradictions in the discourses of other subaltern groups, and have criticized them accordingly. Partha Chatterjee, for example, has described the discourses of Indian subalterns as "disorderly," "irrational," "contrary to the civil etiquette of metropolitan life," incapable of winning "Aristotle's approval" (2004: x, 77–78). Caribbean anthropologists Viranjini Munasinghe has also commented on "the systematicity and ease with which [Caribbean peoples voices] entertain multiplicity and contradiction" (2001: 135). Julio Ortega has described the voice of Puerto Ricans as a "Babel Tower," where individuals "have been forced to opt for a fragmentation, a fracture, of the collective meaning" of their voice (1991: 67). And while all this in many ways may be true, much of the ambiguity and contradiction we find in the voices of the Viequenses dissipates when one recognizes that these discourses are always already crossed by their own historicity: that is, that it is a discourse produced under the knowledge that tomorrow (or five minutes later) one can reflect on the issue, and even retract from everything that has been so far argued. Individuals who enter into the debate do so not with the pretension of having a final and definite position on the subject, but merely wishing to engage in a "negotiation" with others which, hopefully, could help find a collective solution to the dilemma. But the dilemma is never resolved once and for all because ordinary language is a dynamic system, where the dialogic cycle of propositions and responses cannot be stopped, as Wittgenstein so brightly showed. In this broad conversation, the debates don't end when the issue at hand has been resolved, but are rather temporarily abandoned, only to be taken up and continued on some other occasion. This fact might not be able to dissipate ambiguity and contradiction altogether, but it will certainly eliminate much of it.

But eliminating contradiction and ambiguity from the discourse produced by Viequenses does not amount to erasing its *différend*, its own local-specific character, its distance from the discourse produced by North American residential tourists and tourism brokers. This is the reason why it is erroneous to look at the idea of the "lazy Viequense" as simply an "invention" made up by foreigners and then imposed upon the local population. That the idea of a "lazy Viequense" is an "invention" is something that is undeniably true—at least to the extent that all cultural constructs are inventions (including that of the hardworking Protestant). But the danger with this conclusion results only when one wishes to stretch the idea of the "invention" too far, up to a point where, by implication, there remains no difference between the work ethics of Viequenses and that of their foreign employers. Instead, we would argue that there is a significant qualitative difference between the work ethics, "forms of life" and language games of Viequenses and those of their foreign employers, and that stretching too much the "invention" argument would only serve to erase its *différend*. And, in our view, any attempt to erase that *différend* is to be perceived as complicit with the mechanisms of muting the voice of Viequenses that we have been attempting to document.

In any case, the fact remains that the voice of the Viequenses, precisely because it is heteroglossia—and precisely because of its interconnections with discourses about *pasarla bien*, of its employment of third-person-plural propositions, and of its ambiguities in general—will be interpreted either as apologies for laziness or as irrational propositions, and muted on either grounds. Not being understood, they will not be listened to. In the end, what happens to discourses produced by Viequenses in response to accusations of laziness serves as a paradigmatic example of what happens to the voice of Viequenses in general, all the time.

NOTES

1. See *Publicación de la Incubadora de Microempresas Bieke, Inc.*, Vol. 1 (2011).

2. Given that a big portion of the tourism-oriented businesses in Vieques has been established in the town of Esperanza, on the south part of the island, and given that the place was relatively small, we restricted our interviews to the area of Esperanza. Moreover, given the small amount of businesses in the area (we were able to identify twenty-four tourist-oriented businesses in the Greater Esperanza region), we set as our goal to interview 100 percent of business owners/managers of tourism-oriented businesses in the Greater Esperanza region. We were able to interview nineteen of the twenty-four businesses; the remaining five either refused to participate or could not be reached despite repeated attempts to do so. Moreover, we also conducted semi-structured interviews with workers, which were either employees or freelance laborers servicing the tourist population; as well as other people of interest (i.e., community leaders, land squatters, etc.). In total, we conducted forty-one (N=41) recorded interviews. The forty-one persons interviewed are distributed

as follows: nineteen employers or business owners (eleven foreigners, three Puerto Rican and five Viequenses); twelve workers, either employed or working freelance (one North American, one European, two Puerto Ricans and eight Viequenses); and ten additional persons of interest, including community leaders, leaders of land squatting movements, and on. Out of the forty-one interviews performed, thirty-seven were audio-recorded. The remaining four were not recorded at the request of the interviewees. For purpose of reference, and to guarantee confidentiality of our informants, we have assigned numbers to our interviewees, except on those cases where the person being interviewed was a public figure, or was not interested in confidentiality.

3. Many of these tourism investors and managers are not "foreigners" in a literal sense, since they are US citizens living and doing business in a US territory. Yet, in the local scheme of mind, they are perceived as "foreigners," and referred to as such.

4. Many of the employers interviewed recognized that the issues of a problematic work ethics was not an exclusively Viequense problem, and was also a problem of Puerto Ricans in general.

5. Translated from Spanish. Original statement reads: "Porque aquí toda la vida se ha aprendido que si quieres algo ahorra, guarda, y luego lo compras. Aquí es diferente. . . . Parte del encanto de vivir en una isla pequeña es eso, que se vive día a día y se vive el momento."

6. Translated from Spanish. Original statement reads: "El viequense es amable, pero irresponsable. Solo trabaja cuando no le queda más remedio, si pudiese no trabajar . . . no trabajaría."

7. Translated from Spanish. Original statement reads: "Hay un fenómeno real que se dice que la gente de Vieques no les gusta trabajar. . . . No sé si la has escuchado. . . . La gente no entiende que esta es una sociedad donde antes no había trabajo, antes trabajaban 250 personas y las demás personas se acostumbraron a vivir de otra forma sin trabajar, no conocen la disciplina del trabajo, entonces si les dan trabajo, yo no digo que este bien pero yo puedo entender porque veo un poco más allá, que si les dan instrucciones se molestan porque vienen de una sociedad que era sin trabajar, no había oportunidades, no es que sea vago."

8. Nutritional Assistance Plan, or PAN by its Spanish acronym, is a government-funded "food coupons" program.

9. Translated from Spanish. Original statement reads: "Yo he tenido problemas, lo cual es un bochorno para mí decirlo, en cuanto a esta problemática que tenemos en todo Puerto Rico como colonia, veo que han hecho un buen trabajo en criar vagos. Este sistema que tenemos, dándole todos los beneficios sin que tengan que trabajar. Luego los trabajos no los quieren mantener porque pierden todos esos otros beneficios que le dan por no trabajar. Viven mejor sin trabajar que trabajando. Ese es el problema más grande que yo he tenido aquí para mantener la empleomanía. . . . A la que les toca su revisión de las ayudas del PAN—"Me tengo que ir porque me quitan los cupones." Y yo entiendo que si trabajas no necesitas los cupones, y debe de ser un poco más estricto el gobierno en eso, pero no creo que lo vayan a hacer porque con eso es que le meten miedo cada cuatro años."

10. Translated from Spanish. Original statement reads: "No es que sean vagos. Lo que pasa es que no tienen iniciativa para buscar un trabajo mejor o salir un poquito

más alante. Se conforman con lo que tienen. Y eso es bueno también, pero tampoco puedes dejar que vengan otros de afuera y te pisoteen también, tu sabes."

11. Translated from Spanish. Original statement reads: "El problema es que son muy "laid back." Trabajan dos o tres meses. Empiezan con mucho entusiasmo. De momento ya, si uno no está arriba de ellos pues no trabajan. Y ya, dos o tres meses, si no renuncian para irse a colectar [desempleo]."

12. Translated from Spanish. Original statement reads: "Es una cultura de parásitos, en cuanto a los jóvenes tienen una tendencia al ocio, dependencia . . . si lo pueden copiar del compañero para qué hacerlo uno, es lo mismo siempre. Lo que ves en la sociedad en Vieques."

13. Translated from Spanish. Original statement reads: "Yo prefiero coger alguien de aquí, que sé que va a estar aquí, no una persona que viene y se va. Porque después tengo que traer a la persona otra vez. Uno mejor tiene a una persona "treineá" de aquí que, después que sea bueno, pero lo que pasa aquí es que la gente son vaga. Ja! En total, en Puerto Rico, la gente son vaga, de verdad. Incluyéndome a mí también, ja, ja, pero de verdad, los boricuas son vagos. No es mentira. Casi todos son vagos."

14. Translated from Spanish. Original statement reads: "Por lo menos los últimos que hemos tenido son jóvenes y no tienen una responsabilidad de lo que es realmente un trabajo, sinceramente, hay una realidad que son vagos, hay mucho que trabaja y mucho son vagos."

15. These were the words used by Maria Enchautegui (2006), one of the collaborators of the report, and recorded in the "Proceedings from the Brookings Institution Panel on *The Economy of Puerto Rico: Restoring Growth*," that took place at the Brookings Institution on May 25, 2006. http://www.brookings.edu/comm/events/20060525.htm.

16. Translated from Spanish. Original statement reads: "La tasa de participación en la fuerza trabajadora alcanzó su punto máximo en el periodo de la posguerra en 1951, con 55.5 por ciento, y el mínimo en 1983, con 41 por ciento. Esta reducción general indica que la disposición de los trabajadores a entrar en el mercado de trabajo comenzó a declinar justo al momento del despegue del programa de industrialización" (Dietz 2002[1989]: 294).

17. Translated from Spanish. Original statement reads: "Entonces, los viequenses están mirando, el día 30 de este mes el gobierno municipal dejan en la calle a 130 empleados, sin tener una alternativa de donde van a buscar un empleo y el otro mes de junio va a dejar 130 más, o sea, que realmente el desempleo llega a más de 50% sin contar estos despidos de estos dos meses."

18. In terms of their etymology, the Spanish word *vago* comes from the latin *vagus*, but its original usage was more related to the action of wondering the land, walking errand, or rambling—also the root of the anglicized word "vagabond." It was only with the emergence of capitalism that the word will acquire its modern meaning, as work-avoiding. The English concept of "lazy," on the other hand, is of controverted etymological origin, but it dates back to the 16th century. Barnhart has traced the first usage of the word (then spelled "laysy") back to 1549, when it came to replace other concepts like slack, slothful and idle as the main word expressing the notion of "aversion to work." The first usage under its contemporary spelling, with a "z," was by William Shakespeare in his 1590 *A Midsummer Night's Dream* (see Barnhart 1988).

19. Others have argued the same thing about the soliloquies, "internal monologues" and "streams of consciousness" of the characters in the novels of, for example, Gustave Flaubert (Emma Bovary), Marcel Proust (Swann), James Joyce (Molly) or Franz Kafka (Gregor Samsa)—all of whom reflect contradictory feelings, a fragmented consciousness and an uneasiness in adopting a final position (cf. García Peinado 1998). Placing aside the stylistic elements of the literary canon, the individual discourses recorded among Viequenses resemble in many ways those of the characters in these novels—they are bovaristic, their discourse charged with heteroglossia, "a tempest in a teapot."

Chapter 4

Language, the Imaginary, and Tourism

As we had earlier anticipated, while much of the literature within the anthropology of tourism is focused on studying either the "hosts" or the "guests," there are also influential voices in the discipline calling for the need to transcend the dichotomy altogether, and to focus instead on "the relation" between the two; calling at the same time for a new conception of the social field as multiple and fluid, with more than just two groups of stakeholders. The works of tourism researchers working with language and language-related concepts like "imaginaries" or "discourses" have been particularly influential in promoting this movement within the discipline. Even when some of these works center their interests on "the tourist" per se, there will be in them a recognition that the tourist's speech acts and discourses are always framed as "responses" or "contestations" to other discourses with which they have entered in dispute, and with which they are engaged in a "dialectical" or "dialogical" relation inside a "hermeneutic cycle" (Salazar 2010, 2012, 2014; Salazar and Graburn 2014; Di Giovine 2014; Thurlow and Jaworski 2010, 2011; Aledo et al. 2013; Graburn and Gravari-Barbas 2012; Bruner 2005; Hall-Lew and Lew 2014; Moeran 1983; Gmelch and Moeran 2004). The findings and conclusions reached by these researchers greatly coincide with our own findings and conclusions in Vieques, and could be used to support our claim that the subaltern cannot speak.

Salazar and Graburn have outlined an agenda for the anthropology of tourism that, in our view, thoroughly addresses all the sensitive areas of research that this new, multiple and multivocal reality forces us to confront. They propose an anthropology of tourism focused on the "imaginary of tourism," that is, the ideas and images of the host culture that are often reflected in guidebooks, in the explanations of tour guides or in any other marketing propaganda—as well as in the "mind" of the tourist. In generic form, an "imaginary" is defined as a "socially transmitted representational assemblage that interacts with and are influenced by peoples personal imaginings and are used as meaning-making and world-shaping devices" (2014: 1). In terms of its specific content, the "imaginary of tourism" provides a representation of the host culture based on stereotypes, clichés or exaggerations about the local culture that have become hegemonic in the tourism imaginary. They "propagate historically inherited stereotypes that are based on the myths and fantasies that form part of the imaginary" (2014: 8).

In general, the agenda proposed by Salazar and Graburn for an anthropology of the imaginary of tourism can be broken down into three major tasks. The first one is to try to reconstruct the origins and genesis of that tourism imaginary, by "tracing their historical and semiotic makings." This implies—and this would be the second task—recognizing that imaginaries (and the discourses they produce) never exist in a vacuum, but are immersed in a field of multiple imaginaries, and are in fact "dialectically co-constructed" in their interplay with other imaginaries with which they enter in dispute. And it is when the imaginary is translated into discourse that one can come to recognize that they can only be properly understood in their relational dimensions, as inherently engaged "in dialogue" with other discursive imaginaries. "The challenge," then, is to study not only how these imaginaries "are maintained, reproduced, and reinforced, but also how they are challenged, contested, and transformed" (2014: 4–5).

Moreover, there is also a recognition that the interplay of imaginaries is characterized by an imbalance of power and cultural capital between the different actors involved, and of the multiple effects that these power imbalances have in shaping the voice of the different stakeholders. These "imaginaries are embedded with local, national, and global institutions of power," and are therefore never politically neutral. The sociology of Pierre Bourdieu, and particularly his notion of "field of cultural production" (1993), will provide for many of these authors the broad conceptual tool under which the complexity of the discursive and ideational arena will be conceived (Salazar and Graburn 2014; Di Giovine 2014; Thurlow and Jaworski 2010, 2011; Aledo et al. 2013). Di Giovine, for example, will further develop the notion into what he will call the "field of heritage production" or "field of touristic production," which he defines in abstract terms as "a multi-layered, global social structures wherein individuals struggle and negotiate to create, define, and promote formative encounters with place" (2009: 9). In another of his writings, Di Govine will define the field of tourism production in terms similar to those used by Salazar and Graburn, as an *imaginaire dialectic*:

> A structured, totalizing set of relationships, often in conflict, that orders a diversity of "epistemic cultures"—systems of groups with their own culturally specific knowledge, cosmologies, and ritualized practices . . . who struggle to stake their

claim to, define, and ultimately utilize the *imaginaire* of the site or destination. This is thus a much more complex process, as all parties in the touristic experience simultaneously produce, receive, and reproduce these imaginaries—often with much contestation, negotiation, and "position-taking." (Di Giovine 2014: 150)

The need to conceive the *imaginaire dialectic* as a form of "struggle" or "process" (as opposed to a fixed set of ideas and images) will be further emphasized by Di Giovine through the distinction between, on one hand, the *imaginaire* proper, that is, the *imaginaire* as "a thing;" and, on the other hand, the *imaginaire dialectic*, which refers more specifically to "the process by which *the thing* constantly forms and re-forms" (2014: 151, emphasis added). In other words, *imaginaires* cannot be known in independence of their manifestations within the *imaginaire dialectic*, that is, in the context of *living* language and live social interaction.

This second task in Salazar and Graburn's agenda, by itself, already explains the need to go beyond the host/guest divide, or to recognize the multiplicity of voices that are at play inside the "field of tourism production." Salazar and Graburn have been strongly emphatic on this point:

> While anthropologists traditionally analyze tourism in terms of "hosts" and "guess," recent research has reflected the more complex and fluid situation in most contemporary commercial tourism venues . . . In most tourism destinations of any scale, the "locals" and the "visitors" are by no means simple and solidary groups, but are themselves conglomerates of stakeholders. Outsiders include not only tourists, but also investors, travel industry staff, sellers and provisioners, technical and business experts (often expats), the press and the media, and often migrant workers. Locals include the owners and the propertyless, the workers and the uninvolved resident. . . . Moreover, every community and status group has its own ideas about themselves that they wish to convince others, and about the others with whom they necessarily interact. There will always be a dialectic between any one's group set of imaginaries and those of other groups with whom they have important relations. So . . . there are never two groups, "hosts" and "guests." (Salazar and Graburn 2014: 15)

Finally, the third and last task of Salazar and Graburn's agenda for an anthropology of tourism imaginary is to also recognize that these dominant "tourism imaginaries" are "potent propellers of sociocultural and environmental change," therefore requiring that one also "keep the very material effects of the process in view" (2014: 16, 17). Thurlow and Jaworski have also been emphatic on this point, when arguing that "the seemingly innocent here-and-now of tourism-host interactions is rooted in broader historical trajectories of travel, colonization, global inequalities and privilege" (2011: 31), and therefore have both symbolic and material effects.

THE DANGERS OF ESSENTIALISM

Salazar and Graburn's three-tasked agenda for the anthropology of tourism guided many of our methodological and theoretical elections in the Vieques research, and, in our view, sets the field in the direction we believe it should move. If our own work in Vieques deviates from the agenda proposed by Salazar and Graburn, it is only by being more emphatic at pointing out what exactly we mean when we claim that the tourism experience is "blind to whom the Other [i.e., the host] really is" (Salazar and Graburn 2014: 18), or that the representation of the cultures does not reflect them as "what they are in themselves" (Bruner 2005: 5), or that the events that are unfolding in Vieques do not take into consideration the *real* voice, wishes and desires of the Viequenses. For it is in attempting to define whom the other *really is*, what their culture is *really* like *in itself* or what they are *really* attempting to say, that there lies a danger endemic to the discipline of anthropology: constructing monolithic and essentialist accounts of the cultures we are trying to describe, depriving them thus of the diversity and complexity that they naturally harbor. There is always a danger, in the attempt to provide an answer to this question, to forget that these imaginaries "can be altered, changed, and negotiated at all points" (Salazar and Graburn 2014: 17), or that they can only be captured in the form of heteroglossic speech, thus resisting essentialist representations of it.

This issue of essentialism in anthropological writings is of special relevance to the arguments we have been making in this book because, as we will attempt to show, depriving these cultures of their internal complexity and diversity falls within what Spivak has called "epistemic violence"—and in fact forms the backbone to the claim that the subaltern cannot speak. The broken voice of the subaltern is in fact a product of this "epistemic violence." A discussion about anthropological essentialism in the context of heritage tourism will help further illustrate the point.

HERITAGE TOURISM AND AUTHENTICITY

The problem with essentialism becomes particularly acute in the case of heritage tourism sites, for it is there that the question of "authenticity"—and by extension that of "whom the Other really is"—acquires central stage. The issue of authenticity is, in fact, a matter of concern for both locals and tourists: the first ones for identity or nationalistic reasons; the latter because their "tourism imaginary" harbors "an ambivalent nostalgia for the past . . . a fascination with the rare, the endangered, the about-to-disappear," with the "authentic"—what Salazar and Graburn call, following Rosaldo, an "imperialist nostalgia" (2014: 8). In heritage tourism sites, thus, the debate about what is or what is not "authentic" is immersed in a discursive field of heteroglossic struggles which defies monolithic resolutions.

The controversy becomes particularly evident in Edward M. Bruner's (2005) ethnographic work in the New Salem Historic Site: a recreated 19th century village (with live actors interacting with tourists) in central Illinois, and where Abraham Lincoln lived in the 1830s. In here, Bruner's engages in an extensive critique of traditional essentialist notions of authenticity, including not only the "modernist" authenticity claims adopted by anthropologists like MacCannell in his canonic text *The Tourist* (1976); but also, and more emphatically, against "postmodern" theorists who claim to see in these type of tourism heritage sites purely inauthentic representations, pure simulacra. In this latter case, the critique is specifically directed against the interpretations adopted by both Umberto Eco and Jean Baudrillard, and particularly as they relate to North American culture.

Both Eco and Baudrillard are in harmony when they claim that not only the representations found in these types of tourism attractions like the New Salem site are inauthentic, but also such inauthenticity is characteristic of North American aesthetic and ludic values in general. In fact, for both authors, the North American case represents a paradigmatic example of what is increasingly becoming "the postmodern condition" of subalterns everywhere in the globalized world. In their view, heritage sites like the New Salem village are a perfect expression of a system of aesthetic tastes and preferences in which "the simulacra has become the authentic." The North American example is a paradigmatic expression of this because, for North Americans, there is no original or authentic foundation that can be claimed or recovered. All they have is simulacra. The North American singularity or exceptionalism, thus, results from the fact that there is no true history upon which to build a vision of whom they really are. North Americans are, at least according to European standards, a "people without history" or to put it in Baudrillard's words, "the only remaining primitive society."

In direct opposition to this postmodernist version of authenticity, there is also a "modern" interpretation which, while also critical of the banality of the tourism industry, will hold strongly to the idea that there indeed is an "original" or "authentic" to be claimed, and will speak about them in essentialist terms. MacCannell's work is just but one example of this modern version of authenticity within the field of tourism studies. Bruner agrees with MacCannell (and with Eco and Baudrillard for that matter) in his assertion that the authenticity represented in tourism attractions like the New Salem village is a "staged authenticity"—in Bruner's terms, a spectacle "devised . . . specifically for the tourists" (2005: 3). And yet, as his work on Bali will reveal, the assertion can be sustained even when, historically speaking, there is no "original" or "authentic" that can be claimed as a foundation or tradition. This is the case, for example, with the now famous Balinese "dance of the frog." As Bruner explains, in crude historical terms, and despite "appearing traditional," the frog dance dates back only to 1970 when it was "created for foreign visitors in conjunction with Western choreographers." Any attempt at writing the history and evolution of the frog dance as it existed before 1970 will necessarily result in deception, because "it had not existed" before then (2005: 3). Thus, the "inauthentic" origins of the frog dance come to show something MacCannell failed to see. His essentialism consisted in believing "there is always a real and true at the very back" of every heritage tourism attraction. In Bruner's view, on the contrary, there is no need to "look behind, beneath, or beyond anything" in search for the authentic representation, because there is no original. And, by the same token, "there is no simulacrum because there is no original" (2005: 5).

Moreover, and regarding his fieldwork in New Salem, Bruner will argue that in-depth ethnographic work in that heritage site reveals a different picture of the tourist's aesthetic values and imaginaries, and which do not correspond with essentialist interpretations in neither a modern or postmodern version. Both of these versions, Bruner will argue, end up committing essentialism: the first ones (the modernist) by placing authenticity fully on the idea of "the original," the seconds (the postmodernists) by placing it fully on the idea of "the copy." Bruner, on his side, will show that in New Salem the notion of "authenticity" is immersed in a broad debate, and the concept itself is used to mean different things at different times. Bruner will identify at least four major usages of the term: as "verisimilitude," as "genuineness," as "original-ity" and as "authority." Moreover, the multiplicity of positions adopted by the different agents involved will force Bruner to conclude that "tourists are not monolithic, and neither is the meaning of the site" (2005: 165), and to confirm once again what Di Giovine has also claimed: "there are just as many imaginaries as there are tourists" (2014: 149). Thus, Bruner argues for the need to change our traditional understanding of the notion of "authenticity:"

> No longer is authenticity a property inherent in an object, forever fixed in time; instead it is a social process, a struggle in which competing interests argue for their own interpretation of history. (Bruner 2005: 163)

Now, if the problem with defining the authentic is highly conflictive in heritage tourism sites, there is yet another type of tourism attraction which, while not properly related to heritage, does bring the debate of authentic-ity to a different (higher) level: those involving trained animals. We refer specifically to tourism attractions like the Orca show in Sea World, Florida, coincidentally discussed by Eco in his *Travels in Hyperreality* (1986). In here, the "by nature" ferocious and vicious killer Orca has been tamed and trained to do marvelous jumps at the instructions of its trainers. The show is not intended as a representation of the Orca "as it really is" (in its natural state), but rather of "what it can become" in the company of humans. The public, on the other hand, are placed in an environment of extreme physical proximity, where some can even touch the animal, and most get wet with the water splash. Thus, as Eco explains, in the show there is a "naturalization" of humans, concurrently with a "humanization" of animals, which permits the two species to meet halfway and establish communication and communion.

The Orca show can be interpreted in many differing ways, but the divisions greatly depend on whom one believes the "authentic" Orca is, the untamed or the tamed. For those who see the tamed Orca as the more authentic (which is the message Sea World intends to transmit, and what surely forms part of the tourism imaginary of many of the tourists who attend the show), the show can be interpreted as a demonstration of what human ingenuity (in this case North American ingenuity) can achieve in establishing communion with nature, actually making possible the idea of a peaceful coexistence between naturally rival species. The act not only reveals that such forms of peaceful communion between living beings are possible, but also suggests the "evolutionary" possibilities of the relation if this type of "communication" is allowed to continue and intensify in the future. It could also be argued that the show promotes democratic values, welcoming everybody (including ferocious animals) into the great North American "melting pot." For those who, on the other hand, see the untamed Orca as the most authentic, the show can be interpreted as inauthentic, pure simulacra, and, in its most extreme form, an act of animal cruelty. The debate thus extends to include ecologists, animal right activists, as well as so-called pet theorists and circus theorists, among others. But, while the experience is undeniably "hyperreal," the question about which is really the "authentic" Orca (the tamed or the untamed) remains inconclusive, in abeyance, without there being anybody capable of solving the dispute once and for all. This is, indeed, another tourism instance where the wish to establish authenticity is confronted with "the inevitable absence of an impartial judge." It is not the case, as the postmodernists claim, that "the inauthentic has become the authentic," but rather "the inevitable absence of an impartial judge," what characterizes the linguistic field.

In the end, to the question of who defines the authentic in specific historical moments, Bruner will respond: "it is a matter of power, of who has the right to authenticate" (2005: 163).

TYPOLOGIES OF TOURISTS

The problem of essentialism in anthropological representations of cultures is also particularly critical, beyond the field of heritage tourism, in the task of developing typologies—in our case, typologies of tourists. If, as Di Giovine argues, "there are just as many tourist imaginaries as there are tourists" (2014: 149), then the development of typologies, while often useful, may also work to erase the internal complexity and diversity that the field of tourism production harbors. The problem with essentialism could become even more acute when the "types" are arranged along a continuum, implying thus some kind of progression or progress. The case is particularly evident in, for example, Cohen and Cooper's 1986 typology of tourists and tourist's linguistic strategies, or what they call "tourist talk." A critical reading of such work will help further illustrate the point we are trying to put forward here about the dangers of essentialism.

In their "Language and Tourism" (1986), Cohen and Cooper propose a typology/continuum of tourists based on two main variables: the "temporality" or length of the interaction between guests and hosts, as well as on "the degree to which a tourist exposes himself to the strangeness of the host society or, contrariwise, encloses himself within the familiarity of the 'environmental bubble' of his home society provided by the tourist establishment" (1986: 539–540). In this way, the typology runs along a continuum that moves from a touristic experience that is short in duration and more superficial or "banal" (less authentic), to a touristic experience that is longer in duration, and which requires greater exposure to the local culture. The continuum thus begins with the most "institutionalized" experience of the "group mass tourist," followed by the slightly less institutionalized experience of the "individual mass tourist." In these two cases, the touristic experience is very short, and exposure is superficial. In any case, and moving along the continuum, the next type of tourist will be "the explorer" (whose experience already falls within the non-institutionalized experiences of the continuum), immediately followed by the even longer and less institutionalized experience of the "drifter;" the only difference between the two being that the former "makes some limited use of the tourist establishment," while the latter does not.

Moreover, because the different "types" of tourists will employ different types of linguistic strategies in their verbal exchanges with locals, there will also be a parallel typology of "tourist talks," in correspondence with each "type" of tourist. The typology of "tourist talks," moreover, will be based on a different set of variables: the level of competence of the tourist in the local language, as well as the degree of power asymmetry involved between the cultures of guests and hosts. In fact, the general concept of "tourist talk" is itself developed upon the principle that the interactions between hosts and guests are always mediated by asymmetrical power relations. The claim becomes evident in the distinction made between "tourist talk" and "foreign talk"; the latter being a concept more commonly used by anthropologists to refer to the language employed in linguistic exchanges between immigrants (or other type of foreign group) and their hosts (cf. Ferguson 1975). There occurs, Cohen and Cooper argue, a "linguistic reversal" caused by an inversion of the power relations involved between the speakers in each case. As they point out,

> One can . . . formulate the differences between *foreign talk* (FT) generally studied by sociolinguists, and *tourist talk* (TT) in the following manner: in FT *higher* status locals typically talk *down* to *lower* status foreigners [i.e., immigrants] in the *host* language (HL). In TT *lower* status locals typically talk *up* to *higher* status tourists in the *tourist's* language (TL). (Cohen and Cooper 1986: 538)

Thus, if the continuum of tourist types runs from less authentic to more authentic experiences, the continuum of "tourist talks" runs from more to less power asymmetry in the relation between the hosts and the guests. In this way, the lesser the power asymmetry is, the more authentic the experience of the tourist should be, and the more competence in the local language the tourist will gain. When the power imbalance is too steep, linguistic exchanges with locals will be almost exclusively restricted to brief conversations with "tourism brokers" (e.g., tourism guides) who have relatively high competency in the language of the tourist, and whose discourses are often shaped by what Salazar has called "seducation," that is, "the art [of tour guides] of narrating and performing seducing tourism tales" (2014: 111).

Finally, and because the typology/continuum implies the notion of progress, the continuum will assume a progressive, arrow-shaped form which moves from less desirable to more desirable models of tourism. Thus, the typology/continuum will provide, for Cohen and Cooper, not only the basis for an explicit critique of "institutionalized" and power-ridden models of tourism (the "types" located on the bottom part of the arrow), but also a perhaps less explicit apology or defense of less institutionalized models. And, given that the progression of the arrow in its forward movement is left open-ended, the typology/continuum will also suggest the direction the tourism industry should move in the future.

For the purpose of our work on residential tourism in Vieques, a critical review of Cohen and Cooper's typology/continuum can become insightful in two major points. The first one has two do with the linguistic strategies employed by residential tourists. Thus, while it is true that residential tourists are not considered in Cohen and Cooper's typology, something paradoxical emerges when one attempts to determine how they would fit into it—something that is also revealing of what is happening in Vieques. The paradox emerges when one considers that the residential tourists, while having the longest temporality and exposure (which would place them toward the tip of the arrow within the continuum), their "tourist talk" paradoxically resembles that used by the "institutionalized" tourist (which places them now at the extreme opposite side of the continuum). In other words, that while the temporality and exposure of the residential tourist is the greatest among the "tourist types" included in the continuum, their linguistic strategies consist in creating an "environmental bubble" (in many ways similar to the bubble of the institutionalized tourist) in which they can continue to communicate in the language of their country of origin, creating for this a community apart, linguistically and otherwise.

This fact is particularly true of retired residential tourists, and has been amply documented in the literature (Aledo et al. 2012; Hall and Müller 2004; King and Paterson 1998; King, Warnes and Williams 2000; Warnes 1994; William, King and Warnes 1997). Viequenses also constantly complain that residential tourists create their own separate community, and that they make little effort to speak the local Spanish language, often despite residing on the island for extended periods of time. The fact that many Viequenses, after more than a century of North American colonial rule and acculturation efforts, have managed to acquire at least a basic competency in English, strengthens the conditions under which residential tourists never actually have the need to learn Spanish. But for those Viequenses who have little competency in English (or where the topic of conversation is too profound to be elucidated in "tourist talk"), the interactions often resemble the ones described by Cohen and Cooper for the "individual mass tourists," where the tourist continues speaking "in a language in which the locals have no competence, thus becoming incomprehensible to the locals" (1986: 545). This is why, in Vieques, the preference of speaking in either English or Spanish can be in many cases a politically charged act—in the case of locals, even an act of resistance.

Thus, while one could have expected, following Cohen and Cooper's lead, that touristic experiences of longer duration and more exposure would yield maximum levels of competence in the local language, the phenomenon of residential tourists proves that that is not necessarily the case. Perhaps the solution to this paradox of the residential tourism case is to conceive Cohen and Cooper's typology as following a circular pattern, rather than a linear, arrow-shaped continuum, in such a way that the two ends meet at one same point, reflecting thus the similarities in linguistic strategies employed by the two seemingly disparate, even opposing, "tourist types."

Given the connections between linguistic strategies and power asymmetry, what this paradox of residential tourists comes to reveal is that the power asymmetry involved in residential tourism is as wide as, if not wider than, that of "mass institutionalized tourism"—and perhaps the widest to be found in the tourism world. In the case of Vieques, the power asymmetry is further exacerbated by the fact that Puerto Rico is a colony of the United States, and that the residential tourists are Gringos.

Moreover, there are other consequences derived from the election of a progressive (arrow-shaped) model for the continuum—and this would be the second insightful point derived from the typology we wish to highlight. To the extent that the typology/continuum leaves the models of tourism wide open to the imagination, it invites (intentionally or unintentionally) projections of idyllic and utopic tourism arrangements. It might, for example, induce us to believe that there is such a thing as "the authentic" representation of "whom the Other really is," or what their cultures is like "in themselves," or what their voice is *really* saying. It tempts us to commit "epistemic violence," to put it in Spivak's terminology. The point will be further illustrated in connection with a discussion of "pidgin" or "creole" language, and for reasons that will soon become obvious.

THE CREOLE OR PIDGIN METAPHOR

In Cohen and Cooper's typology, while the progressive arrow-shaped continuum is left open to move along the path traced by the continuum, toward more authentic and less power-charged relations between hosts and guests, the farthest the typology actually goes along the continuum is to "the drifter." In this way, if the "mass institutionalized tourist" is the most extreme example of superficial exposure to the host culture, the drifter is the opposite, the most exposed to that same culture, and the one who seems to be deriving more personal growth from the experience, reversing at the same time the power asymmetry between the two groups—in Salazar and Graburn's terms, "going beyond the imaginary." Moreover, regarding the linguistic strategies of "the drifter," in its most extreme cases—they specifically put as example the cases where a drifter romantically befriends a local and develops a "new" language—mixing from the two (or more) languages implicated in the relationship—that Cohen and Cooper define as "patois" or "lingua franca" or, in the context of Thailand, a "Thai-English patois." Thus, the continuum does not culminate with a fully authentic experience of the Other, but rather with an undetermined open space. In strict linguistics terms, it does not culminate with "the drifter" acquiring full competence in the foreign language (as many Viequenses are inclined to believe should be the minimum expected from residential tourists), but rather, with a "patois-" or "creole-like" language.

Now, it is precisely the election of the term "patois" (and more specifically its close relative "creole") that is fortuitous and felicitous to our discussion (even if this was not the intention of the authors), for it serves to remind us that, in the Caribbean, the language that the subaltern speaks is a patois or creole language. More specifically, it serves to remind us that creole languages, as conceived in much contemporary research and theorization on

creole languages and societies in the Caribbean, serve as an ideal metaphor
for the muted voice of the subaltern. A brief review of the work of these
Caribbean creolization theorists—like Kamau Brathwaite, Edouard Glissant,
Wilson Harris, Derek Walcott, George Lamming or Antonio Benítez Rojo,
just to name a few—can help illuminate why exactly the subaltern (or at least
the creole-speaking Caribbean subaltern) cannot speak, and what exactly
does "epistemic violence" entail. And, while it may be argued that the local
version of Spanish that Viequenses speak does not properly fit the canonic
definition of a "creole" language, their language is certainly creole when conceived in the sense outlined by these Caribbean creolization theorists.

In their collective search for the voice of the Caribbean creole subaltern,
these creolization theorists may give the initial impression that their objective
is to provide a "creole" linguistic formula in which the Caribbean subalterns
can speak and be heard. Linguistic formulas like Glissant's *contre poétique*,
or Brathwaite's "nation language," may at first glance seem as attempts to
grant creole subjects the very "language" in which they can retell their own
traumatic history of the middle passage, of slavery and the plantation system
and thus discover "whom they really are." But, a deep exploration of these
formulas will reveal that they merely point to a language that is experienced
more as an absence than as a presence; a language that cannot speak because,
in a deep sense, it attempts to say what cannot be said, what is anterior to
language. Glissant, for example, will speak of his *contre poétique* as a "forced
poetics," that is, what emerges from a person's mouth "whenever a need
for expression confronts something impossible to express" (1981: 236). It
will find its most paradigmatic expression in the "verbal deliriums" of the
mad creole (epitomized in the figure of the madwoman in the attic[1]), or in
the mumbling and bubbling of the possessed in a voodoo trance or in the
traumatic linguistic experience of the recently arrived slave, unable to communicate in the language of his or her new masters—as well as in poetry and
fiction literature, of course.

In claiming this, Glissant's work operates an inversion (in fact, a radicaliza-
tion) of the traditional notion of "resistance," and the related concept of *contre*
(counter). In his work, "counter" no longer means an alternative, opposed
imaginary or discourse—what Evans-Pritchard would have called a "counter-
gaze" (1989); but rather the very absence of one. More to the point, it is the
kind of absence that is experienced when the creole subject is confronted with
a Western exigency for mental and linguistic rationality and transparency; an
indispensable requirement for earning the privilege of being listened to. As Glissant explains, "If we look at the process of 'understanding' beings and ideas as
it operates in Western society, we find that it is founded on an insistence on this
kind of transparency" (1990: 204). And, it is precisely then and there, when
this Western insistence on transparency meets with a creole language (which

is not properly speaking a "language," but rather a *contre poétique*, a "nation language"), that the creole language is radically experienced as a lack—to quote once again Glissant, as an expression of something that is "impossible to express" (1981: 236). And it is here that the two imaginaries or discourses enter "in dispute." And yet it is a dispute of a special kind, for the voice that this *contre poétique* will be able to produce is a broken voice—personified by Dereck Walcott in his poem "Names" (dedicated to Brathwaite), in the figure of the slave speaking "with pebbles under my tongue."

Contrary to, for example, the resistance of the illuminated and full-conscious "black Jacobins" of C. L. R. James, speaking and fighting for the "universal" man and the ideas of the French Revolution, the resistance of the creole-speaking subject in Glissant and Brathwaite is a resistance against the imposition of transparency, and consequently *the imposition of language itself*. Against the Western demand for full transparency, Glissant will propose a demand for "opacity," and will in fact promote opacity to the level of a human right: "the right to opacity" (1990: 204–205).

Thus, while Glissant's idea of a creole *contre poétique*, like Brathwaite's notion of "nation language," might initially and erroneously lead one to believe that these are linguistic formulas that can finally provide creoles with a "language" in which they can proclaim a "counter"-discourse, and thus reverse or erase their condition of muteness, the concepts in fact point in the opposite direction—and much in line with Spivak's assertion that the subaltern cannot speak. For, indeed, negating the subaltern subject their "right to opacity" is no different from what Spivak calls "epistemic violence." Creole languages, as conceived by Glissant, are broken precisely in the same way that the voice of the subaltern is, in Spivak's account. They are impossible to understand under the Western expectation of full transparency.

Along the same line, Spivak will claim that even while one cannot listen to the voice of the subaltern, one can still witness "the itinerary of its silencing;" and, moreover, quoting Pierre Macherey, she adds, "What is important in a work is what it does not say . . . what the work *cannot* say is important, because there the elaboration of the utterance is carried out, in a sort of journey to silence" (1994: 286). What this means, as Britton has so straightforwardly put it, is that "we have to pay as much attention to its omissions and exclusions as to what it includes: [because] the subaltern subject-position may be recoverable only through its negative traces" (1999: 57).

The subaltern's voice, at least in the Caribbean, is "opaque" and "chaotic"—it is *"creole."* And it is in this particular sense (conceived as *contre poétique* or "nation language"), that the notion of the creole/pidgin serves well as metaphor of the muted subaltern voice, and that it can serve to support the claim that the language spoken by Viequenses is de facto a "creole" language—despite the fact that it does not fit the canonic definition of it.

Now, this line of argumentation, we are aware, can also dangerously approach essentialism. For, indeed, what can be more essentialist than pure absence of language, or pure nothingness? The creole language might not be a "language," properly speaking; but it is "something," it is a *contre poétique*. "The elaboration of the utterance is carried out," and it can be witnessed and recorded, although it cannot be fully understood. And the main reason why it cannot be fully understood is because the language of their interlocutors is *contre poétique*, heteroglossia. Anything the subaltern says in the context of "lived" language is something that "can be altered, changed, and negotiated at all points" (Salazar and Graburn 2014: 17), and it is therefore impossible to grasp in its full complexity. In the context of tourism encounters, as Simoni had stated, the discourses produced will "counter univocal readings," in the face of which "we should resist the impulse to find coherence at all cost" (Simoni 2013: 51, 52). For a linguistic anthropologist attempting to document the voice of the subaltern/creole in the Caribbean, what he or she can expect to find is, to put it in Benítez Rojo's terms, "a chaotic system."

> Caribbeaness is a system full of noise and opacity, a nonlinear system, an unpredictable system, in short a chaotic system beyond the total reach of any specific kind of knowledge or interpretation of the world. (Benítez Rojo 1996: 294)

FINAL REMARKS

As critical anthropologists and tourism researchers we can easily envision ideas of how to transform tourism from the inauthenticity and banality, in which it is generally now immersed, to more positive and less power-asymmetrical interaction between hosts and guests—the possibility of tourism becoming "a force for world peace." It is therefore legitimate to criticize the "tourism imaginary" for providing a representation of locals "blind to whom the Other really is," or as misrepresentations of what their cultures "in themselves" really are. But, as Bruner has warned us—and as Salazar and Graburn have also suggested—one must be cautious of stretching this argument too much, that is, up to a point where one ends up attributing to the anthropologist a privileged voice in "objectively" deciding "whom the Other really is," or in deciding what is and what is not really "authentic."

The danger that runs along the anthropological reflection on tourism is that, while aspiring to promote more positive and egalitarian relations between the tourist and locals, we don't end up reproducing and perpetuating "epistemic violence" upon the host communities that we study, becoming thus complicit with the banal representations of that same culture that appear in the same tourist guidebooks and other marketing material that we so strongly criticize.

As Thurlow and Jaworski have argued regarding the glossaries of tour guides, they provide a "codified, fixed regimes of translated truth which . . . promote the literal and denotative, the formulaic and reductive, at the expense of the subtle, the complex, the messy, the 'lived'" (Thurlow and Jaworski 2011: 83). And it is precisely with "the complex, the messy, the 'lived'" that we anthropologists of tourism need to come to terms with.

The irony is that anthropologists are well equipped, both methodologically and theoretically, to assume this challenge. In fact, if there is one privilege that anthropologists should abrogate, it is that of being able to show, through in-depth ethnographic research and anthropological "thick" descriptions, how "the complex, the messy, the 'lived'" defies essentialist representations of it. Anthropologists are more apt to portray the complex and the multivocal through ethnographic writing than, for example, when they engage in the development of all-inclusive typologies and open-ended continuums that create the illusion that it is possible to define in objective manner "whom the Other really is," paying court in this way to essentialism and epistemic violence. This is also Bruner's position when he says that "Grand theorizing [must] thus give way to ethnography" (Bruner 2005: 163). The point also comes to reinforce Valerio Simoni's position (stated earlier) that:

> From the moment that our ethnographies take us in the variety of contexts and spheres of interaction that make up a person's life, the experiences of our research participants, their claims and actions, seem to counter univocal readings, and call instead for a plurality of interpretations. (Simoni 2013: 52)

The natural opacity of "creole" (or "patois") languages and cultures, as conceived by Brathwaite, Glissant and Benítez Rojo, serves as an indication (a metaphor) of how the voice of the subaltern must be interpreted and understood. In this sense, and as Price and Yelvington have already argued, there is a long belated conversation that needs to take place between the anthropologists and these Caribbean thinkers (cf. Yelvington 2001: 235).

NOTE

1. The figure of the madwoman in the attic derives from the creole character of Bertha Mason in Charlotte Brontë's 1847 novel *Jane Eyre*, whose madness forces her husband to lock her up in the attic. While the character of Bertha Mason is hardly given a chance, in Brontë's novel, to tell her side of the story, a sequel to the novel—Jane Rhys's 1966 *Wide Sargasso Sea*—will grant a whole chapter for her to express her complaints. While this act partially empowers the madwoman to some degree, by granting her the opportunity to speak up, the voice that Bertha Mason will produce in Rhy's novel will be almost indecipherable, much in line with Glissant's notion of

contre poétique. One could in fact speak of the voice of the subaltern and the creole as a "feminized" voice, as silenced as the voice of women is in patriarchal societies. The issue of the mad or monstrous female characters in 19th-century novels written by women is deeply explored by Sandra Gilbert and Susan Gubar in their *The Madwoman in the Attic: The Woman Writer and the Nineteenth-Century Literary Imagination* (1984[1979]).

Chapter 5

Race

The process of muting the Viequense voice is not substantially different from processes of muting the voice of other non-white communities in the mainland US context, and elsewhere around the world. As is the case in these non-white communities, in Vieques the social conflicts emerging from tourism in the post-Navy period acquired a strong racial dimension, in this case organized around a gringo-Viequense or gringo-Puerto Rican polarity. And, to be sure, white gringos are not passive actors in this whole social drama.

In general, gringos are held responsible for introducing or raising negative discourses about the moral constitution of Viequenses in the post-Navy period, including negative discourses about their work ethics, their family and reproductive values, their welfare dependency, and so on. It is possible to discern in the discourses of the gringo community the import of what anthropologist Aihwa Ong has called, in the US context, the "bipolar white-black model of American society" (1996: 742), that is, a system of racial classifications characterized by an either/or logic, or under which individuals can only be classified as either white or non-white. This bipolar system of classification, as we will attempt to show, will enter in sharp contrast with locally informed racial classifications used by Viequenses and Puerto Ricans, and under which being black or white becomes something highly negotiable. The end effect of the clash between the two systems will be an increasing racialization of social conflict, or a situation where social conflicts are increasingly being perceived as assuming the form of white gringo-black Viequense conflicts.

THE BIPOLAR BLACK-WHITE MODEL
OF AMERICAN CITIZENSHIP

In her "Cultural Citizenship as Subject-Making" (1996), based on ethnographic work among Asian immigrants into the West Coast of the United States (i.e., Cambodians, Vietnamese, Japanese, Chinese, Koreans), Ong uncovers the existence of a grading system for evaluating immigrants which rests on a continuum between two polarities, or what she calls "the white and black poles of American citizenship" (1996: 743). As she explains,

> Once [Asian] immigrants arrive in the country, whatever their national origin or race, they were ideologically positioned within the hegemonic bipolar white-black model of American society. The racialization of Southeast Asian refugees depended on differential economic and cultural assessment of their potential as good citizens . . . Cambodians . . . were often compared to their inner-city African American neighbors in terms of low-wage employment, high rates of teenage pregnancy, and welfare-dependent families . . . Immigrants situated closer to the black pole are seen as at the bottom of the cultural and economic ranking . . . This positioning of Cambodians as black Asians is in sharp contrast to the model-minority image of Chinese, Koreans, and Vietnamese [including Sino-Vietnamese], who are celebrated for their "Confucian values" and family businesses. (Ong 1996: 742)

This process of "racialization of class" (1996: 739) is then extended, Ong continues, to judge and grade non-white immigrants who enter the United States in an "attempt to discriminate among them, separating out the desirable from the undesirable citizens according to some racial or cultural calculus" (Ong 1996: 741). In the neoliberal world, this "racial and cultural calculus" which helps separate the desirable from the undesirable is based on two major considerations: (a) cultural attitudes toward work; and (b) patterns of dependence on welfare aid. Ong continues:

> In the postwar era, such thinking has given rise to a human capital assessment of citizens . . . weighing those who can pull themselves up by their bootstraps against those who make claims on the welfare state. Increasingly, citizenship is defined as the civic duty of individuals to reduce their burden on society and build up their own human capital—to be "entrepreneurs" of themselves . . . Indeed, by the 1960s liberal economies had come to evaluate non-white groups according to their claims on or independence of the state. (Ong 1996: 739)

To claim, then, that the ethical milieu of the Viequenses is blackened is simply to point to the fact that their attitudes toward work (and family and leisure) are conflated, at a discursive level, with attitudes historically and discursively associated with the blacks in the United States. Thus, there is a big difference between, on the one hand, saying that Puerto Ricans are depicted as having a black skin color or an African heritage, as was indeed often done by the US media for much of the first half of the 20th century (cf. Thompson 2010); and, on the other hand, claiming that certain ethnic populations (i.e., Puerto Ricans, Cambodians) are *ideologically* and *discursively* "blackened" (as Ong's notion attempts to do), that is, in independence of the actual skin color or racial makeup of the ethnic group to which the ascription is targeted. It is in this sense that Ong is able to refer to her Cambodian subjects as "Black Asian," that is, without the concept attempting to imply anything at all about the possible Black or African ancestries of the subject to whom the concept is being applied. And, to be sure, many of the arguments collected by us in our interviews with gringos in Vieques serve the function of framing Viequenses and Puerto Ricans in this way: within the "black pole of American citizenship," where they are seen as falling outside the sphere of "deserving citizens."

The only difference between the Cambodians Ong writes about and the Viequenses is that the latter are already US citizens, while the former are not. But, because Puerto Rico is not an incorporated territory (a state) of the United States, the blackening of Puerto Ricans is not without political implications. In fact, the positioning of Puerto Ricans within the black pole of citizenship is a recurrent tendency among those opposing statehood for Puerto Rico in the mainland US political arena (mainly Republicans, since they fear Puerto Rico would become a Democratic state). Puerto Ricans have stubbornly shown, it is argued, a resistance to switch from the black to the white pole of American citizenship after more than one hundred years of US colonial possession, and after multiple acculturation efforts. The Americanization process, it seems, had failed. This is reason enough, it is finally argued, to negate statehood status to Puerto Rico. Thus, in their struggle for statehood status, Puerto Ricans are being measured and categorized by exactly the same "racial and cultural calculus" that is used to measure and categorize Asian immigrants in the US West Coast. And this is also the racial and cultural calculus that will be used by gringos arriving in Vieques in the post-Navy period to measure and categorize Viequenses as well. The system, as we will attempt to show, will clash with the local system of racial classifications, and will contribute to the muting and blackening of the voice of the Viequenses.

RACIAL CATEGORIZATION SYSTEMS IN VIEQUES AND THE HISPANIC CARIBBEAN

As part of the Spanish Caribbean, the Viequenses are mostly self-reported white Hispanics (58.7 percent as of 2010). Puerto Rico as a whole also shows a relatively small black population, at least in comparative terms within the

Caribbean region, and only 12.4 percent of the population self-reported being black in the 2010 census.[1] The self-reported black population of Vieques is nonetheless bigger than that of Puerto Rico: 28.1 percent versus 12.4 percent in 2010. According to the 2010 census, the total population of Vieques was 9,301, out of which 5,456 self-reported being white, 2,617 black, 62 Native American (Neo-Taino), 509 non-Hispanic (mostly North Americans), and the reminder chose the "other Hispanic" category (i.e., Dominicans, Cubans, Mexicans, etc.). It this sense, the case of Vieques is comparable with those of many other mainland Puerto Rican coastal municipalities, where one finds a higher concentration of blacks (when compared to municipalities from the mountain region).

But being mostly white (according to self-reported census categories) does not erase the fact that, at a more quotidian level, the Viequenses employ a system of racial categorization that accepts multiple grading between black and white, and where racial categorization becomes something highly negotiable. The experience of Vieques is not very different from that of other Spanish Caribbean islands, where individuals are neither "black" nor "white." As Kathleen N. Skoczen has documented for Samana, in the Dominican Republic, the lack of correspondence between local and imported racial categorization systems becomes a major cause of misunderstanding in encounters between locals and tourists.

> Locally, few people would consider themselves "black" . . . , and it is the contact with Europeans and North Americans that has brought these racial categories home for the local Dominican population in a way not experienced before. (Skoczen 2008: 152)

The views of Viequenses about their own racial makeup are also whitened through official discourses about their national mestizo identity, with influx from white Spaniards, African blacks and Taino Indians. This notion of Puerto Rican mestizo identity retains a strong hegemonic hold in the mind of many Viequenses (and Puerto Ricans in general), turning racial divisions along a white/black polarity into something highly negotiable. The terms Viequenses and Puerto Ricans use to define their racial makeup is characterized by what anthropologist Isar Godreau has called a "slippery semantic" (2008).

It will then be the encounter between the two opposed systems of racial classifications: one bipolar, as documented by Ong for mainland US; the other multipolar, as documented by Skoczen and Godreau for the Hispanic Caribbean; that will account for the racialization of social conflicts emerging in Vieques in the post-Navy period, where social tensions increasingly assume the form of Viequense-gringo tensions.

TYPOLOGY OF GRINGOS: THE OLD
ONES AND THE NEW ONES

The initial agents in charge of placing in motion the process of blackening the Viequense's voice in the post-Navy period were the multiple North American tourism investors, managers and workers, as well as residential tourists, that moved to live on the island permanently: what, following Chambers, we will refer to as "tourism mediators" (2009: 32).[2] While there is abundant anthropological literature on the interactions between tourists and the local host populations (the host/guest dynamic), and on the conflictive aspects of these encounters and exchanges (i.e., Smith 1989[1978]; Farrell 1979; Forster 1964; Huit 1979; Sweet 2010[2004]; Abbink 2010[2004]), the literature is less abundant when related to interactions between the local population and these "tourism mediators" and "residential tourists."

The post-Navy period witnessed the arrival of a relatively large group of these foreign "tourism mediators." Although they do not form a big community in absolute numbers, their presence has more than doubled between 2000 and 2010. According to the US Census, residents of Vieques classified as non-Hispanic jumped from 236 in 2000 to 509 in 2010 (a 115 percent increase). The increase in the non-Hispanic population is also evidenced in their percentage share of the whole population, which jumped from 2.5 percent in 2000 (236 non-Hispanic out of a total Vieques population of 9,106) to 5.5 percent in 2010 (509 out of 9,301 Viequenses). While they are not a big community in absolute numbers, many of them are business owners with influential ties to the Municipal Assembly and/or the Vieques Chamber of Commerce, and with powers that go beyond their numerical presence.

In any case, the relationship between locals and "tourism mediators" in the first decade of the post-Navy period has been diverse and complex, and in fact explains why Viequenses often make a distinction between two types of gringos, "the old ones" (*los de antes*) and "the new ones" (*los de ahora*), the former being generally perceived as "cool" and the latter as "economically driven." One of our informants estimated the ratio at 68 percent bad Gringos to 30 percent "cool" ones:

> Sixty-eight percent [are not-cool] . . . I'm telling you, thirty percent [of Gringos] are "cool," and they come and deal with the people and relate with the people . . . Please!. . . [The new ones] don't relate to any Viequense. They have their own groups over there, meetings. (Worker Viequense #11)[3]

Seen in historical perspective, the relationship of Viequenses with Gringos can be divided in four stages arranged in chronological order. The first stage, covering the early Navy period (roughly 1940 to 1973), was conflictive almost from the beginning, and numerous accounts of violent incidents abound for this early period. The immediate threat to the civilian population during this period resulted not so much from the military and bombing activity itself, but rather from the disruption of quotidian life that took place every time hordes of servicemen were given passes to go to the civilian population area, engaging in "public insults, beatings, murders, undignified conduct, drunkenness, disrespectful conduct against women, forced entries, rapes and other" (Cruz Soto 2008: 245). But the situation began to change with the assassination of a local civilian, Pepe Christian, better known as Mapepe, at the hands of four Marines on April 4, 1953 (Holt 2012). The death of Mapepe ignited a long struggle to prohibit Navy personnel from entering the civilian area, a goal which was achieved twenty years later, in 1973. The prohibition was first imposed during the patron-saint fiestas (*fiestas patronales*), but was later imposed with permanent character (Cruz Soto 2008: 245, Fn. 65).

Thus, since 1973 people from Vieques have not had face-to-face contact with military personnel. In the post-Mapepe period, only high-ranked officials were allowed into the civilian zone, and never wearing their military uniform. Viequenses could still recognize them by their haircuts, but they were dressed in civilian clothing and well behaved, and created no trouble in the community. In the post-Mapepe period, then, the conflicts between Marines and the civil population was reduced to practically zero; memories of the pre-Mapepe period survive almost exclusively in the mind of older Viequenses (cf. Fabian 2003).

But the experience of tranquility and peacefulness that characterized the island in the post-Mapepe period also contributed in making the island more attractive to gringos, and brought with it a new wave of North Americans into the island, this time in the form of "residential tourists"—that is, wealthy North Americans who bought vacationing residences in the mountain region of the island, who are only in the island during short periods of time, and who generally keep a low profile in their relationship with the local community. They represent the social actors in the second stage of the Viequense/gringo relations, running from 1973 to the departure of the Navy, in 2003, which we have referred to as the post-Mapepe period. This is also part of the community that the people from Vieques refer to as the gringos *de antes* and, in general terms, the relationship with this community has been non-conflictive. One of our informants describes this sector of the gringo population in the following terms:

> There was also a community of people that was considered much more from . . . more from the mountains, like the richest, millionaires, that, fine, they hired us and all of that, but I wouldn't say that they are in the street with me drinking next to me, in La Nasa, dancing with my wife, I mean, a certain division that was understandable. (Worker Viequense #7)[4]

This group of residential tourists also includes a small group of gringos (not necessarily wealthy) who moved to the island, learned the Spanish language, in some cases married locals, and became active in the community and in the struggle to get the Navy out of the island. Many within this group have, for all practical purposes, "gone native." In fact, the distinction between Viequenses and Non-Viequenses, when referring to this group, gets blurry, and many locals consider them Viequenses. Mark, a Puerto Rican of Viequense origins but born and raised in the United States, himself one of these "adopted" Viequenses, draws from the most obvious examples within this group:

> Although there were already here many North Americans that didn't want the Navy to be here. Including Bob Rabin, Roberto Rabin. I mean, is he not from here? I mean, he is from here. I would also tell you that many people [from Vieques] consider him a Viequense, some may not, but he is North American originally. So now you see, then, equal from my case, he is already a local in his own level. Kathy Gannet! Kathy Gannet is North American . . . important fighter against the Marines, very good keeping and bringing information and all of that, but . . . you know, if you go looking around, it is a minority but it's a lot of people that are North Americans, that are very well respected, and that have done many things for Vieques. And not only those two, you know, you, you have people who have worked in the Society for the Protection of Animals [Humane Society], and all of that. (Mark)[5]

A third stage in the development of the gringo/Viequense relations came after the departure of the Navy, and comprises the very early stages of the post-Navy period. This third stage marks the arrival of part of that group of gringos that Viequenses refer to as "the new ones" (*los de ahora*). Numerous statements were recorded in our interviews emphasizing this distinction, and highlighting the economic thirst of the gringos *de ahora*. Two major complaints dominate in these discourses about the gringos *de ahora*: they create a community apart, and they are money driven.

> Vieques has always had North Americans and Europeans that have cohabited with us. I have some friends here that are friends of ours. But what has arrived now, what I told you, the economic value is what predominates . . . Because they co-habit with us, but they don't co-live with us. They inhabit the same land, but they don't want to live with the Viequense. On the contrary, the worst insults come from them . . . But we are making two societies . . . OK, from one society there has emerged another society inside that society. The American and the European are apart . . . This social reality of cultural distancing allows some people to come from outside and provoke this mess (*revulú*) that we have here with tourism. Because these people don't come here with my perspective, social, of earning something, of opening a business. Those people come here to look for money any way possible. And they create this mess. (Other Viequense #1)[6]

Now you feel it more. The North American "from before" (*de antes*) would hire you, was your friend, because he would give you work and you would clean his swimming pool, backyard. Not anymore . . . The reality is that there is economic competition; the resentment is greater, because you are not from here . . . In my opinion, I believe that there is a lack of respect for the Viequenses on the part of North Americans, because we are different . . . Not all North Americans, but there is racism. North Americans here only meet with [other] North Americans. In Vieques activities very little, and the truth is there is no integration. (Other Viequense #2)[7]

A great part of the problems here is because of that . . . because the population is divided. In here . . . the thing is that in here you have two communities coexisting: the locals and the foreigners. And the foreigner has his world, and then they have these possibilities and professions that the local people don't have. And the Viequense finds himself without provisions, in disadvantage. (Worker Viequense #2)[8]

One of our Viequense informants points to the complex mechanisms and networks that conspire to exclude Viequenses from deriving economic benefits from the tourism industry by arguing that the Gringos *de ahora* create not only their own "community apart," but also their own "tourism apart."

I believe they make a community apart, with a tourism apart. They help each other. For example, if one has a guest house and there is a tourist, they send him to another [Gringo's] place to eat or to make some excursion, and they create this chain. The tourist that goes there, it is very little what they consume outside that chain. Although they are using the resources of Vieques, everything stays within that chain, and money is concentrated in a few people. It is very little what they pay to the municipality for all of that. I heard of a people, a man that placed some moorings (*muertos*) so that people can park their boats and pay him. It is a North American man. And without any permits you go to his bar and pay him for anchoring. I can't say they are all bad, but most of them have this sense of closed business, so that other people from Vieques cannot participate. (Other Viequense #5)[9]

Interestingly, this position held by Viequense about the Gringos *de ahora* was also shared by two non-Viequense tourism workers who we interviewed (one North American and one European), emphasizing once again the tendency to create a community apart and to be money driven:

Before, the Americans would mix with the people of Vieques. But the American that comes now is different. They now come here and take advantage of the Viequenses (*los cogen de pendejos*). Now there are North Americans that hire Viequenses and don't even want to pay them. Before, you would not see that. Before, they would get along better. I think the Americans that are coming here are Jews or something like that. Before, they would come, buy a piece of land and stay to live here. Now they come to look for money . . . , it's different. (Worker European #3)[10]

We [North-Americans] work together [with Viequenses], but we don't play together, you know . . . Not just be friendly with the locals, but make friends with the local. Because there is a big difference between being friendly and being a friend. And, you know, it's not just the Americans, the local Viequenses need to do that too. They are kind of still in this mode where the Americans are coming in and taking over, which is true, you know . . . and now the Viequenses who don't own their businesses have to be employed by the Americans, and this is actually Vieques, this is their land. But a lot could be done with tourism if everybody took that step and start to be friends. (Worker North American #5)

As many of these tourism mediators increasingly settled down to live on the island, the gringo/Viequense conflict slowly extended to residential areas, and Viequenses often talk about conflicts with their gringos-*de-ahora* neighbors. Complaints center heavily on issues related to the noises produced by the multiple domestic animals Viequenses keep in their backyards: dogs, horses and chickens, but particularly roosters. Indeed, the practice of keeping domestic animals in their backyards is widespread among Viequenses, and there are very few places (if any) within the residential zones of Vieques where one can escape the cacophony produced by the barking of the dogs, combined with the crows of the roosters and the snorts and whinnying of the horses (particularly when there is a mare in heat, which is almost always), at night. Trying to go to sleep with this concert going on is an achievement that requires training, and there seem to be some gringos who show a radical incapacity to ever get used to it. But the roosters are the ones that provoke the most complaints. One of our informants reported that she knew of one case where the complaints about roosters had reached the courts of justice:

There was even a case that ended in the courts, of Americans bringing people from Vieques to the court because the roosters they had in their backyard bothered them. And up to this point the situation has turned tense . . . More than anything, the nerve. How are you going to change the form of life, something so natural, not only here but in Puerto Rico . . . in the Dominican Republic, in Mexico . . . you know, some backyard birds. (Worker North American #2)[11]

One of our interviewees also reported having a "crazy gringo" neighbor who shoots her domestic animals with a pellet gun, anticipating what she described as a "class struggle":

I am used to having animals in my house, but a neighbor of mine that is North American, that has a BB gun [pellet gun] and shoots at them [the animals] because he says they bother him . . . it's a constant harassment. The class struggle will be very intense. (Other Viequense #3)[12]

Following in the footsteps of the arrival of tourism investors and managers, there was a fourth and final wave of tourism workers arriving into the island, and competing with Viequenses for low-paying jobs. These are skilled or semiskilled North American workers who come to the island from mainland US for the high season only, and then return to mainland US to work the high season there, which is during the summer. They come from Cape Cod, Martha's Vineyard or The Hamptons (all famous summer vacation destinations in the Eastern Coast of the United States), and come to Vieques to occupy jobs as waiters and bartenders during the winter season. Both employers and employees spoke extensively about this new semiskilled labor force:

The non-Viequenses that we hire come down here to work for the season, so they are here for a purpose: to make as much money as they can in the tourism, and then they get off to the North East and they work off there for the summer, seasonal. So they are predisposed to working harder than people who live in grandma's house, who don't have any rent, don't have any expenses . . . All of it is the fault of the social policies of the United States' government, to tell you the truth. (Employer North American #5)

There is also the transitory North American, that is like: "Look, I come here, I'll stay for a year, I'll stay for the season, for a while, a little while, I come, I work from December to April, I party, I enjoy a beautiful island, I earn enough money, and then . . . It's not that I don't care about Vieques, but I came here to do just that," and that is done in many parts of the world. But Viequenses understand that community . . . what they are and how they function. (Worker Viequense #7)[13]

We have also noticed that there is a market of mostly young people that come over and what they want is to have an experience of six months in the island . . . three or four months, that happens a lot . . . Some of them tell you: "Look, I'm here only for the season, do you have anything to offer me?" OK, since we are in high season maybe we can offer them an opportunity. But they really come for that season . . . for the experience and all of that. . . . But we have interviewed some of these boys and girls, and they have told us that it's becoming less attractive for them to come over because the rent that they are paying where they stay has been also increasing. Then, it used to be very simple because they used to pay very little in rent, and now the rent has doubled or tripled for them. (Employer Puerto Rican #11)[14]

You have the people form Martha's Vineyard, Cape Cod . . . those people work there March, April, May, June, July and August, during the summer, and in the winter they all come here, and workers do the same, and they have the experience and the language that the locals don't speak, and they are the ones that work here in Esperanza . . . They are many and if Viequenses get a job it's washing dishes, cleaning . . . and they are not given the opportunity, they are in disadvantage. They compete with people that come from working in luxury and expensive tourist places, and they have an incredible experience. The one to be blamed is also the owner of the business, that doesn't have the sensibility and hires them and doesn't give the opportunity to the locals. (Worker Viequense #2)[15]

Yes, because they come for the winter season . . . see, because a lot of them have a summer season, whether in Maine, in Massachusetts, in Cape Cod, or work in The Hamptons in New York, for the summer there, that's where the big money is . . . and then in their winter season they don't have anything to do, so they come down here, and they're all in their twenties, you know, they're already finishing school, and they come here for six months, and they work as a waiter, bartender, waitress, you know, in the hotels, front-desk maybe, if they need somebody, and then they leave, in the summertime. They come when I need them, and they are skilled. (Employer North American #7)

The impact of this fourth and final wave of gringos extends not only to waitresses, bartenders and cooks, but also to a whole network of support for the tourism sector that includes construction workers, gardeners, landscapers, plumbers, electricians, mechanics, private guards and so on. These were jobs that had traditionally been, within the cultural arrangements Viequenses had with the gringo community before 2003, reserved almost exclusively for Viequenses. So one of the things that many locals perceive as having undergone significant change in the post-2003 period is the entry of gringos into the sector traditionally reserved for Viequenses. The insertion of this gringo workforce has occurred in one of either two ways: either directly replacing Viequenses or by pushing themselves in as middlemen in the operation and sub-hiring Viequenses to do the actual job.

In the past they looked for Viequenses to work in construction and so on, but what the big companies are doing is . . . for example, they get the contract from a person, American with American, and then they sub-hire Puerto Ricans and pay them a salary to work for them. But the people who are working in the construction as such are the Puerto Ricans . . . All the employees are Puerto Ricans, all of them . . . I mean, the big money is going to the Americans, what we get is the crumbs . . . all right, people here that work in construction can get by, but they don't have the mentality to see things as a big business, you know. They go, they work in construction, whatever, and they earn some bucks . . . but they are not seeing the "big picture," they don't see the big potential that exists. (Worker Viequense #1)[16]

There is little chance of finding a job here, neither Viequenses nor anybody. The Americans that have come over have replaced the labor of Viequenses. Viequenses used to be the ones who would clean the backyards, built a house, paint, etcetera, those jobs that don't require much skill. Now it is North Americans who do those jobs . . . Let's say, cleaning a backyard, that is a simple job, and there are tons of North Americans cleaning backyards . . . and then Viequenses that could be doing that as a job have to fight. (Other Viequense #2)[17]

The new panorama for Vieques in the post-Navy period is that the practice of having jobs traditionally reserved for Viequenses is quickly disappearing, and that Viequenses are having to compete with this new migrant labor force in unfavorable conditions, given their language and service skills and experience. One of our informants, while being interviewed, suddenly came to the realization that there is actually only one line of job that is still completely in control of Viequenses: "The *públicos* (collective taxis)! The *público* drivers are all from here" (*¡Los públicos! Los públicos son de aquí todos*). In all this, Vieques is once again following the pattern of so many other tourism beach destinations around the globe. As Chambers points out:

> The major obstacle to fully realizing these benefits [of tourism employment] in a local area is that potential employers might find that the local population lacks the skills necessary for employment. This is often the case when tourist development occurs in regions where the local population has had limited access to education and little previous experience in dealing with outsiders. While it is entirely possible to provide local residents with the kinds of trainings that would prepare them for tourism employment, employers often decide that it is easier to import already-skilled labor from other places. (Chambers 2009: 41)

STRUGGLE FOR THE CONTROL OF ESPERANZA AND THE MALECÓN

One of the places where the gringo/Viequense conflict acquires a more public character is in the area of Esperanza. Esperanza is one of the two major urban centers in Vieques (Isabel II being the other one), and it is the area where most of the tourism business is concentrated, particularly along the beachfront road that runs through it, and which is usually referred to as "el Malecón" (boardwalk or esplanade). It consists of a road approximately one fourth of a mile long, with the beach and the esplanade on one side and tourism businesses on the opposite. This boardwalk is also the place where both tourists and Viequenses from Esperanza hangout during their free time, particularly on weekends and holidays. Viequenses speak with nostalgia of a time when the businesses in the Malecón were all owned by Viequenses, before they were sold out to gringos.

> Look, I tell you that when I was growing up all these were businesses from Boricuas only. La Concha, el Quenepo, were from Boricuas. El Amanchi was from Boricuas . . . La Amanchi . . . and now that is no more. And all we have left is that, that right there [pointing to Mucho Gusto, a Puerto Rican restaurant owned by a Viequense] . . . There are no more Boricuas anymore . . . There are more Gringos than Puerto Ricans here, ain't that right?, than Viequenses? Not

one Puerto Rican. All Americans, and they don't even speak Spanish or nothing. Let them go to hell. (Worker Viequense #9)[18]

You have seen all that area of the Malecón, all that area where the Malecón is used to be residential houses, there were no businesses there. There, the only business in those times—I remember when I was small—was that one over there [points to El Quenepo], and it was a shack with its owner, who was the one that ran the business, and his wife that was the cook, and he remained there until, three or four years ago, he started receiving his social security, he decided to retire and sold to a North American, as it happened also with Bananas. All those businesses, if you go to the Malecón, one single residential house is the most you'll find. (Worker Viequense #4)[19]

All the business for tourists are owned by people who are not from here, in the Malecón. Except [for] . . . el Bili [owned by a non-Viequense Puerto Rican], they are all from Americans. (Worker Viequense #2)[20]

Look at all these restaurants, owned by North Americans . . . Only one from here, and the rest are, 90% or something like that of the rest, are from North Americans. (Worker Viequense #7)[21]

Moreover, Viequenses remember a time when the Malecón was their hangout place, when the price of food was within their reach, and when the type of food was Puerto Rican/Viequense. While they are already familiar with North American hamburgers and tacos, they speak with disdain about the few *nouvelle cuisine* restaurants that are now opening.

You know where it's really expensive? Look, you even have to make a reservation. If you don't, you can't go in. El Quenepo. Do you know how much is worth a small plate of a little fish, this big [measures with his finger a 5 in. fish]? A little fish! A *colirubia* fish this small, this small, a *chopita* [small fish]. Well decorated, something that looks like a painting. Eighty dollars. Some mashed potatoes, a few vegetables, but like well sticking up, as if it was a pyramid. Eighty. A flan, a coconut flan, six dollars . . . I don't pay that much. (Worker Viequense #9)[22]

While it is true that most of the business on the Malecón are dedicated to tourism, and most are in fact owned and run by foreigners, mostly North Americans, the same is not true for the few shacks and ambulant businesses that operate on the beach side of the road, toward the Eastern end of the Malecón. While part of the beach side of the Malecón is restricted to a boardwalk with benches and gazebos facing the water, as one walks down this boardwalk from West to East one encounters, halfway along the strip, a small wooden structure that has been reserved by the municipality for the Esperanza fishermen, along with a small pier and a big fenced space devoted to parking. The wooden structure is the fish market (*pescadería*). In the present, though, it operates as a bar called "La Nasa."

La Nasa is a picturesque place, operated by Dominicans but run by a well-known Viequense called Toñito Silva (a.k.a. Ñito), that belongs to the Silva family. The Silva family is well known in Vieques for their *independentista* ideology and militancy. Many in Vieques claims that "the Silvas" are all *Macheteros* (the name of a Puerto Rican freedom-fighting group), which is just another way of saying that they are very much pro-independence. When talking about his business, La Nasa, Ñito claims he is not interested in making a profit, but instead turns the business into a statement about the symbolic "ownership" of the Malecón, which belongs to the Viequenses. He sells beer very cheap, waging a war of prices with the Americans. He also plays Dominican *Bachata* music very loud, as if entering into a competition with the North American pop-rock music that emerges from the American restaurants and bars across the street. Stories abound about attempts by Americans to have the business shut down.

> Ah, La Nasa, that now they want to take it out of here those Gringos, saying to give visibility to the water, to give visibility to the businesses over there, ah, because it makes ugly the view of the Malecón. Some balls! (Worker Viequense #9)[23]

Others claim the place is reserved for the sale of fish, and cannot be used to sell alcohol. Many also claim Ñito doesn't have a license for the sale of alcohol. But the truth is that, as of 2015, La Nasa is still there and operating, and there are no indications that it will be shutting up in the near future. The place remains, without a doubt, a paradigmatic symbol of the struggle of Viequenses to retain symbolic control of the Malecón, and of Vieques in general.

But once the spot granted to the fishermen comes to an end, further east along the beach side of the Malecón, one encounters a group of seven or eight shacks devoted to either the sale of food or beach equipment rental, and with the side of the street occupied by artisans during weekends. The spot is part of a bigger property owned by a corporation named Sun Bay Properties, Inc. In any case, many of these artisans and food vendors are Viequenses, and much of the food and artisanal work they sell is Puerto Rican or locally made. So, the spot beyond La Nasa is still somewhat controlled by Viequenses, and remains as the last strip of land under their control—in a pragmatic sense, of course, since food vendors and artisans do not own the land on which they operate. In this strip of land, there is "Rana's Place," operated by Ranita and his wife, both Viequenses. They have a movable aluminum structure, and sell *bacalaitos* (cod fritters) and *pastelillitos de chapin* (fish-stuffed turnovers) only during weekends. There is also Sombra's spot, a Viequense Rasta who can cook almost anything, always accompanied by the typical Puerto Rican staple: *arroz con habichuelas* (rice and beans). If told in advance, he can cook his speciality: lobster tail cooked over wood-fire for $15. He adorns his shack with Taino Indian symbols, and when asked about it he says: "That's what I am."[24] There is also a bigger food truck that comes from Fajardo on the ferry every weekend, and sells almost every Puerto Rican fritter one can imagine: *pastelillitos de chapín, bacalaitos, alcapurrias, tacos, sorullitos de maiz, rellenos de papa, piononos* among others. Besides the food stands, there is also a snorkeling and kayak rental shack in the area, and multiple ambulant artisans who set up tables on the side of the road bordering the area selling seashell jewelry, hats, T-shirts and many other things. Among all the food vendors located in this area, there is only one that is gringo-owned: Danny's Burger. Danny, the owner, has a movable aluminum structure that sells specialty hamburgers for $10 each.

But the dynamics of the Malecón began to change in 2009, with the arrival of the new (often perceived as "pro-tourist" or "pro-American") NPP party mayor, Evelyn Delerme, who won elections for mayor of Vieques in that same year. A series of new municipal laws were immediately approved that restricted the activities of Viequenses in the Malecón. Once Delerme was in office, Municipal Ordinance 28 was released "prohibiting" vendors from selling their souvenirs in the Malecón, among other things.[25] Moreover, there would be a reorganization of state and municipal police. But the measure that most infuriated Viequenses was the creation of a vigilante patrol made up of North American civilians working on a voluntary basis. Many complaints from locals were recorded in our interviews regarding the reforms implemented by the police, Municipal Ordering 28 and the vigilante patrol. One of our informants said the following about these changes, exemplifying at the same time the "way with words" and outspokenness that is characteristic of many Viequenses, and of the Vieques voice in general—the same voice that will later be muted.

The last idea they came up with was that they want to buy the municipal police their equipment, and that they become their police. But, what is that? And I told one of the policemen:"You mean to tell me that you are not anymore my police? Are you a private police working for them?" . . . They even collected money to train the municipal police . . . when you go to Esperanza you will notice a group of people with a yellow jacket. The last thing that could happen to us was that the North Americans now do vigilance of the Malecón . . . Thank god a group of us protested, because that would mean turning the municipal police into the private security police of the North American sector. The last thing they did was that the mayor, who gives in more easily than a Polo cigarette, took out the artisans from the Malecón. But, that is cultural . . . Do you know why she took them out? Because the Americans across the street didn't like them to be there. This mayor has turned out to be the mayor of the Americans. (Other Viequense #1)[26]

As for the vigilante patrol, the idea had a short life, and lasted until the first violent confrontation took place between local guys and the "yellow jackets," as they were called. One eye-witness related the details of the confrontation:

> Last week, here, two or three Americans came as if they were policemen, I don't know if you saw them, with yellow jacket that said patrol, in a patrol car, this and that . . . North Americans that are not from here . . . can you imagine . . . they parked right there . . . Community Patrol. The thing is that the guy who organized that was the guy whose house was robbed in La Hueca, a Gringo who came from outside, he moved here, and was [retired] Lieutenant from the New York police. Then he said that things in the Malecón will get fixed, because he was going to fix them . . . Not one of them was Puerto Rican. All Americans, and they didn't even speak Spanish or anything. Let them go to hell . . . They see you around and they stop you. They stand here [pointing right next to him] and there they stay. They wait until somebody attempts to do a hit or something. They stay there, *posteaos* [like light posts], and they don't move from there . . . That didn't last long. They stoned them . . . [Interviewer asks: Who did?] The guys [*Los muchachos*]. They were coming from the beach side. When they [the patrollers] saw the stones coming at them they took that road up the Malecón. Uhhh! They were running. Ja, ja! (Other Viequense #6)[27]

THE HISTORY OF DANNY'S BURGER

Beyond the managers and investors related to the tourism industry who came to Vieques, there is also a concern about the wave of North American workers also coming to the island in search of jobs and opportunities within the tourism industry.

> You are also going to find many North Americans that are broke, that come without a cent, that are surviving here, in a town with 50% unemployment. I would like the Viequenses to be the ones hired, but there is also a reality: the immigration of North Americans that is coming is not the immigration of the seventies, eighties: people with money, they would build houses in the mountain, with swimming pools, and would every now and then come to a restaurant. Now all sorts of people are coming. Not all the ones that are coming have a job, have a preparation, economic resources, so there is pure competition between the locals, that cannot go anywhere else, and them. (Other Viequense #2)[28]

In fact, this group of foreign workers constitutes, within our typology of gringos, the fourth and last group of North Americans to appear in the history of the gringo/Viequense relations, and which Viequenses classify within the broader category of "the new ones" (*los de ahora*). Viequenses' complaints about this fourth group center on the belief that they exhibit an extreme form of greed that is often shocking to Viequenses, and which fills the Viequenses with indignation. The tragic events surrounding the history of Danny's Burgers serve to illustrate the type of greedy behavior exhibited by this group of gringos, as well as, in somewhat tragic manner, the level of violence that the gringo/Viequense conflict has already reached in Vieques.

Danny is a gringo who came to the island after 2003, and opened a food shack on the beach side of the Malecón, where most of the food shacks were owned by locals. He sold hamburgers for $10 each (a price that Viequenses saw as excessively high), and had an ambulant cart equipped with kitchen. He also arranged the surroundings of the cart with a canopy and tables and chairs, which also served the function of marking his territory in no-man's-land.

But the problem Viequenses had with Danny had nothing to do with his business, but rather with the fact, which was gossip all over Vieques, that Danny was selling his business on Craig's List (on the internet) for 62,500 dollars. Danny did not own the land on which he conducted his business, and therefore all he could really sell was the burger cart, plus any goodwill he wished to add. Moreover, he would advertise the business with "bathrooms across the street," that is, bathrooms that belonged to another private business on the other side of the road. The owner of that business, during a recorded interview, said this about the issue:

> Yes, and he also had bathrooms, had bathrooms "across the street" . . . They were My Bathrooms!—"With bathroom access" it said, "bathroom access across the street" . . . Without asking me or anything. (Employer Puerto Rican #12)[29]

In any case, this attempt to sell his business on Craig's List for 62,500 dollars was seen by Viequenses as equivalent to "trying to get something for nothing," and criticized accordingly. Viequenses were well aware that there was nothing illegal behind Danny's actions but, in their minds, anybody who pays 62,500 dollars for Danny's Burgers would be robbed, and in this equation Danny would be the robber.

The history of Danny's Burger took a tragic turn when Danny began to claim "exclusive use" over a municipal trash bin that was located close to his shack. Danny had a dispute with Sombra, a Rastaman from Vieques that occupied the shack immediately next to his, claiming the trash bin was closer to his shack, so it was for the exclusive use of his customers. The dispute never evolved into any form of physical violence between Danny and Sombra, but on the night of Saturday, April 25, 2008 the events took a tragic turn: Danny's Burger cart was set on fire and burned down to ashes.

The site of the burning immediately became a "must visit" site for many Viequenses and gringos alike. It was the most exciting thing that had happened on the island in those days, and the word was out that "they burned Danny's Burger." One "cool" Gringo (*de los de antes*) who visited the place the next day also showed support for the action, making a sign of approval with his hand while saying: "The *pueblo*, baby!" In general, not even "cool" Gringos are fond of the Grinos *de ahora*.

The next day, Danny went to the police accusing Sombra of burning his business. The accusation apparently didn't go anywhere, but by 2011, neither Danny's nor Sombra's shacks were there anymore, and nobody had reoccupied their spots either. We spoke with Sombra the day after the incident, and he claimed full innocence, but meditates on the causes of the gringo/Viequense confrontation with half-joking speculations as it having been caused by the Navy's Raytheon Radar that still operates from the island:

> The radar that is right there . . . If you get to the end of La Hueca, in the end, there, there is a gate there and some antennas, that is a radar. It is called the ROTHR radar. It was made by Raytheon, Rytheon the company, and that they say it can even change the weather, they can use it for that . . . Look, four hurricanes they got to Cuba, four hurricanes this year, four. Do you know where they have another one? In Virginia. They [the Navy] have yet another one in Texas, and they have one in Vieques. What they are doing is shooting to Venezuela, to all those countries around here. The excuse is that it is for [control of] drug trafficking. Go to hell, if you have boats passing through here every day packed with bags of drugs. In 1998 they finished that radar. It is called "relocateable over-the-horizon." What is the meaning of "relocate?" That you can point the signal . . . if I want to locate Venezuela I point it to Venezuela. If I want to go to Colombia I go to Colombia. I mean, that that has a radio that can go one way or another . . . And that radiation over people, what is it causing? We don't know. Maybe that euphoria of [Gringo/Viequense] confrontation that we have in Vieques. (Sombra)[30]

Criticisms of the ultra-greedy attitudes of some foreign investors, like the one exhibited by Danny, are also very common when talking about the archaic and unreliable car-rental infrastructure of Vieques. Perhaps one of the most problematic aspects of tourism development in Vieques is the scarcity of rental cars, and in high season it is very difficult to find one available. There are no big car-rental chains in Vieques, and all the twelve car-rental businesses that exist are individually owned, mostly by foreigners. There is also a significant abundance of rundown and defective cars. But criticism of the irregular practices of car-rental businesses in Vieques is common, and can also be evidenced through a search of car-rental reviews on the internet. This exercise will lead the reader to hours and hours of horror stories about the experience of customers with car rentals in Vieques, particularly the practice by car-rental owners of charging several hundred dollars to your credit card one month after the car has been returned, collecting damages presumably done to the car while under your possession. Some of these reviews are worth quoting:

Vieques Car Rental, by James (New York City) I rented a JEEP in Vieques in November of 2009 with my Husband. The JEEP was an older model, 99 I believe. It was good enough to get around in but during the middle of our stay the left rear tire fell off while we were, luckily just turning onto pavement and driving slowly. As well, we were lucky enough to pass a bar where the town seemed to come and help along with the Police Chief Edina. All were very helpful. The police chief saw that one of the lug nuts had been broken off and rusted meaning that tire was missing a lug nut. The owner denied responsibility, of course and slapped us with a $440 bill to our surprise when we got home. At this point we are enlisting the support of the police chief and our credit card is investigating. I, of course, am not renting from Vieques car rental again and urge others not to. It is one thing to take care of your business, it is another to prey on renters.[31]

"Do not use Maritza's Car rental" Aug 05, 2008, 5:28 PM. I cannot even begin to tell you how stressful Maritza's made our trip to Vieques. We had Hacienda Tamarindo reserve the cheaper car which we knew would be old but we thought it would function. They dropped it (a Chevy Tracker) off at the hotel in the afternoon and in the morning when we got in to go to the beach it would not start. About an hour later they showed up and decided we would need a new car. We were then driven to Maritza's. They gave us a new Jeep for the day but told us we needed to have it back by 3pm b/c someone else had rented it. Keep in mind that we have just lost 2.5 hours of our beach day and did not want to rush back to return the car. They also refused to give us any kind of discount. We reluctantly agreed—went to the beach and returned the car. They then gave us the original car which they said was fixed. The next day we took it to the beach and when we finally found our beautiful deserted beach . . . the car wouldn't turn off! We had to drive all the way back to Maritza's—again—losing valuable sun/beach time. They refused to give us any discount and actually charged us for three full days. They said we were lucky we weren't being charged for the other two days we had reserved the car for. The staff there are completely rude and do not care about their customers. Larissa from Connecticut.[32]

"Vieques is Very Nice—Except for Martineau Car Rental" New York City, Aug 19, 2010. Dear Travelers: We were recently defrauded by Martineau Car Rental, souring our one year wedding anniversary trip to Vieques. They are trying to steal $300 from us and we are fighting it with our credit card company. Please don't rent from them. They completely lied and said we did something to their car that we did not do. They provided a receipt to the credit card company that is dated two years prior to our visit. They screamed at my husband and me on the phone. I've filed a police report, from New York City no less. I am not making this up. Save yourself the hassle. They seemed nice. They are not. They pretty much ruined Puerto Rico for us. Nice job.[33]

While there was always a rumor going around that big car-rental companies were looking into opening branches in the island, the rumor became real in 2013 with the opening of an Avis branch. In general, the absence of rental cars in Vieques is certainly a factor preventing even more tourists from choosing Vieques as their vacation destination.

In any case, the Gringo/Viequense conflict that is emerging in social relations in Vieques during the post-Navy period[34] is a conflict that takes place particularly between Viequenses and the gringos *de ahora*, those who came after 2003. It is this group who, in the eyes of the Viequenses, exhibit an unethical conduct in their business dealings, and an extreme form of greed in their economic ambitions—as well as a culture of speedy wealth acquisition.

FINAL REMARKS

In the post-Navy period, the tendency among Viequenses (and residential tourists) is to increasingly view social conflict in racial terms, that is, as a conflict between Gringos and Viequenses. But, as we have attempted to show, the conflict is actually being racialized in a double sense. First, it is being racialized in the sense that it is increasingly being perceived as assuming an us/they division along racial/ethnic lines (Gringos vs. Viequenses); but also, and more importantly, in the sense that the discourses of Viequenses are being framed as ideologically and discursively belonging to "the black pole of American citizens," and therefore condemned to not be listened to. And this is what, in practical terms, being blackened entails.

NOTES

1. Interestingly, this 12 percent represented an increase from 8 percent in the 2000 census. Moreover, it was coupled with a decrease in the self-reported white population from 80.5 percent in 2000 to 75.8 percent in 2010.
2. While the chain of "tourism mediators" can be quite broad, and could include personnel physically far removed from the tourism destination (e.g., travel agent), the concept can also be used to categorize the foreign tourism investors who operate on the island, and are residential tourists, immersed with the local population of Vieques in face-to-face and permanent interactions (many of whom were our interviewees).

3. Translated from Spanish. Original statement reads: "El 68 porciento . . . Te lo digo yo. 30 por ciento son "cool," y van y bregan con la gente y se relacionan. Pero personas que llevan 30 años aquí, no saben decir hola, hola, hola. H.O.L.A. Mira que fácil. 35 años tu llevas aquí y tú no sabes decir hola. Por favor! No te relacionas con ningún viequense. Tienen sus grupitos ellos de allá, reuniones."

4. Translated from Spanish. Original statement reads: "Y hubo una comunidad de gente que se consideraba como muchos más . . . más de la loma, como que los más ricos, millonarios, que está bien, nos contratan y todo eso, pero no te diría que están en la calle conmigo bebiendo al lado mío, en La Nasa, bailando con mi esposa, o sea, una cierta división que se entendía."

5. Translated from Spanish. Original statement reads: "Compleja, bien compleja. Porque había una . . . primero que nada, cuando estaba la Marina pues ya creaba un pequeño, un pequeño, una inmensa confrontación. Aunque habían aquí mucha gente norteamericana que no quería que la Marina estuviera. Inclusive, Bob Rabin, Robert Rabin, o sea, él es de aquí, también te diría que mucha gente lo considera viequense, algunos no, pero él es estadounidense originalmente. Y ya, pues, igual que yo, ya es de acá hasta en su nivel. ¡Kathy Gannet! Kathy Gannet es estadounidense . . . amplia luchadora en contra de la Marina, tremenda llevadora de información y todo eso, pero . . . tú sabes, que si vas buscando por ahí, hay una minoría pero hay un montón de gente que sí son estadounidenses, que son muy bien respetados, y que han hecho muchas cosas para Vieques. Y no solamente esos dos, tu sabes, tienes gente que ha trabajado con la Sociedad Protectora de Animales, y todo eso."

6. Translated from Spanish. Original statement reads: "Vieques siempre ha tenido norteamericanos y europeos que han cohabitado con nosotros. Tengo unos amigos aquí que son amigos nuestros. Pero lo que ha llegado ahora, lo que te dije, el valor económico es lo que permea . . . Porque ellos cohabitan con nosotros, pero no conviven. Ellos habitan la misma tierra, pero no quieren convivir con el viequense. Al contrario, los peores insultos vienen de ahí . . . Pero estamos haciendo dos socie-dades . . . Ok, de una sociedad se ha hecho otra sociedad dentro de esa sociedad. El americano y el europeo está aparte . . . Esta realidad social de aislamiento cultural hace que vengan unas personas de afuera, y que provoquen este revulú que hay aquí con el turismo. Porque esa gente no viene con la perspectiva mía, social, de ganarme algo, de que abra una empresa. Esa gente lo que viene es a buscar chavos a como dé lugar. Pues forman un reguero."

7. Translated from Spanish. Original statement reads: "Ahora se siente más. El norteamericano de antes te contrataba, era tu amigo, porque te daba trabajo y le lim-piabas la piscina, patio. Ahora no . . . La realidad es que hay competencia económica, el rencor es mayor, porque tú no eres de aquí . . . En mi opinión, yo entiendo que hay un falta de respeto hacia el viequense por parte de los norteamericanos, porque somos distintos . . . No todos los norteamericanos, pero hay racismo. Aquí los norteameri-canos se reúnen con los norteamericanos. En actividades de viequenses muy poco y realmente no hay integración."

8. Translated from Spanish. Original statement reads: "Gran parte de los prob-lemas de aquí es por . . . porque la población está dividida. Aquí, es que aquí están coexistiendo dos comunidades: los locales y el extranjero. Y el extranjero tiene su

mundo, y entonces tiene unas posibilidades y unas profesiones que la gente local no tiene. Y el viequense se ve desprovisto, se ve en desventaja. Y yo pienso que todo lo que está sucediendo aquí tiene que estar vinculado con eso que está sucediendo."

9. Translated from Spanish. Original statement reads: "Yo creo que hacen una comunidad aparte, como un turismo aparte. Ellos se ayudan unos con otros. Por ejemplo, si uno tiene un guest house y hay un turista, y lo mandan a otro lugar [de Gringos] a comer o hacer excursiones y crean como una cadena. Esos turistas que llegan ahí, es muy poco lo que consumen fuera de esa cadena. Aunque están usando los recursos de Vieques todo se concentra en esa cadena, el dinero se concentra en pocas personas. Es muy poco lo que le pagan al municipio por todo eso. He escuchado de gente de un señor que puso unos "muertos" boyas para que metan los botes y le paguen a él, es un señor norteamericano. Y sin permiso tú vas a su bar y le pagas a él por anclar. Yo no te puedo decir que todos son malos pero en su mayoría tienen este sentido del negocio cerrado, que las otras personas de Vieques no pueden participar."

10. Translated from Spanish. Original statement reads: "Antes los americanos se mezclaban con la gente de Vieques. Pero el americano que viene ahora es distinto. Ahora vienen aquí y les cogen de pendejos (a los viequenses). Ahora hay norteamericanos que contratan viequenses y ni tan siquiera les quieren pagar. Antes eso no se veía, antes se llevaban mejor. Yo creo que los americanos que vienen para acá son judíos o algo así. Antes venían, se compraban un pedazo de tierra y se quedaban a vivir aquí. Ahora vienen a buscar dinero . . . ., es diferente."

11. Translated from Spanish. Original statement reads: "Porque inclusive aquí hubo un caso que fueron a tribunal, de unos americanos llevando a personas de Vieques a la corte porque los gallos que tenían en el patio les molestaban. Y hasta ese punto la situación ha llegado a ser tan tensa . . . Más que nada el descaro. ¿Cómo tu vas a cambiar la forma de vivir, algo natural, no tan solo aquí en Puerto Rico . . . en Santo Domingo, en México . . . tu sabes, unas aves del patio. Y como que hay una total separación de las cosas de lo que se está viviendo aquí, y yo pienso que es una de las principales raíces de los problemas que están sucediendo."

12. Translated from Spanish. Original statement reads: "Yo estoy acostumbrada a tener animales en casa, pero mi vecino es un norteamericano que tiene una escopeta de "bibis" (perdigones) y les tira porque dice que le molestan . . . es un hostigamiento constante. La lucha de clases va a ser bien intensa."

13. Translated from Spanish. Original statement reads: "Y también estaban la comunidad estadounidense transitoria, que es que: "Mira, yo vengo aquí, me quedo un año, me quedo "for the season," una temporada, vengo, trabajo de diciembre a abril, party-seo, me disfruto una isla muy bella, gano bastante dinero, y pues, no es que no me importe Vieques, pero vine a hacer eso," y eso se hace en muchos sitios del mundo." Pero esa [comunidad] también los viequenses entienden lo que son y cómo funcionan."

14. Translated from Spanish. Original statement reads: "También hemos notado que hay como un mercado de más que nada jóvenes que vienen y lo que quieren es tener una experiencia de seis meses en la isla . . . Tres o cuatro meses, eso pasa mucho. Muchos te lo dicen. Unos te lo dicen: "Mira, estoy aquí más que por la temporada, tienes algo que ofrecerme. OK, como estamos en temporada alta quizás

podamos ofrecerle esa oportunidad. Pero realmente vienen por esa temporada . . . por la experiencia, y eso es todo. Fíjate, hemos entrevistado algunos de esos muchachos o muchachas, y entonces nos han dicho que cada vez es menos atractivo para ellos venir aquí, porque la renta que ellos pagan en el lugar donde se queden ha ido aumentando también. Entonces, antes era bien sencillo porque pagabas bien poco de renta, cobrabas lo mismo, y ahora la renta se ha duplicado o triplicado para ellos."

15. Translated from Spanish. Original statement reads: "Tienes la gente de Martha's Vineyard, Cape Cod . . . . esa gente trabaja allí marzo, abril. mayo, junio, julio y agosto, en el verano, y para el invierno todos vienen para acá, y los trabajadores también, y tienen la experiencia y el idioma que la gente local no habla, y son los que trabajan aquí en Esperanza . . . . Son muchos y si trabajan los de Vieques son lavando platos, limpiando . . . y no se les da la oportunidad, están en desventaja compiten con personas que vienen de trabajar en un lugar fino turístico de mucho dinero, y tienen una experiencia increíble. También el culpable es el dueño del negocio que no tiene sensibilidad y los contrata y no le da oportunidad al local."

16. Translated from Spanish. Original statement reads: "Antes pues se buscaban los locales que bregan en construcción y eso, pero las compañías grandes lo que están haciendo es . . . está bien, ellos cogen el contrato con la persona, americano con americano, entonces ellos básicamente subcontratan a los puertorriqueños y les pagan un salario por trabajar con ellos. Pero los que están haciendo la construcción como tal son los puertorriqueños . . . Todos los empleados son puertorriqueños, todos . . . O sea que el dinero gordo se lo llevan los americanos, nosotros lo que cogemos son las migajas . . . está bien, aquí la gente que trabaja en construcción se defienden, pero no tienen la mentalidad para verlo de una manera más grande como negocio, tu sabes. Ellos van, trabajan en construcción, lo que sea, y se ganan par de pesos . . . pero no están viendo el "big picture," no están viendo el potencial grande que hay."

17. Translated from Spanish. Original statement reads: "Aquí hay muy poca posibilidad de encontrar trabajo ni para los viequenses ni para nadie. Los americanos que han venido han reemplazado la mano de obra de los viequenses, los viequenses eran los que te limpiaban el patio, construían una casa, pintaban, etc. Ese trabajo que no necesita mucha destreza ahora son los norteamericanos los que lo hacen . . . Para decirte que una limpieza de patio que es una tarea sencilla y hay montones de norteamericanos limpiando patios . . . .. y entonces el viequense que pudiera tener eso como su negocio tiene que pelear."

18. Translated from Spanish. Original statement reads: "Mira, te digo a ti que cuando yo estaba creciendo todo esto eran negocios de boricuas nada más. La Concha, el Quenepo era de boricuas. El Amanchi era de boricuas . . . La Amanchi . . . y ahora no hay más na.' Ah, La Nasa, que ahora hasta la quieren sacar de aquí esos gringos, y que pa' darle visibilidad pa' allá [para el agua], para darle visibilidad a los negocios de ahí, ah, que afea la vista del malecón. Qué cojones. Y lo único que tenemos es eso, eso ahí, aquí no hay más nada boricua . . . Aquí los gringos, eso es una comunidad gringa en Esperanza. Hay más gringos que puertorriqueños aquí, ¿verdad?, que viequenses. Ni uno puertorriqueño. Tos americanos, y ni hablan español ni na.' Que se vayan pal' carajo."

19. Translated from Spanish. Original statement reads: "Usted ha visto todo ese área del Malecón. Todo ese área del Malecón lo que eran casas de residencia, ahí no eran negocios. Ahí el único negocio que para aquel tiempo—yo recuerdo cuando yo pequeño—era aquel, y era una choza con su dueño, que era el que atendía, y su esposa que era la cocinera, y así estuvo hasta, tres o cuatro años atrás, recién empezó a coger su seguro social, decide retirarse del negocio, entonces le vende a un norteamericano, que eso pasa como en Bananas. Todos estos negocios, si usted va al Malecón, si ve una casa de vivienda es mucho."

20. Translated from Spanish. Original statement reads: "Todo los negocios para turistas los tienen personas que no son de aquí, en el malecón. Excepto [por] . . . Bili, todos son de americanos."

21. Translated from Spanish. Original statement reads: "Mira todos estos restaurantes son de estadounidenses . . . Uno de aquí, y los demás son, un 70% o algo así de los demás . . . son norteamericanos."

22. Translated from Spanish. Original statement reads: "Tú sabes dónde está bien caro de verdad, mira, que tú tienes que hacer reservación. Si no, no puedes entrar. El Quenepo. ¿Tú sabes cuánto te cuesta un platito de un pescaito así? Un pescaito! Una colirubita así de chiquita, asi de chiquita, una chopita. Bien decorá, una cosa que parece un cuadro. Ochenta pesos. Papita majadita, vejetalitos así pero bien trepaitos, así como pirámides. Ochenta. Un flan, un flan de coco, seis pesos . . . Yo no pago eso."

23. Translated from Spanish. Original statement reads: "Mira, te digo a ti que cuando yo estaba creciendo todo esto eran negocios de boricuas nada más. La Concha, el Quenepo era de boricuas. El Amanchi era de boricuas . . . La Amanchi . . . y ahora no hay más na.' Ah, La Nasa, que ahora hasta la quieren sacar de aquí esos gringos, y que pa' darle visibilidad pa' allá [para el agua], para darle visibilidad a los negocios de ahí, ah, que afea la vista del malecón. Qué cojones. Y lo único que tenemos es eso, eso ahí, aquí no hay más nada boricua . . . Aquí los gringos, eso es una comunidad gringa en Esperanza. Hay más gringos que puertorriqueños aquí, ¿verdad?, que viequenses. Ni uno puertorriqueño. Tos americanos, y ni hablan español ni na.' Que se vayan pal' carajo."

24. The Tainos were the Indians who inhabited the island of Puerto Rico at the time of the arrival of Columbus in 1493. In the present, Puerto Ricans integrate the inheritance of Taino culture into their national mestizo identity, and Taino symbols are widely used by Puerto Ricans in T-shirts, tattoos, drawings and in decoration of artisanal products and so on. In more contemporary times, neo-Taino movements have also emerged fueled significantly by the proven fact that 61.3 percent of Puerto Ricans have Taino mitochondrial DNA. See, for example, Martinez-Cruzado et al. 2005.

25. See *Ordenanza 28* (2008–2009), signed April 2, 2009 by the Municipal Legislature of Vieques. It reads: "Queda terminantemente prohibido por parte de los ciudadanos y/o visitantes lo siguiente: Ventas de cualquier tipo; Ruido o música en tono estridente; Correr cualquier tipo de vehículo de motor; Amarrar o pasear animales."

26. Translated from Spanish. Original statement reads: "Lo último que se les ocurrió es que ahora ellos quieren ellos comprarle a la guardia municipal las cosas, y que sea su guardia. Pero, ¿qué es eso? Y se lo dije a uno de los guardias:"Tú me quieres decir que tú ahora no eres guardia mío. ¿Tú eres policía de seguridad de ellos?" . . .

Inclusive que ellos recogieron dinero para y que adiestrar la Policía Municipal. Suerte que un grupo protestamos, porque eso significa convertir la Policía Municipal en la guardia de seguridad privada de ese sector norteamericano . . . Lo último que hicieron fue que la alcaldesa, que está más floja que los tabacos de polo, sacara a los artesanos del malecón. Muchacho, si eso es cultural . . . ¿Tú sabes porque los sacó? Porque a los americanos de al frente les molesta que eso este allí. La alcaldesa nos ha resultado ser la alcaldesa de los americanos."

27. Translated from Spanish. Original statement reads: "Aquí la semana pasada, este, entraron dos o tres Americanos como si fueran guardias, no sé si tú los vistes, con sweater amarillo, decía Patrol, patrulla, que si esto que si lo otro . . . norteamericanos que no son de aquí . . . Imagínate tu . . . ahí se parquearon . . . Patrulla comunitaria. Es que el que se montó eso fue el que le tumbaron en la casa en La Hueca. Un Gringo que vino de afuera, se mudó pa' aca, era teniente de la policía en Nueva York. Entonces dijo que aquí se va a arreglar el Malecón, porque él lo va a arreglar . . . Ni uno puertorriqueño. To's Americanos, y ni hablan español ni na.' Que se vayan pal' carajo . . . Te ven por ahí y te paran. Se para aquí y ahí se quedan. Esperan que alguien venga a dar un golpe o algo. Se quedan ahí posteaos, y no se mueven de ahí. No, eso no duro mucho. Le entraron a pedra's. [Entrevistador pregunta: ¿Quién le entró a pedradas?] Los muchachos. Desde la playa venían por ahí. Cuando ellos vieron las pedra's cogieron por ahí pa' arriba por ese Malecón, Uhhh! Corrían. Ja, ja!"

28. Translated from Spanish. Original statement reads: "Vas a encontrar mucho norteamericano que esta "pela'o," que vinieron sin un centavo, que está sobreviviendo, en un pueblo del 50% de desempleo. Yo me gustaría que fueran los viequenses los empleados pero también hay una realidad, la inmigración que vienen de norteamericanos acá, no es la inmigración que venían en los setentas, ochentas, era gente con dinero, hacían casas en la montaña, con piscina y venían de vez en cuando a algún restaurante. Ahora está viniendo todo tipo de persona, no todos los que vienen tienen trabajo, no tienen preparación, recursos económicos, así que hay una competencia pura entre los locales que no se pueden ir a ningún lado y ellos."

29. Translated from Spanish. Original statement reads: "Si, y tenía baños también, tenía baños "cruzando la calle" . . . ¡Eran los míos!—"With bathroom access," decía: "bathroom access across the street" . . . Sin preguntarme a mí ni nada."

30. Translated from Spanish. Original statement reads: "El radar que está ahí al lado . . . Si llegas a ese final de La Hueca, al final, ahí, vistes que hay unos portones y hay unas antenas, eso es un radar. Se llama el radar Rothr. Lo creo Raytheon, la compañía Raytheon, y eso dicen que puede cambiar hasta el tiempo, pueden utilizarlo pa' eso . . . . Mira cuanto huracanes no metieron a Cuba, cuatro huracanes este año, cuatro. Sobes donde tienen uno, en Virginia. Tienen otro en Texas, y tienen el otro en Vieques. Lo que hacen es tirando a Venezuela, a todos esos países de aquí. La excusa es que es para el narcotráfico. Váyase al carajo, si por aquí pasan lanchas todos los días cargados de sacos de droga. (Sombra) En el 98 terminaron ese radar. Se llama radar relocalizable sobre el horizonte. ¿Qué significa relocalizar? Que la señal puede ir . . . Si quiero localizar a Venezuela lo pongo pa Venezuela. Si quiero ir pa Colombia lo pongo pa Colombia. O sea, que eso tiene un radio que puede ir pa allá, puede ir pa

allá . . . Y esa radiación sobre las personas, ¿qué está causando? No sabemos. A lo mejor esta misma euforia de confrontación."

31. See http://www.viequestravelguide.com/vieques-car-rental.html.

32. See http://www.tripadvisor.com/ShowTopic-g147326-i649-k2164424-Do_ not_use_Maritza_s_Car_rental-Isla_de_Vieques_Puerto_Rico.html).

33. Source: http://www.tripadvisor.com/ShowUserReviews-g147326-r75971026- Isla_de_Vieques_Puerto_Rico.html.

34. The burning of Danny's Burgers can be taken as a signal of how Gringo/ Viequense relations can unexpectedly take a violent and confrontational turn. The anthropological literature on tourism is flooded with examples of community movements organized against tourism development, and movements where local population have chosen to mount their political protests in the forms of attacks on tourists and tourist facilities. In the Philippines and Bali, for example, politically motivated terrorists attacks have included the bombing of tourist hotels, and in Egypt they have involved assaults on Western tour groups. In Colorado, "ecoterrorists" have burned vacation homes in protest for what they perceive to be overdevelopment of tourist areas (see Ness 2005; Hitchcock and Putra 2007). In the Darien region of Panama, Kuna Indians have also participated in the burning of hotels (see Martínez Mauri 2010). The threat of violence becomes more urgent in places where there is a history of struggle and mobilization, and a historical conscience of participation in these mobilizations. This is, to be sure, the case with Vieques.

Chapter 6

Decontamination, Reparations, Health, and Crime Issues

When we claim, as we have been doing, that Viequenses cannot speak, we do not mean to say that they cannot physically speak. Viequenses do speak, and speak a lot. They have also managed to commission the voice of very influential politicians, civic and religious leaders, as well as artists and intellectuals, to speak on their behalf, or in defense of Vieques' cause. But the most important effect resulting from the blackening/silencing process that we have attempted to describe is that, even when the subaltern attempts to speak through his powerful interlocutors, and using the language dictated by metropolitan etiquette, it won't be listened to. A definite closure over what can and cannot be said has already been accomplished. Nowhere does this become more evident than in the struggle for decontamination of the island, and the related struggles for reparations.

Thus, if Vieques is better known for its struggle to expel the Navy out of the island, the actual exit of the Navy in 2003 led way to what Baver has called "stage two" (2006: 92) of the struggle: the environmental struggle; which in Vieques implies mainly the cleanup of munitions left behind by the Navy. As such, the struggle was transformed from one conceived, in the pre-Navy period, as a struggle for the defense of human rights, to the one conceived, in the post-Navy period, as a struggle for environmental justice. The issue is not unrelated to the development of the tourism industry, since any upscaling of the tourism activity would require additional "decontaminated" beaches.

Effective decontamination of Vieques began in 2005. In February of that year the Environmental Protection Agency (EPA) listed the island on the National Priorities List (NPL) of most hazardous waste sites on the nation, and included Vieques in the Superfund National Priority List of zones that must be decontaminated. Later that year, the US Navy assigned 76 million dollars for the initial stages of the cleanup, and cleanup activities began soon afterward. Eight years later, in 2013, the amount of devices extracted dramatically serves to show the magnitude of the environmental disaster that was left behind: the US Navy had already invested 183.1 million dollars in the decontamination process, and it was estimated that an additional 350 million dollars will be required to complete the task. It had already completed the cleaning of 2,578 of the 3,706 acres that were contaminated, from where it had removed 38,275 explosive devices and recycled thirteen million pounds of metal. The cleanup is expected to be completed by 2024, only for the land portion. The sea bed also needs to be decontaminated, but that would require an estimated fifteen additional years.

Many observers of the Vieques cleanup are suspicious that the process might never be completed, and make reference to the Kaho'olawe bombing range, in Hawaii, as the most apt case for comparison (e.g., Klein 2001; Baver 2006). Also used as a training ground and bombing range by the US Armed Forces, the Kaho'olawe range was abandoned in 1994, and it took ten years and 460 million dollars to finish its cleanup. Yet, while the original goal was to remove 100 percent of surface ordnance and 30 percent of subsurface munition, the military only accomplished 77 percent and 9 percent of the work, respectively. Even after the decontamination was supposed to have been "completed," in April 2004, the island remained contaminated and off-limits to the general public. The experience of the Kaho'olawe range was discouraging for many Viequenses; they believed they will receive the same treatment, or worse. As Baver has suggested, the people from Vieques should probably expect to receive even less than what was given to Kaho'olawe, given that "the Kaho'olawe cleanup was done with considerably more powerful brokers in Washington pushing for its completion than is the case for Puerto Rico" (2006: 101).

But beyond the similarities that might exist between Vieques and Kaho'olawe, there is also one big difference between the two that makes the whole idea of comparison irrelevant: namely, the fact that human civil population in Kaho'olawe was zero, while that of Vieques was 9,301 (as of 2010). And indeed, if there is an issue that is almost intrinsically interwoven with the Vieques' decontamination struggle, it is the human cost resulting from the long-term exposure of the civilian population residing in the island to metals and other contaminants. Vieques' human health profile is saddening, with health disparities in almost every health category one could think of, the most critical being asthma, kidney failure, diabetes, hypertension and various types of cancer. Without a doubt, one key motivation behind the cleanup struggle is the presence of a significant civilian population living within kilometers of the contaminated areas, and the critical health problems and health disparities present in the island when compared to both Puerto Rico (Big Island) and mainland US. Thus, if the concept of "environmental justice" defines the second stage of the Vieques struggle, the term "environment" needs to be understood here in a broader sense, that is, one that includes humans as part of the environment, part of what needs to be protected. In here, environmental justice and human rights are inevitably interwoven.

But it is cancer, above all other illnesses suffered disproportionately by Viequenses, that evidences in drastic form the true dimensions of the Vieques health nightmare. According to data from the Puerto Rico Comprehensive Cancer Center and the Cancer Registry, the cancer incidence rate decreased from 339.67 (per 100,000 persons) in 2005 to 183.58 in 2008, and increased from there to 224.57 in 2009 (last year for which statistics are available). The Big Island cancer rate remained relatively static at around 285 (average of 284.5 for the period 2005–2009). Cancer death rate reveals even more critical figures: the rate went from 882.29 (per 100,000 persons) in 2004, down to 709.92 in 2006, up again to 807.58 in 2007, and then down again to 605.49 in 2008. The Big Island's cancer death rate, on the other hand, decreased from 717.27 in 2004 to 648.68 in 2006, and slightly decreasing from there to 605.49 in 2008 (last year for which there are data available). The average for the Big Island was 676.09 for the period 2004–2008. In fact, it was in 2008 that, for the first time in its history, the Vieques cancer death rate went below that of the Big Island, with 605.49 and 653.17 respectively.

This means that, roughly estimated, seventeen new persons are diagnosed with cancer, and eight persons die from cancer, each year in Vieques. Given the tiny size of the island and the population, this is equivalent to saying that in Vieques cancer is everywhere. There is absolutely no one who has not been a victim of cancer, either as a diagnosed patient or otherwise. Everybody has one or several significant-others, often relatives, who have suffered from this ailment, and emotions run high when talking about this issue. An overwhelming majority of Vieques cancer patients are convinced their illness is related to military activities of the Navy. For them, this is simply "common sense."

In 2007 Vieques resident Juanita Sánchez, on behalf of her daughter and some 7,125 other residents of the island (out of a total population of 9,300), filed lawsuit against the US Government asking for reparations for health

Table 6.1   Cancer Statistics for Vieques and Puerto Rico

	Average 1990–1994 (VQS/PR)	Average 1995–1999 (VQS/PR)	Average 2000–2004 (VQS/PR)	Average 2005–2009 (VQS/PR)
Cancer incidence rate	297.8/281.3	351/277.8	297.7/282.7	263/284
New cases	131	170	176	164
Cancer death rate	68	85	84	80

Source: Puerto Rico Comprehensive Cancer Center, and the Cancer Registry of Puerto Rico.

problems caused by military activities in Vieques. Working against the interests of the plaintiffs was the existence of a 2003 report issued by the Agency for Toxic Substances and Disease Registry (ATSDR) which found no scientific evidence linking military activities with the health problems of Viequenses. The public health assessments in the report noted that residents of the island were exposed to environmental contamination at such low levels that no harmful health effects were expected, and the agency concluded that there was "no apparent public health hazard." In any case, when the lawsuit reached the Puerto Rico Federal District Court, Judge Daniel Domínguez dismissed it. The decision was then appealed by Juanita Sanchez et al. at the Court of Appeals in Boston.

While the Court of Appeals was busy examining the case, the events took an unexpected turn, and one with great potential for advancing the reparations struggle. In 2009 Dr. Howard Frumkin, executive director of the ATSDR, agreed to take a "fresh look" at the 2003 data, after strong criticism by a congressional commission—the subcommission for Investigations of the Science and Technology Commission of the House of Representatives. Members of the commission urged Dr. Frumkin to reexamine his agency's studies on Vieques taking into consideration the many scientific studies by Puerto Rican researchers and others that indicate high levels of heavy metals in the environment and in the people of Vieques. The ATSDR conducted open dialogues with the people of Vieques on August 12, 2009, and in November 2009 Puerto Rican researchers were invited to present their findings to the ATSDR, among them were Jorge Colón, Cruz María Nazario, Carmen Ortiz Roque, Carmen Colón de Jorge, Imar Mansilla Rivera, Carlos Rodríguez Serra and Arturo Massol Deyá.

And yet, when the "fresh look" had been completed, by March 2011, the ATSDR issued a report reaffirming the absence of scientific evidence linking poor health with Navy activities on the island; enraging at once the Puerto Rican scientific community and the people of Vieques. Daniel Colón Ramos, a Puerto Rican professor and researcher from the Department of Molecular Biology at Yale University, went as far as to accuse the ATSDR of practicing "pseudoscience":

> The pseudoscientific studies that the ATSDR has conducted in Vieques have been criticized by scientists from the University of Puerto Rico, the University of Georgia and . . . Yale University, precisely because they suffer from foul sampling and inappropriate controls. It is almost as if the studies, by omission or incompetence, had been designed to fail. The international scientific community has referred to studies from this federal agency as "inconclusive by design." . . . In the United States, it is widely known that the studies from the ATSDR are designed to reach predictable results. (Colón Ramos 2013: 69)

Only days after the ATSDR issued its report, the First Circuit Court of Appeals in Boston ruled that the court has no jurisdiction in the case of Juanita Sánchez et al., siding with the decision of Judge Daniel Domínguez in the lawsuit originally filed in 2007. Puerto Rican Judge Juan R. Torruella (one of the three Supreme Court judges overlooking the Juanita Sanchez et al. case) issued a vehement dissent.

> Nowhere does the medieval concept of 'the King can do no wrong' underlying the doctrine of sovereign immunity sound more hollow and abusive than when an imperial power applies it to a group of helpless subjects. This cannot be a proper role for the United States of America. . . . In this latest chapter to the ongoing Culebra/Vieques saga, this court blocks plaintiffs' access to the courts of the United States, depriving US citizens who live in Vieques of the only effective remaining forum in which to seek redress for their alleged wrongs. . . . I for one, protest this intolerable and undemocratic situation in the strongest of terms. (Judge Juan R. Torruella)

With this decision from Boston, the only remaining forums left to Viequenses seeking reparations for health problems are supranational or international courts. And indeed, on September 23, 2013, The National Lawyers Guild (NLG), together with the Caribbean Institute for Human Rights (ICADH), the Inter-American University of Puerto Rico, the Western New England School of Law and the *Alianza de Mujeres Viequenses*, filed a petition against the US before the Inter-American Commission on Human Rights (IACHR), on behalf of ten Viequense cancer patients. The possibility of seeking reparations within the US judicial system has been blocked off permanently.

But the morale behind the story is that, even when the voice of complaint of the Viequenses transcends the contexts of living language, even when they are able to formalize their requests using the language of western rationality and of power, in written form, and aided often by influential non-Viequense lawyers and scientists speaking on their behalf, they will remain unheard. Discourses about cleanup and reparations, even when they adopt forms that fall within "the etiquette of metropolitan life," will not be listened to.

What is perhaps unique to these two specific 2011 events (i.e., the publication of the 2011 ATSDR's report and the Court of Appeals' ruling) is the fact that, in them, Viequenses have been told quite explicitly that their voice will not be listened to. This is unique in at least two ways: first, in that in here Viequenses have a response from colonial administrators, a rare and significant event in and of itself; and, second, that they are explicitly being told that they will not be listened to. There is, to be sure, a qualitative difference between "not being listened to" and "being told that you won't be listened to."

But there is also something else unique to the requests for decontamination and reparations, and that separates them from most of the other voices produced by Viequenses (regarding work, land, etc.): that the latter do not transcend the sphere of quotidian life, while the former does. Discourses about working conditions, about the laziness and lack of work ethics of Viequenses, about land speculation and the Dracula Plan, or about the dissatisfaction with the social transformations resulting from the introduction of the tourism economy, are "cultural hot buttons" that rarely leave the sphere of everyday intersubjectivity and dialogue in quotidian life. Rarely do they leave a direct textual trace (e.g., in the form of legal documents or scientific reports), as do the struggles for decontamination and reparations.

This fact, to be sure, can help us understand why the voice of the Viequense assumes the form that it often assumes in living language. The voice of the Viequenses is often broken and contradictory precisely because it is a voice that is produced in the anticipation that it will not be listened to, and therefore feels no reason or need to adhere to the formalities of metropolitan etiquette. If it needs to adhere to any etiquette at all, it would be the etiquette of a language game in which the subjects can give free rein to their ideas, knowing that whatever they say is always already open for reconsideration the next day (or five minutes later) and in anticipation that it won't be listened to.

CRIME

Another major topic of concern for Viequenses during the post-Navy period was the drastic increase in crime. All modalities of criminal offenses saw an increase during the period 2004–2013: offenses against the person reflected an upward spiral, going from twenty-three in 2004 to fifty-three in 2012; homicides increased from zero in 2004 to sixteen in 2013; property crimes went from 204 in 2004 to 250 in 2012, with a low peak of 130 in 2006 and high peaks of 322 in 2009 and 2010.

The fluctuations reflect not only a significant increase in all modalities of offenses in the years after the departure of the Navy, but also (and particularly) in the years during and immediately after the US and global financial crisis, that is, roughly the years from 2008 to 2010. This period also coincides with a plummeting of the tourism occupancy rate as was stated earlier.

But, without a doubt, the worst year of the decade was 2013, given the drastic increase in homicides registered in that year. A fight between two rival drug dealing *pandillas* (gangs) unleashed a series of assassinations, raising the number of homicides to sixteen. This is not only the highest homicide rate in the history of Vieques, but also the highest in the world, when compared to bigger nations.

Table 6.2   Crime Statistics for Vieques, 2004–2013

Year	Offenses Against The Person	Homicides	Property Crime
2004	23	0	204
2005	21	1	142
2006	24	1	130
2007	15	1	134
2008	34	4	228
2009	42	1	322
2010	28	8	322
2011	40	4	230
2012	53	3	250
2013	Not available	16	Not available

Source: see Vieques 2008.

No doubt drug trafficking is related to the crime spree affecting Vieques in 2013. The island is often used as a port of entry of drugs that are later transported to the Big Island and to the mainland US. The magnitude of the drug dealing industry in Vieques is reflected by the huge amount of drugs confiscated by the Caribbean Border Interagency Group and the Caribbean Corridor Strike Force from the ferry boats (on which it was usually transported) during the nine-month period between January and September 2013—they confiscated 138 kilos (304 pounds) of cocaine, two weapons and approximately 21,400 dollars in currency. Six individuals were arrested in connection with these interventions.

Several factors may account for this increase in crime and drug trafficking during the post-Navy period: joblessness, the introduction of the tourism industry and the restructuring of the welfare state. As has been common in many places around the world, when welfare states cease to assume their "pastoral functions" (as Foucault called them), they leave a void in the social fabric that will most likely be replaced, when the conditions become extreme, by criminal organizations (mafia, gangs) operating in the informal and illegal economy. The events taking place in Vieques in 2013 perhaps serve as a revelation of how Vieques is moving in this direction (cf. Hernandez and Colón 2013).

In the end, crime statistics continue to be on the rise without there being much Viequenses can do or say about it as is the case with so many other Caribbean islands after the introduction of tourism economies. In this way crime resembles the land speculation phenomenon, in the sense that both assume the form of unstoppable forces resulting from the tourism development packages and a situation where there is so little Viequenses can do to stop or regulate them. And, when this happens, the last recourse locals are left with to resist it is living language, simply because it is possible.

FINAL REMARKS

If the voice of the Viequenses has been muted (is being muted) on issues related to work or land, this is in part due to the ambivalent and often contradictory character that the voice often adopts in live contexts. Perhaps one could claim that it is precisely because there is an anticipation that the voice will be muted, based on the experience of having been muted innumerable times before, that the voice acquires this ambivalent and contradictory character.

But it was particularly when talking about cancer and crime—as also happens with the land speculation bacchanal—that Viequenses will truly discover how hard it is to struggle against structural forces that seem unstoppable and uncontrollable, that seem to have a life of their own; and, also, how little colonial powers are willing to listen to one, despite the human suffering and loss of lives that are at stake. If before the 2011 Court of Appeals' ruling, the voice of Viequenses was produced in the anticipation and suspicion that it would not be heard or will not be listened to, in the post-2011 period that suspicion dissipates altogether. For even when the discourses transcend the sphere of quotidian life, when the attempt is made to speak directly to colonial powers, even then they will be muted.

The beforehand knowledge that the voice will not be heard, even if it shouts, has as one of its effects the creation of a *language game* through which individuals express their desires and construct self-respect. But, because the act of talking is a futile act, much like talking to oneself (Spivak compares it to the experience of Robinson Crusoe talking to Friday), the subject is left free to say anything that comes to mind. In this manner, the voices of Viequenses multiply, adopt innumerable forms and positions, put forward innumerable arguments and counterarguments, up to a point where one is left in confusion. In other words, what emerges from our interviews, taken collectively, is very distant from anything resembling a "unified" voice. Taken collectively, the message acquires a structure that resembles more a predicament, where the individuals don't really know what they want, or seem to want two incompatible things at the same time. And this cacophony of voices that are produced in quotidian life threatens to deprive the signifier of a coherent signified, or to lead to a situation where the signifier *becomes* the signified.

Chapter 7

The Future of Vieques

The future of Vieques already exists in paper: for example, in legal documents, in area plans, in declarations of environmental impacts, in architectural blueprints, drawings and miniature models, in construction permits and land titles and so on. If everything works according the wishes and expectations of governmental planners and tourist investors, by 2025 Vieques will have a population of 30,000 (more than three times the actual population); 5,000 hotel rooms (ten times the room capacity of 2015); one marina (there are no marinas now); two golf courses (there are no golf courses now); three additional tourism-oriented mega-hotels and residential projects which already exists in blueprints and mockups, and which already have names (Sun Bay Resort, Dos Palmas and Mosquito Village); as well as a cruise ship dock. And, if the voice of the Viequenses revealed, still in 2015, an unconformity with the transformations taking place in the island after the introduction of a tourism economy, one could only wonder how they will feel when the transformations that are in the agenda for the near future become a reality. If many of the post-Navy Vieques complaints result from the introduction of tourism, a mental picture of the nearby islands of St. Thomas and St. John serve to remind Viequenses of what could happen to Vieques in the perhaps not so distant future.

The introduction of a more massive form of tourism into Vieques had already begun in 2001, with the opening of the 156-room luxury Martineau Bay Resort. Financial problems forced its closing soon after, and after several failed attempts to reopen, it finally did in 2009 as a W hotel, an exclusive line of hotels owned by the Starwood chain. Beyond the W, the rest of the hotels in Vieques are much smaller, and no hotel of the size of the W has opened in Vieques as of 2015. After the W, the second-largest new hotel built on the island in the post-Navy period was a 21-room hotel named El Blok, on the Esperanza strip, which opened in 2013.

A very rough estimate of the number of hotel rooms in Vieques by 2003 revealed a figure of approximately 300–400 (before the W opened). With the construction of El Blok and several other smaller hotels and guest houses, the total number of rooms in Vieques probably reached the 500 figure by 2014, plus the 156 rooms at the W Hotel (excluding the villas). Nonetheless, with the several new projects that are in the horizon, it is uncertain how long Vieques will be able to hold on to its prestige as the last untouched territory in the Caribbean. The 2008 Area Plan for Vieques considers an increase to 1,000 rooms by 2010 (a goal which had not been reached by 2015), and to 5,000 rooms by 2020 (Area Plan, p. 84).

And there are, as we had already anticipated, three major big tourism complexes projected for the island, and in different stages of getting construction approval by the Puerto Rican government: a huge 360-room complex in the southern side of the island named Sun Bay Resort; a second-home 66-apartment complex in the southwestern side of the island named Dos Palmas; and a huge complex on the northern side of the island named Mosquito. All of these projects are mired in controversies, and many wonder if Vieques can realistically hold a tourism development of this magnitude.

SUN BAY RESORT

Sun Bay Resort is set for construction in a huge area of land near the Esperanza region, which includes an old plantation house known as *Casa del Francés* (Frenchman's House). The land was purchased by an Italian, New York-based architect named Roberto Branvilla, with the intention of building a mega-resort on the property. Being promoted as an ecotourism project, the dimensions of this project are way above anything Vieques has experienced in the past, and the environmental impact of a project this big would be unquestionably enormous. An excerpt from the "1999 Project Description" says it will require an investment of $150 million and includes:

> a wide spectrum of residential condos, a 200-room beach front hotel, a 75-cabin "ecological village" . . . a 45-room hilltop inn, and a 40-room golf club . . . an 18 hole golf course . . . a marina . . . and polo fields. (Project Description, Sunbay Resorts Development, 1999)[1]

The Committee for the Rescue and Development of Vieques (CRDV) stated that "this type of project is completely contrary to the sustainable-community development articulated in the Guidelines for Sustainable Development currently being used by the government to prepare the Master Plan for future development of Vieques." The Puerto Rico Legislature's Natural

Resources Commission Director, Jorge Fernández Portuondo, was even more direct: "it is madness . . . totally out of proportion" (*es una locura . . . fuera de toda proporción*).

Moreover, the Sun Bay project contemplates the construction a golf course, which is already a highly controversial issue, given the fact that most of Vieques land is highly contaminated: first by intensive agriculture and, after the arrival of the Navy, by the bombings. The construction of a golf course would be controversial because, as Chambers has explained, "[t]he maintenance of golf courses not only requires the expenditure of vast amounts of water resources but also the use of inordinately high amounts of environmentally harmful fertilizers and pesticides, much more than is generally required for agricultural uses." (Chambers 2009: 72)

DOS PALMAS

There is also a smaller project of second-home or vacation-apartments in the southwestern side of the island, under the name of Dos Palmas. It consists of sixty-six luxury apartments, and various amenities: two infinity swimming pools, beach access, swim-up bar and an onsite restaurant. The developers of the project had projected construction beginning in the spring of 2010, but as of the end of 2015 no construction had begun on the site. The web page for the project describes it as follows:

> Dos Palmas is a unique resort of beachfront condominiums located on the secluded Southern coast of the Island of Vieques. With pure white sand beaches, pristine, crystal waters, untouched natural beauty and outstanding sunrise and sunset views, Dos Palmas is the premiere location for those seeking a luxurious vacation home retreat. With construction slated to begin in Spring of 2010, we are already 50% booked; there are only thirty units left.[2]

The Dos Palmas project became highly controversial due to irregularities in the approval of permits by the Puerto Rico Water and Sewage Company (*Administración de Acueductos y Alcantarillados*, or AAA). The *Junta de Permisos* did not grant construction permits because the AAA had placed the objection that the Río Blanco of Naguabo, which supplies the water for Vieques, didn't have the capacity to supply enough additional water for a project of that magnitude.

Vieques, it should be clarified, has no source of water of its own. All the water wells that exist in Vieques have been declared contaminated (high in metals and nitrate) and sealed. Moreover, with a 30-inch rainfall per year, it is improbable for cisterns to recover rainwater (*acuíferos*) which could produce enough water to supply the needs of major water-demanding hotel facilities like Dos Palmas or Sun Bay Resort. Thus, Vieques receives all its potable (drinking) water through an underwater pipe that feeds from the Río Blanco Water Treatment Plant in Naguabo, in mainland Puerto Rico. The water enters Vieques through the Punta Arenas region, where it is then stored in six tanks located throughout the island. According to data from the Puerto Rico Natural Resources Administration (*Administración de Recursos Naturales y Ambientales, or* DRNA),[3] Vieques receives approximately one million gallons per day (1 mgd) in this way, out of which 0.20 mgd continue on through the pipe to the nearby island of Culebra, where the pipe ends (for a detailed history of the water conflict in Vieques up to 2011, see Rodríguez Arroyo 2011).

In any case, in 2000 the AAA "miraculously" changed its position regarding the Dos Palmas case, and approved the project with some restrictions (it required the developer to make improvements to the water-capturing facilities in the Río Blanco source). And, while it is true that by 2016 construction of Dos Palmas had not yet begun, and that by that same year the web page of Dos Palmas had been closed and the project showed no signs of life (they are neither constructing nor preselling), the permits have already been granted.

MOSQUITO VILLAGE

Finally, and in addition to the Sun Bay and Dos Palmas projects, which are private initiatives, there is a public plan for the construction of a tourism village. The 2008 Area Plan for the Municipality of Vieques contemplates, as part of a governmental initiative to preserve the land through the system of zoning and land trusts, the construction of a third large urban center, in addition to the already existing two: Isabel II and Esperanza. The new center, named Mosquito Village, would be developed in 1,515.42 acres of land located in the north-eastern side of the island, relatively distant from the two other urban centers. The plan contemplates space for 2,564 residential units, with capacity for an estimated residential population of 7,694. Ownership of all residential units would remain in the hands of the municipality in perpetuity, through a system of zoning and land trusts.

Moreover, the 2008 Area Plan for Mosquito Village explicitly states that the village to be constructed is designed mainly for providing housing to "a population from the outside" which, in the absence of such a village, would thus proceed to buy land from Viequenses and aggravate even further the problem of hoarding and speculation with the land. The Area Plan states:

Mosquito is conceived as a new urban settlement of the complexity and the scale of a town. The town would be built on land belonging to the Municipality. . . . This place could provide housing for the increasing population of retired persons that are in their third age and are looking for the vitality and habitability of the natural environment in an urban context. . . . There is an increasing need on the part of a population *from the exterior* and in their old age, that could represent . . . an effective demand for residences. Their presence integrated into the community would contribute to the diversity of urban life, would increase the demand for services and products and would stimulate the internal economy.[4]

The Mosquito Village would strategically be located right in front of the Mosquito Pier, because it is destined to become (in the future) the main port of entry by sea to the island. The origin of the pier dates back to the early years of the Navy period. The US Navy began construction of the Mosquito pier in 1941, with the purpose of creating a sea wall that extended from Vieques all the way to the town of Ceiba, on the main island of Puerto Rico, where the Roosevelt Roads Naval Base was located. The purpose was to build a massive man-made harbor capable of housing the US and British fleets simultaneously. But the construction was interrupted in 1943 (after the attacks on Pearl Harbor), and the wall was left incomplete, although it can function as a pier. Later on, in 2003, the Department of Defense of the United States ordered and started the remodeling of the old pier of Mosquito, locally known as *Rompeolas* (it was renamed "Puerto de la Libertad David Sanes Rodríguez" in 2003).

The location of Mosquito Village, right in front of the Mosquito Pier, is strategic in several ways. The Area Plan for Mosquito contemplates moving the ferry and cargo route, which now runs from Fajardo to Isabel II, to run instead from Bahia La Puerca in Ceiba to Mosquito Pier. This is, in fact, what is known as the "natural route," because it is the shortest route between Vieques and the island of Puerto Rico (19 km, instead of the 37.8 km that separates Fajardo from Isabel II) (cf. Maldonado 2011). Moreover, the tourism-oriented infrastructure that would be developed there (the plan contemplates space for a commercial village right at the entrance of the port, as well as the construction of hotels and restaurants, and other tourist-oriented facilities in the area) would make Vieques an attractive port-of-call for cruise ships wishing to dock on the island, as the Mosquito Pier is capable of providing anchorage to ships that size. The Area Plan reads: "The space is provided as a reserve for a location for export sectors to the minor islands and/or as attraction for the cruise ship industry" (Area Plan, p. 62).[5] Although Vieques had already berthed its first small cruise ship (starting from 2007, the 110-passenger luxury cruise ship Sea Dream I anchors in Esperanza every two weeks), bigger cruise ships haven't yet ventured into Vieques.

According to the Area Plan, there is one major uncertainty with the viability of the Mosquito Village project: water—as was in the case of Dos Palmas. The Area Plan "infers" that there will be enough water available for the project, but it also points to "a virtual deficit of 0.6 mgd" (Area Plan 2008, p. 93) based on the standard consumption statistics for residential houses.[6]

But what is of relevance here is that the future of Vieques already exists in paper (e.g., in legal documents, in area plans, in architectural blueprints, drawings and miniature models, in construction permits and land titles), but one despairs of finding the slightest presence of the voice of the Viequenses in them. To what extent and for how long will Vieques be able to remain as an "unspoiled," "untouched," "pristine," "undeveloped" tourist destination only time will tell. Even some of the foreign tourism investors and managers we interviewed adopted a fatalistic (perhaps more realistic also) view of the future of Vieques, one that sees the excesses of capitalism and neoliberalism as irremediably unstoppable. One of them, after arguing for an ecotourism model for Vieques, and that it should "stay small," added:

> Where do *I want* [Vieques] to go and where *I think* it's going to go are two different things. But where I think it's going to go . . . it's just the inevitability of politics and money, going hand in hand, and I think they might overdevelop it. (Employer North American #7)

FINAL REMARKS

Thus, if everything works according to plans, the cleanup of Vieques will be completed by 2024. By 2025, moreover, "the inevitability of politics and money" will overdevelop Vieques, and the negative effects that result from this overdevelopment will increase and accentuate. The mental picture of what Vieques will look like after these several touristic projects that are "in the pipeline" have been developed is devastating. In few places is the often-quoted image of Walter Benjamin's "Angel Novus" fighting against "progress" more apt than in here.

> A [Paul] Klee drawing named "Angelus Novus" shows an angel looking as though he is about to move away from something he is fixedly contemplating. His eyes are staring, his mouth is open, his wings are spread. This is how one pictures the angel of history. His face is turned toward the past. Where we perceive a chain of events, he sees one single catastrophe that keeps piling ruin upon ruin and hurls it in front of his feet. The angel would like to stay, awaken the dead, and make whole what has been smashed. But a storm is blowing from Paradise; it has got caught in his wings with such violence that the angel can no longer close them. The storm irresistibly propels him into the future to which his

back is turned, while the pile of debris before him grows skyward. This storm is what we call progress. (Benjamin 1968[1955])

But the greatest fear of Viequenses is that, by then, their voice will no longer need to be muted because there will be no Viequense voice any longer. The *New* Dracula Plan will have been carried to full completion. By then, the words of Viequense novelist Carmelo Rodríguez Torres—in his 1971 *Veinte siglos después del homicidio*—will have become prophetic. In the novel two characters are having a conversation over the weird-sounding croaking of a specific Coquí, a species of frog native and unique to Puerto Rico and which Puerto Ricans have turned into one of the most important icons of their national identity. The Coquí represents, in the novel, one of the few remaining Viequenses left in the island. The conversation evolves as follows:

[The Coquí's croaking was] a broken croaking, as if someone had it grabbed by the throat. «Why does it croaks like that?» «It is locked up in a can. There are very few of them left. One of these days there will be none left. Pedro told me he would find me a female [frog] . . . The greatest danger is that it comes out gay (*pato*). That could be the end. (Rodríguez Torres 1980[1971]: 69–70)[7]

It is instructive noticing that, in Rodríguez Torres's literary imagination the situation of survival is so urgent, that even homosexuality needs to be considered a threat to the "national" interests of the group, and to its mere survival as a distinctive group. This urgency is also present in the minds of many of our Viequense informants. Their fear is that, by the time the touristic development planned for Vieques is carried to its completion, Vieques will have become, perhaps, the Vieques that Rodríguez Torres envisioned.

NOTES

1. See also documentary in Youtube: http://www.youtube.com/watch?v=Fvr42e7ftOo. Accessed December 15, 2009.

2. http://www.dospalmasbeachclubandresort.com/Accessed December 15, 2009. By 2014, the site no longer existed.

3. Extracted from the *Departamento de Recursos Naturales* (DRNA) web page: http://www.drna.gobierno.pr/oficinas/saux/secretaria-auxiliar-de-planificacion-inte-gral/planagua/inventario-recursos-de-agua/cuencas-hidrograficas/Cuenca%20del%20Rio%20Blanco.pdf.

4. Translated from Spanish. Original statement reads: "Mosquito se concibe como un Nuevo asentamiento urbano de la complejidad y la escala de un pueblo. El poblado se construye en tierras propiedad del municipio . . . Este lugar puede albergar a la creciente población de retirados que se encuentran en su tercera edad y que buscan la

vitalidad y habitabilidad del ambiente natural en un contexto urbano . . . Existe una necesidad creciente de parte de una población del exterior y de edad avanzada, que puede representar . . . una demanda efectiva residencial. Su presencia integrada a la comunidad contribuiría a la diversidad de la vida urbana, aumentaría la demanda por servicios y productos y estimularía la economía interna" (Area Plan, p. 65).

5. Translated from Spanish. Original statement reads: "Se provee el espacio como reserve para la localización de sectores de exportación a las islas menores y/o como atracción a la industria de cruceros" (Area Plan, p. 62).

6. Translated from Spanish. The Area Plan (in Spanish) reads: "Sin embargo, según el censo del 2000, Vieques cuenta con alrededor de cuatro mil viviendas (4,000), a base del estándar [de consumo de agua], la capacidad disponible para servir esta [sic] demanda es de uno punto seis millones de galones diarios (1.6 mgd). Es decir existe un déficit virtual de 0.6 mgd." The problem is aggravated by the fact that the "virtual deficit" would even be higher when one considers that tourists require, on the average, three times more water than a local inhabitant (Hunter and Green 1995), and thus, estimates of water consumption by tourist-oriented developments like Mosquito Village should be based on a different "standard" for measuring consumption than that used to estimate local housing consumption.

7. Translated from Spanish. Original statement reads: "un canto roto, como si lo apretaran por la garganta. «¿Por qué canta así?» «Está encerrado en una lata. Quedan muy pocos. Un día de estos nos quedamos sin ninguno. Pedro me dijo que me conseguiría la hembrita . . . El peligro mayor es que salga pato. Se pueden acabar»" (Rodríguez Torres 1980: 69–70). The Word "pato" (literally, duck) is widely used by Puerto Ricans to designate gay or homosexual men.

Conclusion

During the decade-long period when we were doing research in Vieques, 2004–2015, several things were happening in the international scene that were of relevance to the topic of our research. Among them was the emergence, beginning in 2010, of multiple social movements around the globe: from the casserole bangers in Argentina, through the Arab Spring movements in Tunisia and throughout the Middle East, to the *Indignados* movements in Plaza del Sol in Madrid and throughout Europe, to the "Occupy Wall Street" movements throughout the cities of North America, to the multiple anti-globalization riots taking place around the world. During this decade, many subaltern groups around the globe seemed to want to express their dissatisfaction with the actual social arrangement. Some academic observers have looked at these series of global movements as a positive sign, hoping to see in them the moment when subalterns are finally able to make their voice heard.

How could we then be claiming (with Gayatri Spivak) that the Viequense subaltern cannot speak? Can such thing be claimed in a historical moment like this? Surely, it is controversial to claim that the subalterns cannot speak well into the second decade of the 21st century: that is, in a time and age when civil unrest had acquired global dimensions. Moreover, it is controversial to claim that the voice of the subaltern is muted *in* the context of Vieques, when it was precisely these same Viequenses who managed "to have their voice be heard" in their David-versus-Goliath struggle to expel the Navy from their island back in 2001. Were they not then able to make their voice heard?

With the intensity of these international social movements waning down by 2016, it is uncertain where they may lead us in the future. Nevertheless, there is something about the collective voices of these rebellious groups which is worth highlighting, for in this they resemble the voice of the Viequenses collected by us. By adopting a strong commitment to nonpartisan politics and to democratic free-expressionism, and refusing to adopt official leaders or spokespersons, these movements run the risk of saying nothing; more specifically, by saying so many things at one and the same time, some contradictory, they run the risk of rendering their message unintelligible. The issue became ironically evident in the 2011 "Occupy Boston" movement, where activists gathered in Dewey Square decided to issue a statement about their commitment to a collective all-inclusive voice by designating as their spokesperson a stray dog that lived in the square they were occupying.[1] Thus, the multiplicity of voices emerging from the Occupation Boston movement produced a message that was as intelligible as the barking of a stray dog. In here, the signifier is devoid of a signified; in here, more precisely, the signifier *is* the signified. Like the voice of these various global social movements, the voice of the Viequenses is also a fractured voice, a voice that runs the risk of being interpreted as unintelligible, as pure noise (like the barking of a dog, or the noise produced by casseroles being banged with kitchen spoons), and thus muted.

A specific event occurring in 2007 (while engaged in fieldwork) is symptomatic of the actual state of affairs at the beginning of the 21st century, as we see it. The event occurred during the XVII Ibero-American summit in Santiago, Chile, on November 10, 2007, when the then king of Spain, Juan Carlos I, scolded the then democratically elected Venezuelan president Hugo Chavez, asking him "why don't you shut-up?" (*¿Por qué no te callas?*) in the middle of an open session. The fact that the request was made more than 200 years after Venezuelans gained independence from Spain reflects in a dramatic manner how the struggle to determine who can and who cannot speak, or what can or cannot be said, continues well on within postcolonial politics. When, in 2011, the First Circuit Court of Appeals in Boston ruled that "the court has no jurisdiction" in the case of Juanita Sánchez et al., it was simply reenacting in a more "diplomatic" form—with "the civil etiquette of metropolitan life," as Chatterjee would have put it (2004: x)—what King Juan Carlos I could not help, in the middle of a Quixotic fit, but sputter in unfortunate terms, to say the least.

Now, this process of muting, we are well aware, extends to include our own publication as well, as no written or spoken word can break free from it. Moreover, and as Spivak reminds us, it is precisely when intellectuals attempt to speak for or on behalf of the subalterns, to give a voice to the voiceless, that the voice acquires its maximum level of muteness—then, Spivak argues, the subaltern voice becomes "as mute as ever" (1994: 295). This is also the reason why we, in documenting the voice of the Viequenses, cannot attribute to ourselves the role of the engaged anthropologist attempting to speak for those who have no voice of their own; not out of lack of willingness or desire, but rather out of the conviction that our own voice, being a reflection of the voice of the Viequenses, is as muted as theirs.

In any case, there are several additional things that should be clarified about what exactly we mean when we say, with Spivak, that the subaltern cannot speak. First, the proposition does not imply that, because subalterns won't be listened to, they might as well not speak at all. It would be ludicrous to argue such a thing, given that it would imply proposing an end to history and to the free flow of "living" language, and to human/social life in general—something we are not interesting in doing. Moreover, we believe the proposition that the subaltern "should" not speak would be counterproductive to the Viequenses' struggles; as we do not negate that the unintelligible noise that the subalterns produce might also have its effects on history. Finally, the proposition that the subaltern cannot speak is not meant to be taken as a categorical imperative of history. History and time, we are aware, have yet to do their part and, as is sometimes the case, to contradict all reasonable expectations and prove us wrong. In fact, we publish this book with the desire that, even while muted, it will perhaps increase the level of noise, and perhaps contribute to the struggle for a tourism development in Vieques different from what all reasonable predictions might indicate, and closer to that experienced by other tourism destinations where "ecotourism" and "revitalization" models have proven that another road is possible (cf. Stronza 2001; Honey 2008; Di Giovine 2009a, 2010; Jamal and Robinson 2009). Thus, our best hope is to be part of a broader voice that is, as poet René Char once put it, simply "asking of the unforeseeable to frustrate the expected."

What we do know is that Viequenses, in general, are not happy with the effects of residential tourism, and that the first ten years of living without the Navy has left a feeling of disappointment—a feeling aptly characterized by local newspaper *El Nuevo Dia* Special Issue ten years after the departure of the Navy as a "truncated dream" (*sueño trunco*) (2013: 1).

In the end, then, the assertion that the subaltern cannot speak is only intended as a statement about the general condition of subalterns everywhere in the modern globalized world, and of Viequenses in particular, at the beginning of the 21st century; and about the manner in which global forces increasingly delineate what can and cannot be said. Moreover, the proposition is also intended as a statement about the general condition of Puerto Ricans under US colonial rule, as what is "expected" to happen in Vieques is not much different from what is "expected" to happen in broader Puerto Rico, where tourism is increasingly becoming a central pillar of the economy. If, as Julio Ortega has argued, "whatever happens in Puerto Rico . . . will be a rehearsal of what's going to happen in Latin America" (1991:67); in the same manner, we contend that whatever happens in Vieques will be a rehearsal of what's going to happen (and perhaps what is already happening) in broader Puerto Rico.

NOTE

1. I am grateful to Nicole Young, a student from the University of Massachusetts-Boston doing research in Vieques, but also actively involved in the Occupy Boston movement, for recounting this story to me.

Bibliography

Abbink, Jon. 2010[2004]. "Tourism and Its Discontents: Suri-Tourist Encounters in Sothern Ethiopia." In *Tourists and Tourism: A Reader*, edited by Sharon Bohn Gmelch, 115–36. Long Grove, IL: Waveland Press.

Ahearn, Laura A. 2011. *Living Language: An Introduction to Linguistic Anthropology*. Hoboken, NJ: Wiley-Blackwell.

Aledo, Antonio. 2008. "De la tierra al suelo: la transformación del paisaje y el Nuevo Turismo Residencial [From land to soil: The transformation of the landscape and the new residential torurism]." *Arbor: Ciencia, Pensamiento y Cultura* 729: 99–113.

Aledo, Antonio, Jens Kr. Steen Jacobsen and Leif Selstad. 2012. "Building Tourism in Costa Blanca: Second Homes, Second Chances?" In *Culture and Society in Tourism Contexts*, edited by A. M. Nogués-Pedregal, 111–39. Bingley, UK: Emerald Group Publishing Limited.

Aledo, Antonio, Tristan Loloum, Guadalupe Ortiz and Hugo García-Andreu. 2013. "El turismo residencial internacional en el nordeste de Brasil: un análisis de partes interesadas." *Revista Española de Investigaciones Sociológicas* 142: 3–24.

Alvarado Vega, José, and Alex Díaz. 2011. "The real story behind Puerto Rico's low 40.6% labor-participation rate." *Caribbean Bussines* 39(18). http://www.caribbeanbusinesspr.com/prnt_ed/ news 02.php.

Ateljevic, Irena, and Stephen Doorne. 2000. "Staying within the fence: Lifestyle entrepreneurship in tourism." *Journal of Sustainable Tourism* 8(5): 378–92.

Ayala, César J., and José L. Bolivar. 2011. *Battleship Vieques: Puerto Rico from World War II to the Korean War*. Princeton: Markus Wiener Publishers.

Bakhtin, Mikhail. 1981. *The Dialogic Imagination: Four Essays*. Austin: University of Texas Press.

Baldacchino, Godfrey. 1997. *Global Tourism and Informal Labor Relations: The Small Scale Syndrome at Work*. London: Mansell.

Barnhart, R. K. 1988. *The Barnhart Dictionary of Etymology*. New York: The H. W. Wilson Company.

Barreto, Amilcar A. 2002. *Vieques, the Navy, and Puerto Rican Politics*. Gainesville: University Press of Florida.

Baver, Sherrie L. 2006. "Environmental justice and the cleanup of Vieques." *Centro Journal* XVIII(1): 91–107.

———. 2012. "Environmental Struggles in Paradise: Puerto Rican Cases, Caribbean Lessons." *Caribbean Studies* 40(1): 15–35.

Benítez Rojo, Antonio. 1996. *The Repeating Island: The Caribbean and the Postmodern Perspective*, translated by J. E. Maraniss. Durham: Duke University Press.

Benjamin, Walter. 1968[1955]. *Illuminations*. New York: Schocken Books.

Benson, M. C. 2013. "Postcoloniality and privilege in new lifestyle flows: The case of North Americans in Panama." *Mobilities* 8(3): 313–30.

———. 2015. "Class, race, privilege: structuring the lifestyle migrant experience in Boquete, Panama." *Journal of Latin American Geography* 14(1): 19–37.

Benson, M., and K. O'Reilly 2009. "Migration and the search for a better way of life: a critical exploration of lifestyle migration." *The Sociological Review* 57(4): 608–25.

Berman Santana, Déborah. 2006. "La lucha continua: Challenges for a Post-Navy Vieques." *CENTRO Journal* 18(1): 109–23.

Boschken, H. L. 1975. "The second home subdivision: Market suitability for recreational and pastoral use." *Journal of Leisure Research* 7: 63–75.

Bourdieu, Pierre. 1993. *The Field of Cultural Production*. New York: Columbia University Press.

Boyer, William W. 2010[1971]. *America's Virgin Islands: A History of Human Rights and Wrongs*. Durham, NC: Carolina Academic Press.

Britton, Celia M. 1999. *Edouard Glissant and Postcolonial Theory: Strategies of Language and Resistance*. Charlottesville and London: University Press of Virginia.

Browne, Katherine E. 2004. *Creole Economics: Caribbean Cunning Under the French Flag*. Austin: University of Texas Press.

Bruner, Edward M. 2005. *Culture on Tour: Ethnographies of Travel*. Chicago, IL: University of Chicago Press.

Buller, H., and K. Hoggart. 1994. "The social integration of British home owners into French rural communities." *Journal of Rural Studies* 2: 197–210.

Bunten, Alexis C. 2008. "Sharing Culture or Selling Out?: Developing a Commodified Persona in the Heritage Industry." *American Ethnologist* 35(3): 380–95.

Burge, Tyler. 2007. "Philosophy of Language: 1950–2000." In *Columbia Companion to Twentieth-Century Philosophies*, edited by Constantin V. Boundas, 186–209. New York: Columbia University Press.

Burtner, Jennifer, and Quetzil E. Castañeda. 2010. "Tourism as a 'Force for World Peace:' The Politics of Tourism, Tourism as Governmentality and the Tourism Boycott of Guatemala." *The Journal of Tourism and Peace Research* 1(2): 1–21.

Carrier, James G., and Donald V. L. Macleod. 2005. "Bursting the Bubble: The Socio-cultural Context of Ecotourism." *Journal of the Royal Anthropological Institute* 11: 315–34.

Casado-Díaz, María A. 1999. "Socio-demographic Impacts of Residential Tourism: A Case Study of Torrevieja, Spain." *International Journal of Tourism Research* 1(4): 223–37.

————. 2006. "Retiring to Spain: An Analysis of Differences among North European Nationals." *Journal of Ethnic and Migration Studies* 32(8): 1321–39.

Casado-Díaz, María A., Claudia Kaiser and Anthony M. Warnes. 2004. "Northern European retired residents in nine Southern European areas: Characteristics, motivations and adjustment." *Aging and Society* 24: 353–81.

Chambers, Erve. 2009. *Native Tours: The Anthropology of Travel and Tourism.* Long Grove, IL: Waveland Press.

Chatterjee, Partha. 2004. *The Politics of the Governed: Reflections on Popular Politics in Most of the World.* New York: Columbia University Press.

Cohen, Erik. 1979. "A phenomenology of tourist experiences." *Sociology* 13(2): 179–201.

Cohen, Erik, and Robert L. Cooper. 1986. "Language and tourism." *Annals of Tourism Research* 13(4): 533–64.

Collins, Susan M., Barry Bosworth and Miguel A. Soto-Class, eds. 2006. *The Economy of Puerto Rico: Restoring Growth.* Washington, DC: Brookings Institution Press.

Colón Ramos, Daniel. 2013. "Vieques y la pseudociencia." *El Nuevo Día,* May 11.

Coppock, J. Terry, ed. 1977. *Second Homes: Curse or Blessing?* Oxford: Pergamon.

Crang, Mike. 2004. "Cultural Geographies of Tourism." In *A Companion to Tourism,* edited by Alan A. Lew, C. Michael Hall and Allan M. Williams, 74–84. Oxford, UK: Blackwell Publishing, Ltd.

Crouch, David. 2004. "Tourist Practices and Performances." In *A Companion to Tourism,* edited by Alan A. Lew, C. Michael Hall and Allan M. Williams, 85–95. Oxford, UK: Blackwell Publishing, Ltd.

Crouch, David, Lars Aronsson and Lage Wahlström. 2001. "Tourist encounters." *Tourist Studies* 1(3): 253–70.

Cruz Soto, Marie. 2008. *Inhabiting Isla Nena, 1514–2003: Island Narrations, Imperial Dramas and Vieques, Puerto Rico.* PhD diss. University of Michigan.

D'Amore, L. J. 1988a. "Tourism: A Vital Force for Peace." *Annals of Tourism Research* 15(2): 269–71.

————. 1988b. "Tourism: The World's Peace Industry." In *Tourism: A Vital Force for Peace,* edited by L. J. D'Amore and J. Jafari, 7–14. Montreal: L. J. D'Amore and Associates.

Dann, Graham M. S. 1996. *The Language of Tourism: A Sociolinguistic Perspective.* Wallingford, Oxon, UK: CAB International.

Denvir, Ann, and Frank McMahon. 1992. "Labour turnover in London hotels and the cost effectiveness of preventative measures." *International Journal of Hospitality Management* 11(2): 143–54.

Derrida, Jacques. 1982[1968]. *Margins of Philosophy.* Chicago: University of Chicago Press.

Dewhurst, Peter, and Helen Horobin. 1998. "Small Business Owners." In *The Management of Small Tourism and Hospitality Firms,* edited by Rhodri Thomas, 19–38. London: Cassell.

Díaz Román, Miguel. 2012. "Otro mal síntoma económico: la tasa de participación de 39.6% en septiembre es la más baja en la historia" *El Nuevo Día,* November 23.

————. 2013. "Predios en contrabando." *El Nuevo Día,* April 29.

Dietz, James L. 2002[1989]. *Historia Económica de Puerto Rico.* San Juan, Puerto Rico: Ediciones Huracan.

Di Giovine, Michael A. 2009a. "Revitalization and Counter-Revitalization: Tourism, Heritage and the Lantern Festival as Catalysts for Regeneration in Hội An, Việt Nam." *Journal of Policy Research in Tourism, Leisure, and Events* 1(3): 208–30.

————. 2009b. "Re-Presenting Saint Padre Pio of Pietrelcina: Contested Ways of Seeing a Contemporary Saint." *Critical Inquiry* 35(3): 481–92.

————. 2009c. *The Heritage-scape: UNESCO, World Heritage and Tourism.* Lanham, MD: Lexington Books.

————. 2010 "Rethinking Development: Religious tourism to St. Padre Pio as material and cultural revitalization in Pietrelcina." *Tourism* 58(3): 271–88.

————. 2014. "The Imaginaire Dialectic and the Refashioning of Pietrelcina." In *Tourism Imaginaries: Anthropological Approaches*, edited by N. B. Salazar and N. H. H. Graburn, 147–71. New York and Oxford: Berghahn Books.

Eco, Umberto. 1986. *Travels in Hyperreality: Essays.* San Diego: Harcourt Brace Jovanovich.

Escobar, Arturo. 1995. *Encountering Development: The Making and Unmaking of the Third World.* Princeton: Princeton University Press.

Estrada Torres, Michelle. 2013. "Descartado un aumento en las lanchas: El director de la ATM asegura que esa alternativa no es considerada." *El Nuevo Día*, September 2.

Evans-Pritchard, Deirdre. 1989. "How 'They' See 'Us:' Native American Images of Tourists." *Annals of Tourism Research* 16: 89–105.

Fabián, Ana M. 2003. *Vieques en mi memoria: testimonios de vida.* San Juan: Ediciones Puerto.

Farrell, Bryan. 1979. "Tourism's Human Conflicts: Cases from the Pacific." *Annals of Tourism Research* 6: 122–36.

Ferguson, Charles A. 1975. "Towards a characterization of English foreigner talk." *Anthropological Linguistics* 17(1): 1–14.

Ferguson, James. 1994. *The Anti-Politics Machine: Development, Depoliticization and Bureaucratic Power in Lesotho.* Minnesota: University of Minnesota Press.

Forster, John. 1964. "The Sociological Consequences of Tourism." *International Journal of Comparative Sociology* 5: 217–27.

Galanes-Valldejuli, Luis. 2007. "Are we there yet?: The Tension Between Nativism and Humanism in Fanon's Writings." *Human Architecture* V: 59–70.

Gallent, Nick and Mark Tewdwr-Jones. 2000. *Rural Second Homes in Europe: Examining Housing Supply and Planning Control.* Aldershot: Ashgate.

García Muñiz, Humberto. 2001. "Goliath Against David: The Battle for Vieques as the Last Crossroad?" *CENTRO Journal* 13(1): 126–41.

García Peinado, Miguel A. 1998. *Hacia una teoría general de la novela.* Madrid: Arco Libros, S. L.

Geertz, Clifford. 1973. "Thick Description: Toward an Interpretive Theory of Culture." In *The Interpretation of Cultures: Selected Essays*, 3–30. New York: Basic Books.

Gilbert, Sandra and Susan Gubar. 1984[1979]. *The Madwoman in the Attic: The Woman Writer and the Nineteenth-Century Literary Imagination.* New Haven and London: Yale University Press.

Glissant, Edouard. 1981. *Caribbean Discourses: Selected Essays [Le discourse antillais]*, translated by J. Michael Dash. Charlottesville: University Press of Virginia.

———. 1990. *Poétique de la relation*. Paris: Guillemard.

Gmelch, George. 2003. *Behind the Smile: The Working Life of Caribbean Tourism*. Bloomington and Indianapolis: Indiana University Press.

Gmelch, Sharon Bohn, ed. 2010[2004]. *Tourists and Tourism: A Reader*. Long Grove, IL: Waveland Press.

Gmelch, Sharon Bohn, and Brian Moeran. 2004. "Rereading the Language of Japanese Tourism." In *Tourists and Tourism: A Reader*, edited by S. B. Gmelch, 111–25. Long Grove, IL: Waveland Press.

Godreau, Isar P. 2008. "Slippery Semantics: Race Talk and Everyday Uses of Racial Terminology in Puerto Rico." *CENTRO Journal* XX(2): 5–33.

Goldthorpe, John H., David Lockwood, Frank Bechhofer and Jennifer Platt. 1969. *The Affluent Worker in the Class Structure*. Cambridge: Cambridge University Press.

Graburn, Nelson H. H. 1977. "Tourism: The Sacred Journey." In *Hosts and Guests: The Anthropology of Tourism*, edited by Valene L. Smith, 17–32. Philadelphia: University of Pennsylvania Press.

Graburn, Nelson H. H., and Maria Gravari-Barbas. 2012. "Tourist Imaginaries." *Via@ - International Interdisciplinary Review of Tourism* 1. www.viatourismreview.net/Editorial1_ES.php.

Greenwood, David. 1989[1978]. "Culture by the Pound: An Anthropological Perspective on Tourism as Cultural Commodification." In *Hosts and Guests: The Anthropology of Tourism*, edited by Valene L. Smith, 127–38. Philadelphia: University of Pennsylvania Press.

Guerrón Montero, Carla. 2011. "On tourism and the constructions of 'paradise islands' in Central America and the Caribbean." *Bulletin of Latin American Research* 30(1): 21–34.

Hall, C. Michael, and Dieter Müller, eds. 2004. *Tourism, Mobility and Second Homes: Between Elite Landscape and Common Ground*. Clevedon, UK: Channelview Publications.

Hall-Lew, Lauren A., and Alan A. Lew. 2014. "Speaking Heritage: Language, Identity and Tourism." In *The Wiley Blackwell Companion to Tourism*, edited by Alan A. Lew, C. Michael Hall and Allan M. Williams. Hoboken, NJ: John Wiley & Sons, Ltd.

Hernández, Maribel, and Javier Colón. 2013. "La Mafia Domina Vieques." *Primera Hora*, October 23.

Hirsh, Edward. 1985. "The Art of Poetry: Derek Walcott." In *Conversations with Derek Walcott*, edited by William Baer, 95–121. Jackson, Mississippi: University Press of Mississippi.

Hitchcock, Michael and Nyoman Darma Putra. 2007. *Tourism, Development and Terrorism in Bali*. London: Ashgate Publishing Co.

Honey, Martha. 2008[1999]. *Ecotourism and Sustainable Development: Who Owns Paradise?* Washington, Covelo, London: Island Press.

Hopgood Dávila, Eugenio. 2013. "La Épica del Monte Carmelo." *El Nuevo Día*. http://vieques.elnuevodia.com/.

Hughes, George. 1995. "The cultural construction of sustainable tourism." *Tourism Management* 16(1): 49–59.

Huit, Groupe. 1979. "The Sociocultural Effects of Tourism in Tunisia: A Case Study of Sousse." In *Tourism: Pasport to Development?*, edited by Emmanuel de Kadt, 285–304. New York: Oxford University Press.

Hunter, Colin, and Howard Green. 1995. *Tourism and the Environment: A Sustainable Relationship*. New York: Routledge.

Jackiewicz, Edward L., and Jim Craine. 2010. "Destination Panama: An examination of the migration-tourism-foreign investment nexus." *Recreation and Society in Africa, Asia and Latin America* 1(1): 5–29.

Jafari, Jafar. 1989. "Tourism and peace." *Annals of Tourism Research* 16: 439–43.

Jamal, Tazim, and Mike Robinson. 2009. "Introduction: The Evolution and Contemporary Positioning of Tourism as a Focus of Study." In *The SAGE Handbook of Tourism Studies*, edited by Tazim Jamal and Mike Robinson, 1–16. London: SAGE Publications, Ltd.

Johnson, Keith. 1981. "Towards an understanding of labor turnover." *The Service Industries Journal* 1(1): 4–17.

———. 1985. "Labour turnover in hotels – revisited." *The Service Industries Journal* 5(2): 135–51.

Kaltenborn, Bjørn P. 1997. "Nature of place attachment: A study among recreation homeowners in Southern Norway." *Leisure Sciences* 19: 175–89.

———. 1998. "The alternate home: Motives of recreation home use." *Norsk Geografisk Tidsskrift* 52: 121–34.

King, Russell, and Guy Patterson. 1998. "Diverse paths: The elderly British in Tuscany." *International Journal of Population Geography* 4(2): 157–82.

King, Russell, Tony Warnes and Allan M. Williams. 2000. *Sunset Lives: British Retirement Migration to the Mediterranean*. London: Berg Publishers.

Klein, Deborah. 2001. "For the Future of Vieques, Look to Hawaii." *New York Times*, June 16.

Lafargue, Paul. 1883. *The Right to be Lazy*. http://www.marxists.org/archive/lafargue/1883/lazy/index.htm.

Lamont, Michèle. 1992. *Money, Morals, and Manners: The Culture of the French and American Upper-Middle Class*. Chicago: University of Chicago Press.

———. 2000. *The Dignity of Working Men: Morality and the Boundaries of Race, Class and Immigration*. Cambridge, MA: Harvard University Press.

Lashley, Conrad, and A. Chaplain. 1999. "Labor turnover: Hidden problem, hidden cost." *Hospitality Review* 1(1): 49–54.

Leite, Naomi, and Nelson Graburn. 2011. "Anthropological Interventions in Tourism Studies." In *The SAGE Handbook of Tourism Studies*, edited by Tazim Jamal and Mike Robinson, 35–64. London: SAGE Publications, Ltd.

Levitan, Sar A., and Clifford M. Johnson. 1982. *Second Thoughts on Work*. Kalamazoo, Michigan: The W. E. Upjohn Institute for Employment Research.

Lewis, Oscar. 1975[1959]. *Five Families: Mexican Case Studies in the Culture of Poverty*. New York, NY: Basic Books.

———. 1968. *La Vida: A Puerto Rican Family in the Culture of Poverty*. New York, NY: Vintage Books.

Little, Cheryl. 1996. "Principles of Sustainability." *Environmental Action* 28(1 & 2): 9.

Lockwood, Andrew, and Yvonne Guerrier. 1989. "Flexible working in the hospitality industry: Current strategies and future potential." *Journal of Contemporary Hospitality Management* 1(1): 11–16.

Lyotard, Jean–François. 1989. *The Differend: Phrases in Dispute.* Minnesota: University of Minnesota Press.

MacCannell, Dean. 1976. *The Tourist: A New Theory of the Leisure Class.* Oakland: University of California Press.

Maldonado, Ricardo J. 2011. "What is the short Route?" *Vieques This Weekend* II (February 2011): 20–22.

Marqués, René. 1977[1962]. "El puertorriqueño dócil." In *El puertorriqueño dócil y otros ensayos (1953–1971)*, 153–210. Rio Piedras, Puerto Rico: Editorial Antillana.

Martínez-Cruzado, J.C., Toro-Labrador, G., Viera-Vera, J., Rivera-Vega, M.Y., Startek, J., Latorre-Esteves, M., Román-Colón, A., Rivera-Torres, R., Navarro-Millán, I.Y., Gómez-Sánchez, E., Caro-González, H. and Valencia-Rivera, P. 2005. "Reconstructing the population history of Puerto Rico by means of mtDNA phylogeographic analysis." *Am. J. Phys. Anthropol.* 128: 131–155.

Martínez Mauri, Mónica. 2010. "El tesoro de Kuna Yala: Turismo, inversiones extranjeras y neocolonialismo en Panama." *Cahiers des Amériques Latines* 65(3): 73–88.

Mazón, Tomás, and Antonio Aledo. 2005. "El dilema del turismo residencial: ¿turismo o desarrollo inmobiliario?" In *Turismo residencial y cambio social: nuevas perspectivas teóricas y empíricas*, edited by Tomás Monzón y Antonio Aledo. Alicante: Aguaclara.

McCaffrey, Katherine. 2002. *Military Power and Popular Protest: The U.S. Navy in Vieques, Puerto Rico.* New Brunswick: Rutgers University Press.

McWatters, Mason R. 2009. *Residential Tourism: (De)constructing Paradise.* Bristol: Channel View Publication.

MD: 6-foot shark bit tourist in Vieques. 2012. *Caribbean Business*, September 1712.

Mintz, Sidney. 1956. "Cañameral: The Subculture of a Sugar Plantation Proletariat." In *The People of Puerto Rico: A Study in Social Anthropology*, edited by Julian Steward. Chicago: University of Illinois Press.

———. 1992[1960]. *Taso: trabajador de la caña.* Rio Piedras, Puerto Rico: Ediciones Huracán.

Moeran, Brian. 1983. "The language of Japanese tourism." *Annals of Tourism Research* 10(1): 93–108.

Müller, Dieter K. 1999. *German Second Home Owners in the Swedish Countryside: On the Internationalization of the Leisure Space.* Umeå: Department of Social and Economic Geography.

———. 2002. "Second home ownership and sustainable development in northern Sweden." *Tourism and Hospitality Research* 3: 343–56.

———. 2004. "Mobility, Tourism, and Second Homes." In *A Companion to Tourism*, edited by Alan A. Lew, C. Michael Hall and Allan M. Williams, 387–98. Oxford, UK: Blackwell Publishing, Ltd.

Munasinghe, Viranjini. 2001. *Callaloo or Tossed Salad? East Indians and the Cultural Politics of Identity in Trinidad.* Ithaca, NY: Cornell University Press.

Ness, Sally Ann. 2005. "Tourism–terrorism: The landscaping of consumption and the darker side of place." *American Ethnologist* 32(1): 118–140.

Myers, Erick S. 2009. *What Becomes of Boquete: Transformation, Tension, and the Consequences of Residential Tourism in Panama.* Master's Thesis, Ohio University.

Nowak, Jean-Jacques, Sylvain Petit and Mondher Sahli. 2010. "Tourism and globalization: the international division of tourism production." *Journal of Travel Research* 49(2): 228–45.

Ong, Aihwa. 1996. "Cultural Citizenship as Subject-Making: Immigrants Negotiate Racial and Cultural Boundaries in the United States." *Current Anthropology* 37(5): 737–61.

———. 2006. "Mutations in Citizenship." *Theory, Culture and Society* 23(2–3): 499–531.

Ortega, Julio. 1991. *Reapropiaciones: Cultura y nueva escritura en Puerto Rico.* Rio Piedras: Editorial de la Universidad de Puerto Rico.

Ortman, Jennifer M., Victoria A. Velkoff and Howard Hogan. 2014. *An Aging Nation: The Older Population in the United States, Population Estimates and Projections, Current Population Reports.* US Census Bureau. http://www.census.gov/prod/2014pubs/p25–1140.pdf.

Pattullo, Polly. 2005. *Last Resort: The Cost of Tourism in the Caribbean.* New York: Monthly Review Press.

Pearce, Philip L. 1993. "Fundamentals of Tourist Motivation." In *Tourism Research Critiques and Challenges*, edited by Douglas G. Pearce and Richard W. Butler, 113–34. London/New York: Routledge.

Pedreira, Antonio S. 2001[1934]. *Insularismo: Ensayos de interpretación puertorriqueña.* San Juan: Editorial Plaza Mayor.

Picard, David, and Michael A. DiGiovine, eds. 2014. *Tourism and the Power of Otherness: Seductions of Difference.* Bristol, UK: Channel View Publications.

Rabin, Robert. 2011. "Military Expropriation Documents: Playa Grande Central Inventory - 1941" *Vieques Events* 10(3): 33–38.

———. n/d. "Vieques: Five Centuries of Struggle and Resistance." Vieques-Island.com webpage. Accessed November 29, 2016. http://www.vieques-island.com/navy/rabin.html#ENGLISH

Recanati, François. 2004. *Literal Meaning.* Cambridge: Cambridge University Press.

Riley, Michael. 1990. "The labor retention strategies of UK hotel managers." *The Service Industries Journal* 10(3): 116–19.

———. 1999. "Redefining the debate on hospitality productivity." *Tourism and Hospitality Research* 1(2): 182–6.

———. 2004. "Labor Mobility and Market Structure in Tourism." In *A Companion to Tourism*, edited by Alan A. Lew, C. Michael Hall and Allan M. Williams, 135–45. Oxford, UK: Blackwell Publishing, Ltd.

Riley, Michael, Adele Ladkin and Edith Szivas. 2002. *Tourism Employment: Analysis and Planning.* Clevedon: Channel View Publications.

Rist, Gilbert. 2013. *The History of Development: From Western Origins to Global Faith.* London, UK: Zed Books, Ltd.

Rodríguez Arroyo, Myraida. 2011. *Historia del Agua en Vieques: Un estudio de la contaminación del agua y de las luchas comunitarias sobre el agua desde el periodo de ocupación militar hasta el presente.* Honors Program Thesis, University of Puerto Rico at Cayey.

Rodríguez Juliá, Edgardo. 2002. *Caribeños.* San Juan: Editorial del Instituto de Cultura Puertorriqueña.

Rodríguez Torres, Carmelo. 1980[1971]. *Veinte siglos después del homicidio.* Rio Piedras, Puerto Rico: Editorial Antillana.

Roland, L. Kaifa. 2011. *Cuban Color in Tourism and La Lucha: An Ethnography of Racial Meanings.* New York: Oxford University Press.

Rust, Jon. 2004. "Life in Vieques after the Navy's Departure." *San Juan Star,* May 2.

Sachs, Wolfgang. 1996. Introduction to *The Development Dictionary: A Guide to Knowledge as Power,* 1–6. London: Zad Books.

Safa, Helen I. 1974. *Urban Poor of Puerto Rico.* Oxford, UK: Holt Rinehart & Winston.

———. 1995. *The Myth of the Male Breadwinner: Women and Industralization in the Caribbean.* Oxford, UK: Westview Press.

Salazar, Noel B. 2010. *Envisioning Eden: Mobilizing Imaginaries in Tourism and Beyond.* Oxford, UK: Berghahn Books.

———. 2012. "Tourism Imaginaries: A conceptual approach." *Annals of Tourism Research* 39(2): 863–82.

———. 2014. "Seducation: Learning the Trade of Tourist Enticement." In *Tourism and the Power of Otherness: Seductions of Difference,* eds. David Picard and Michael A. Di Giovine. Bristol: Channel View Publications.

Salazar, Noel B., and Nelson H. H. Graburn. 2014. "Introduction: Toward an Anthropology of Tourism Imaginaries." In *Tourism Imaginaries: Anthropological Approaches,* edited by N. B. Salazar and N. H. H. Graburn, 1–28. New York and Oxford: Berghahn Books.

Santiago Ríos, Miguel Ángel. 2007. *Militarismo y clases sociales en Vieques: 1910–1950.* San Juan: Ediciones Huracán.

Sen, Amartya. 2000. *Development as Freedom.* New York: Anchor Books.

Shaw, Gareth. 2004. "Entrepreneurial Cultures and Small Business Enterprises in Tourism." In *A Companion to Tourism,* edited by Alan A. Lew, C. Michael Hall and Allan M. Williams, 122–34. Oxford, UK: Blackwell Publishing, Ltd.

Shucksmith, D. M. 1983. "Second homes: A framework for policy." *Town Planning Review* 54(2): 174–93.

Simoni, Valerio. 2013. "Revisiting Hosts and Guests: Ethnographic Insights on Touristic Encounters from Cuba." *Journal of Tourism Challenges and Trends* VI(2): 39–62.

Skoczen, Kathleen N. 2008. "Almost paradise: The cultural politics of identity and tourism in Samaná, Dominican Republic." *Journal of Latin American and Caribbean Anthropology* 13(1): 141–67.

Smith, Valene L., ed. 1989[1978]. *Hosts and Guests: The Anthropology of Tourism.* Philadelphia: University of Pennsylvania Press.

Spalding, Ana K. 2013. "Lifestyle migration to Bocas del Toro, Panama: exploring migration strategies and introducing local implications of the search for paradise." *International Review of Social Research* 3(1): 67–86.

Spivak, Gayatri Chakravorty. 1994. "Can the Subaltern Speak?" In *Colonial Discourse and Post-Colonial Theory: A Reader*, edited by Patrick Williams and Laura Chrisman, 66–111. New York: Columbia University Press.

Strachan, Ian Gregory. 2002. *Paradise and Plantation: Tourism and Culture in the Anglophone Caribbean*. Charlottesville: University of Virginia Press.

Stronza, Amanda. 2001. "The Anthropology of Tourism: Forging New Grounds for Ecotourism and Other Alternatives." *Annual Review of Anthropology* 30: 261–83.

Sweet, Jill D. 2010[2004]. "'Let'em Loose': Pueblo Indian Management of Tourism." In *Tourists and Tourism: A Reader*, edited by Sharon Bohn Gmelch, 137–50. Long Grove, Illinois: Waveland Press.

Taylor, Frank Fonda. 1993. *To Hell With Paradise: A History of the Jamaican Tourist Industry*. Pittsburg: University of Pittsburgh Press.

Telfer, David J. 2009. "Development Studies and Tourism." In *The SAGE Handbook of Tourism Studies*, edited by Tazim Jamal and Mike Robinson, 146–65. London: SAGE Publications, Ltd.

Thompson, Lanny. 2010. *Imperial Archipelago: Representation and Rule in the Insular Territories Under U.S. Dominion After 1898*. Honolulu: University of Hawaii Press.

Thurlow, Crispin and Adam Jaworski. 2010. *Tourism Discourse: The Language of Global Mobility*. Basingstoke: Palgrave Macmillan.

———. 2011. "Tourism Discourse: Languages and Banal Globalization." *Applied Linguistics Review*. https://doi.org/10.1515/9783110239331.285.

Torres Bernier, Enrique J. 2003. "El Turismo Residenciado y sus Efectos en los Destinos Turísticos." *Estudios Turísticos* 155–156: 45–70.

"Trouble on Welfare Island." 2006. *The Economist*, May 25. Accessed December 23, 2015. http://www.economist.com/node/6980051.

Urry, John. 1990. *The Tourist Gaze: Leisure and Travel in Contemporary Societies*. London: Sage Publications.

van Noorloos, Femke. 2011a. "Residential tourism causing land privatization and alienation: New pressures on Costa Rica's coasts." *Development* 54(1): 85–90.

———. 2011b. "A transnational networked space: tracing residential tourism and its multi-local implications in Costa Rica." *International Development Planning Review* 33(4): 429–44.

———. 2013. "Residential tourism and multiple mobilities: Local citizenship and community fragmentation in Costa Rica." *Sustainability* 5(2): 570–89.

Vélez Rodríguez, Evelyn. 2002. *Plan Drácula: Proyecto V-C: Negociaciones Secretas entre Luis Muñoz Marín y La Marina*. Rio Piedras, Puerto Rico: Editorial Edil.

Vieques: 10 Años Sin La Marina: Sueño Trunco. *El Nuevo Día*, April 28.

Warnes, Anthony M. 1994. "Permanent and seasonal international retirement migration: The prospects for Europe." *Nederlandse Geografische Studie* 173: 68–80.

Wearing, Stephen, Deborah Stevenson and Tamara Young. 2010. *Tourist Cultures: Identity, Place and the Traveller*. London: SAGE Publications, Ltd.

Weber, Max. 2009[1905]. *The Protestant Ethics and the Spirit of Capitalism*. New York: W. W. Norton & Co.

Williams, Allan M. 2004. "Towards a Political Economy of Tourism." In *A Companion to Tourism*, edited by Alan A. Lew, C. Michael Hall and Allan M. Williams, 61–73. Oxford, UK: Blackwell Publishing, Ltd.

Williams, Allan M. and C. Michael Hall. 2002. "Tourism, Migration, Circulation and Mobility: The Contingencies of Time and Place." In *Tourism and Migration: New Relationships between Production and Consumption*, edited by C. Michael Hall and Allan M. Williams, 1–52. Dordrecht, the Netherlands: Kluwer Academic.

Williams, Allan M., Russell King and Tony Warnes. 1997. "A place in the sun: International retirement migration from the UK to Southern Europe." *European Urban and Regional Studies* 4: 115–34.

Wittgenstein, Ludwig. 1922. *Tractatus Logico-Philosophicus*, translated by C. K. Ogden. London: Routledge & Kegan Paul.

———. 1953. *Philosophical Investigations*, translated by G.E.M. Anscombe. Oxford: Blackwell.

———. 1958. *The Blue and Brown Books*. Oxford: Blackwell.

Wong, Brian, and Ghazali Musa. 2015. "Challenges of international retirees in second home destination: A phenomenological analysis." *Tourism Management Perspectives* 15: 81–90.

World Trade Organization. 1994. *Recommendations on Tourism Statistics*. WTO: Madrid.

Yelvington, Kevin A. 2001. "The anthropology of Afro-Latin-America and the Caribbean: Diasporic dimensions." *Annual Review of Anthropology* 30: 227–60.

Young, Iris Marion. 1998. "Unruly Categories: A Critique of Nancy Fraser's Dual Systems Theory." In *Theorizing Multiculturalism: A Guide to the Current Debate*, edited by Cynthia Willett, 50–67. Malden, MA: Blackwell.

Author Index

Abbink, Jon, 95
Ahearn, Laura A., xv
Aledo, Antonio, 3, 5, 10, 75, 76, 84
Alvarado Vega, José, 63
Aronsson, Lars, 4
Ateljevic, Irena, 60
Ayala, César J., ix

Bakhtin, Mikhail, xiv–xv, xviii, 69
Baldacchino, Godfrey, 8, 40
Barnhart, R. K., 73n18
Barreto, Amilcar A., ix
Baudrillard, Jean, 79
Baver, Sherrie L., ix, 117–18
Bechhofer, Frank, 51
Benítez-Rojo, Antonio, xi, 86, 88, 89
Benjamin, Walter, 130–31
Benson, M., 3
Benson, M. C., 3
Berman Santana, Déborah, ix
Bolivar, José L., ix
Boschken, H. L., 3
Bosworth, Barry, 61–63
Bourdieu, Pierre, 76
Boyer, William W., 50
Brathwaite, Kamau, 86–87, 89
Britton, Celia M., 87
Browne, Katherine E., 34, 47–48

Bruner, Edward M., 4, 5, 75, 78–80,
    88–89
Buller, H., 3
Bunten, Alexis C., 41
Burge, Tyler, xviii
Burtner, Jennifer, 6, 8

Casado-Díaz, María A., 3
Castañeda, Quetzil E., 6, 8
Chambers, Erve, 39–40, 49, 95, 102,
    127
Chaplain, A., 35
Char, René, 135
Chatterjee, Partha, 70, 134
Cohen, Erik, 4, 82–85
Collins, Susan M., 61–63
Colón, Javier, 123
Colón Ramos, Daniel, 120
Cooper, Robert L., 82–85
Coppock, J. Terry, 3
Craine, Jim, 3
Crang, Mike, 8
Crouch, David, 4
Cruz Soto, Marie, ix, 96

Denvir, Ann, 35
Derrida, Jacques, xv
Dewhurst, Peter, 60

Díaz, Alex, 63
Díaz Román, Miguel, 13, 14, 65
Dietz, James L., 62
Di Giovine, Michael A., 3–4, 5, 7,
    75–77, 80, 82, 135
Doorne, Stephen, 60

Eco, Umberto, 79–81
Escobar, Arturo, 6
Evans-Pritchard, Deirdre, 4, 86

Fabián, Ana M., 96
Farrell, Bryan, 95
Ferguson, Charles A., 83
Ferguson, James, 6
Forster, John, 95
Foucault, Michel, 123

Galanes Valldejuli, Luis, 61
Gallent, Nick, 3
García-Andreu, Hugo, 3, 75
García Muñiz, Humberto, xxn3
García Peinado, Miguel A., 74n19
Geertz, Clifford, 34, 52
Gilbert, Sandra, 89n1
Glissant, Edouard, 86–87, 89
Gmelch, George, 40
Gmelch, Sharon Bohn, 4, 5, 75
Godreau, Isar P., 94
Goldthorpe, John H., 51
XX Graburn, Nelson H. H., 4, 5, 8, 41,
    75–79, 85, 88
Gravari-Barbas, María, 5, 75
Green, Howard, 7, 132n6
Greenwood, David, 4
Gubar, Susan, 89n1
Guerrier, Yvonne, 40
Guerrón Montero, Carla, 3

Hall, C. Michael, 3, 84
Hall-Lew, Lauren A., 5, 75
Harris, Wilson, 86
Hernández, Maribel, 123
Hirsh, Edward, 50
Hitchcock, Michael, 116n34

Hogan, Howard, 2
Hoggart, K., 3
Holt, Eden, 96
Honey, Martha, 6, 7, 135
Hopgood Dávila, Eugenio, 18
Horobin, Helen, 60
Hughes, George, 7
Huit, Groupe, 95
Hunter, Colin, 7, 132n6

Jackiewicz, Edward L., 3
Jacobsen, Jens Kr. Steen, 3, 84
Jamal, Tazim, 135
James, C. L. R., 87
Jaworski, Adam, 5, 75, 76, 77, 89
Johnson, Clifford M., 50
Johnson, Keith, 35

Kaiser, Claudia, 3
Kaltenborn, Bjørn P., 3
King, Russell, 3, 84
Klein, Deborah, 118

Ladkin, Adele, 40
Lafargue, Paul, 67–68
Lamming, George, 86
Lamont, Michèle, 47, 51
Lashley, Conrad, 35
Leite, Naomi, 4, 8
Levitan, Sar A., 50
Lew, Alan A., 5, 75
Lewis, Oscar, 38–39, 43
Little, Cheryl, 7
Lockwood, Andrew, 40
Lockwood, David, 51
Loloum, Tristan, 3, 75
Lyotard, Jean-François, xv, xviii, 68

MacCannell, Dean, 4, 79–80
Maldonado, Ricardo J., 129
Marqués, René, xiii, xxn6
Martínez Cruzado, Juan, 114
Martínez Mauri, Mónica, 8, 116n34
Marx, Karl, 66–68
Mazón, Tomás, 3

McCaffrey, Katherine, ix
McMahon, Frank, 35
McWatters, Mason R., 3
Mintz, Sidney, 46–47
Moeran, Brian, 5, 75
Müller, Dieter K., 2, 3, 84
Munasinghe, Viranjini, 70
Musa, Ghazali, 3
Myers, Erick S., 3

Ness, Sally Ann, 116n34

Ong, Aihwa, 91–94
O'Reilly, K., 3
Ortega, Julio, 70, 135
Ortiz, Guadalupe, 3, 75
Ortman, Jennifer M., 2

Patterson, Guy, 3, 84
Pattullo, Polly, x–xi
Pearce, Philip L., 4
Pedreira, Antonio S., xiii, xxn6, 61
Picard, David, 3–4
Platt, Jennifer, 51
Putra, Nyoman Darma, 116n34

Rabin, Roberto, ix, 17–18
Recanati, François, xviii
Riley, Michael, 35, 40
Rist, Gilbert, 6
Robinson, Mike, 135
Rodríguez Arroyo, Myraida, 128
Rodríguez Juliá, Edgardo, 61
Rodríguez Torres, Carmelo, 131
Roland, L. Kaifa, 47, 48

Sachs, Wolfgang, 6
Salazar, Noel B., 4, 5, 41, 75–79, 83,
    85, 88
Santiago Ríos, Miguel Ángel, 17
Selstad, Leif, 3, 84

Sen, Amartya, 6
Shaw, Gareth, 60
Shucksmith, D. M., 3
Simoni, Valerio, 5, 8–10, 41–42, 88–89
Skoczen, Kathleen N., 94
Smith, Valene L., 2, 95
Soto-Class, Miguel A., 61–63
Spalding, Ana K., 3
Spivak, Gayatri Chakravorty, xix, 85,
    87, 124, 133–35
Stevenson, Deborah, 4
Strachan, Ian Gregory, 39, 49
Stronza, Amanda, 5, 7, 135
Sweet, Jill D., 95
Szivas, Edith, 40

Taylor, Frank Fonda, 39, 49
Telfer, David J., 7
Tewdwr-Jones, Mark, 3
Thompson, Lanny, 93
Thurlow, Crispin, 5, 75, 76, 77, 89
Torres Bernier, Enrique J., 2

Urry, John, 4

van Noorloos, Femke, 3
Vélez Rodríguez, Evelyn, 20, 29n12
Velkoff, Victoria A., 2

Wahlström, Lage, 4
Walcott, Derek, xi, 50, 86–87
Warnes, Anthony M., 3, 84
Wearing, Stephen, 4
Weber, Max, 36, 60, 66–67
Williams, Allan M., 3, 84
Wittgenstein, Ludwig, xv–xix, 69, 70
Wong, Brian, 3

Yelvington, Kevin A., 89
Young, Iris Marion, xix, 69
Young, Tamara, 4

Subject Index

agriculture, 62
Angel Novus, 130
aplatanamiento, 61
Area Plan for the Municipality of
    Vieques, 26, 126, 128–30
attrition, 35, 40

baby-boomers, 2
Bahamas, 44
Bali, Thailand, 79–80, 116n34
Balinese frog dance, 80
Bioluminescent Bay. *See* Mosquito
    Bioluminescent Bay
black/white poles of American
    citizenship, 91–93
Bocas del Toro, Panama, 3
Boquete, Panama, 3
Borneo, 44
Brazil, 3

cancer. *See* Vieques, cancer and health
    indicators
Chomski/Sausserian approach to
    language, xv
citizenship, 91–93
Colorado, 116n34
Committee for the Rescue and
    Development of Vieques, 126
contemporary social movements,
    133–34

contextualism, xviii
contre poétique, 86–88
Costa Rica, 3
creole economics, 47–48
creole languages, 85–89
creolization, theories of, 85–89
crime, 122–24, *123*
cruise ships, x, 125, 129
Cuba, x, 41–42
Cuban Revolution, x
Culebra, 14
cultural hot button, 34, 63, 122
culture of poverty, 38–39

débrouillard, 48
decontamination, 117-19, 122
development:
    theorization about, 6–7;
    tourism development, 6–10, 125–30
le différance, xv
differénd, xv–xviii, 68–71
discourses:
    about dissatisfaction with tourism,
        xi–xii;
    about *pasarla bien*, 50–60, 70–71;
    about work and laziness, 33–43,
        61–69
Dominican Republic, 94
Dos Palmas. *See* development in
    tourism

Dracula Plan. *See* V-C Navy Plan
drug trafficking, 123

ecoterrorism, 116n34
ecotourism, 6–7, 135
Egypt, 116n34
enjoyment of life. *See* discourses, about
    pasarla bien
entrepreneurship, 48, 60
environmental justice, 117–19
epistemic violence, 78, 85–89
erosion thesis, 8
essentialism, in anthropology, 78–81, 89

family resemblance, theory of meaning
    of words, xv, xix
field of cultural production, 76
field of touristic production, 5, 76–77
flexibility, 40
force for world peace, tourism as, 6, 88
foreign talk, 82–83
forms of life, xv

golf, 125, 126–27
Guanacaste, Costa Rica, 3

Havana. *See* Cuba
having a good time. *See* discourses,
    about *pasarla bien*
Hawaii, 44
health, 118–20
heritage tourism, 1, 78–81
heteroglossia, xiv–xv, 9, 69, 89n1
Hôi An, Viêt Nam, 7
host/guess dichotomy, 4, 75–77
La Hueca. *See* land, squatting and
    recovery movements
human rights, 117, 119, 121

Ibiza, x
ideal language, philosophical theory
    of, xv
imaginaire dialectique, 76–77
imaginary of tourism, 4–5, 75–78,
    80–88

Indonesia, x
Italy, 7

Japan, 44
Java, x
jineteros, 41–42, 47–48
joie de vivre. *See* discourses, about
    pasarla bien

Kaho'olawe, Hawaii, 118
Kuna Indians, 116n34

labor mobility, 35
labor participation rate. *See* Puerto Rico,
    labor participation rate
labor turnover. *See* labor mobility
land:
    squatting and recovery movements,
        17–27.
    See also real-estate boom
language game, xiv–xviii, xix, 70,
    123–24
langue, xv
lifestyle:
    factors and entrepreneurship, 60;
    migration, 2.
    See also residential tourism
living language, xv, xix, 9, 69, 88, 124,
    135
luchadores. See jineteros

Mallorca, x
Martinique, 48
Marxism, 66–68
Master Plan for the Sustainable
    Development of Vieques, 26,
    126
migration movements:
    of migrant workers, 50, 100–102;
    of retired persons. *See* residential
    tourism
El Monte. *See* land, squatting and
    recovery movements
Monte Carmelo, 18
Mosquito Bioluminescent Bay, 1, 44–50

Mosquito Village. *See* development

La Nasa, 103–4
nation language, 86–88
neoplantation, 39, 49
New Salem Historic Site, 79–80

Operation Bootstrap, 62

Panama, 3, 116n34
parole, xv
pasarla bien. See discourses, about
        pasarla bien
patois. See creole languages
phenomenology, 4
Philippines, 116n34
phrases in dispute, xv, xviii, 5, 69
pidgin. *See* creole languages
Pietrelcina, Italy, 7
PIIGS, 68
Pipa, Brazil, 3
plantation system, 17–18, 39, 49, 86
poverty. *See* Vieques, economic
        statistics of
pragmatism, in philosophy of language,
        xiv–xviii
pro-poor tourism, 7
Protestant Reform, 67–68
Protestant work-ethics, 47, 60, 67–68
Puerto Rico:
        cancer statistics, *119*;
        census data, 93–94, 110n1;
        labor participation rate, 62–63, 65

real-estate boom, 13–18, 123–24, 128
rental villas, 16
reparation movements, 119–22
residential tourism, 1–4, 95–96
retired migrants. *See* residential tourism
revitalization paradigm, 7, 135
rural gentrification, 3

Samana, Dominican Republic. *See*
        Dominican Republic
sampling data, xix, 71n2

second-home tourism. *See* residential
        tourism
seducation, 83
seduction of difference, 3
semantics, in philosophy of language,
        xiv–xviii
social movements, contemporary,
        133–34
Spain, x
speculation bacchanal. *See* real-estate
        boom
St. Croix. *See* USVI
St. John. *See* USVI
St. Lucia, xx–xi
St. Thomas. *See* USVI
subaltern voice, theory of the, xix, 27,
        75, 85–89, 117, 121–22, 124,
        133–35
Sumatra, x
Sun Bay Resort. *See* development in
        tourism

Taino Indians, 114n24
Taso (Anaustacio Zayas), 46–47
tourist talk, 82–83
traditionalism, 36
typology of gringos, 81–110
typology of tourists, 81–85, 89

unemployment. *See* Vieques, economic
        statistics of
unruly categories, xix, 69–70
USVI, United States Virgin Islands,
        14–15, 18, 50, 125

V-C Navy Plan, 20, 27, 47
Verde Vieques. *See* land, squatting and
        recovery movements
Vieques:
        cancer and health indicators, *119*;
        census data, 93–94, 95, 110n1;
        crime statistics, 122–23, *123*;
        decontamination of, 117–19, 122;
        economic statistics of, xi, 33;
        geographical information of, ix;

real-estate boom, 13–18, 123–24,
  128;
tourism infrastructure in, 1, 10n2,
  125–26
vigilante patrol, 105–6

villas. *See* rental villas

water, 127–28, 130
weekend homes, 2
work ethics. *See* Protestant work-ethics

About the Author

Luis Galanes Valldejuli is full professor of anthropology in the Department of Social Sciences of the University of Puerto Rico at Cayey. His research and theoretical interests have centered on highlighting the complexity of local discourses about identity, nationalism and nativism, as they emerge at the intersections between race, gender, colonialism and tourism. At a geographical level, his research has mainly centered on the Caribbean region, and particularly on the area comprised by Puerto Rico and the Virgin Islands (both the US and British).